TOWARD A PENTECOSTAL THEOLOGY OF RELIGIONS

ENCOUNTERING CORNELIUS TODAY

TOWARD A

PENTECOSTAL THEOLOGY
OF RELIGIONS

ENCOUNTERING CORNELIUS TODAY

TONY RICHIE

CPT

CPT Press
Cleveland, Tennessee

Toward a Pentecostal Theology of Religions
Encountering Cornelius Today

Published by CPT Press
900 Walker ST NE
Cleveland, TN 37311
email: cptpress@pentecostaltheology.org
website: www.pentecostaltheology.org

Library of Congress Control Number 2013930948

ISBN-10 1935931342
ISBN-13 9781935931348

DEDICATION

To my wife Sue, without whose many contributions, support, and partnership I would be able to accomplish nothing. I am completely assured both that apart from the Lord Jesus Christ I can do nothing (Jn 15.5) and that my full confidence in Sue Richie is well placed (Prov. 31.11). Thank you for everything, Sweetheart. I love you!

TABLE OF CONTENTS

ACKNOWLEDGEMENTS

Obviously, no book comes into being entirely as the result of the labors of one person. I am grateful to CPT Press, especially Chris Thomas and Lee Roy Martin, for their invitation to write this book and for their encouragement and expertise throughout the writing process without which this book would not have become a reality. I am deeply indebted to President Steven Jack Land and the faculty of the Pentecostal Theological Seminary for providing an environment conducive for spiritual transformation and intellectual stimulation, including many engaging conversations through which I have learned much from many, first as a student and later as a faculty member, especially Jackie David Johns. I am particularly grateful for the commitment of Sang-Ehil Han, Vice President for Academics, to provide venues for Pentecostals to engage in academic conversation on Christian theology of religions and dialogue with neighbors living together in a multi-faith world, and for the enlightening personal conversations I have enjoyed having with him on this topic. Special thanks are owed to Lee University systematic theology professor Christopher 'Crip' Stephenson who provided critical reading and creative input on Chapters 5 through 7. Wide-open discussions with students in my theology of religions class at PTS during the Fall semester of 2012, especially Chris Brewer, David Johnson, Kevin Snider, and Dennis Purvis, have directly influenced key portions of this monograph, especially Chapter 1. The prayers, support, and friendship of the good people of New Harvest Church of God in Knoxville, Tennessee, where Sue and I have been blessed to serve as senior pastors for fifteen years, as of this writing, have been crucial. While the aforementioned persons, along with others too numerous to mention, have been particularly helpful in producing this book, I own up to whatever imperfections it may (and does, I am sure, in fact) contain as my own responsibility.

ABBREVIATIONS

ACCS	*Ancient Christian Commentary on Scripture*
AJPS	*Asian Journal of Pentecostal Studies*
ATJ	*Asbury Theological Journal*
COGE	*Church of God Evangel*
CWJW	*Complete Works of John Wesley*
ERT	*Evangelical Review of Theology*
FLBCNT	*Full Life Bible Commentary to the New Testament*
GDT	*Global Dictionary of Theology*
IRM	*International Review of Mission*
JES	*Journal of Ecumenical Studies*
JEPTA	*Journal of the European Pentecostal Theological Association*
JPT	*Journal of Pentecostal Theology*
NIBC	*New International Biblical Commentary*
NIDPCM	*New International Dictionary of Pentecostal-Charismatic Movements*
Pneuma	*Pneuma: The Journal for the Society for Pentecostal Studies*

INTRODUCTION

Many years ago, before becoming president of Pentecostal Theological Seminary, Pentecostal theologian Steven Jack Land wrote in
the inaugural issue of what has since become a major publishing
venue, the *Journal of Pentecostal Theology*, that 'Theology is concerned
with the relations between God and creation, and Pentecostal theology conceives that relation to be a living dynamic, requiring discerning reflection or discursive reasoning that is gifted by and at-
tuned to the things of the Spirit'.[1] The present volume is written
with that astute observation firmly in mind. Among other things,
this statement suggests that Pentecostal theology is not merely theoretical; it involves the living out of faith in everyday life. For another, it implies that matters which profoundly affect everyday life
in this world should receive sustained theological attention by Pentecostals. In this case, a pressing topic of contemporary lived reality
requiring Spirit-gifted and Spirit-attuned reflection and reasoning is
Pentecostal theology of religions. Accordingly, that is the thrust of
this volume. It is offered in the hopeful prayer that the Holy Spirit
will indeed anoint it for the glory of God.

Some Diverse Precedents

From very early in its history and ministry the Pentecostal movement frequently interacted directly with other religions. For example, Elizabeth Brown lived and worked among Arab Muslims in
Jerusalem and Jordan as early as 1895 and then later with Jews in

---

[1] Steven J. Land, 'A Passion for the Kingdom: Revisioning Pentecostal Spirituality,' *JPT* 1 (October 1992), p. 28.

the State of Israel.[2] For another out of many possible examples, Robert F. Cook went to South India as early as 1913, enjoying exceptional results among the Hindu population.[3] Subsequently, Margaret Gaines spent a half century ministering among Jews, Christians, and Muslims in the Middle East.[4] Pentecostal missions of various sorts have continued steadily, with varying degrees of resistance and success, among Muslims and others in Lebanon, Iran, Iraq, Syria, Turkey, Pakistan, and Afghanistan – and including Asian Pentecostal activity in the Arabian Peninsula.[5] Again, in the Philippines, in spite of interreligious challenges and tensions, a long-time Pentecostal presence has produced an impressive yield.[6]

However, there has often been much misunderstanding by those of other religions about what Christians and especially Pentecostals really believe and practice. In predominately Muslim populated nations, such as, for example, Guinea, misunderstanding has at times been extreme.[7] In such cases traditional evangelism approaches have not been effective. Furthermore, frequently Pentecostal presence among those of other faiths, such as Islam, has been beclouded with political and cultural confusion.[8] At times outright religious persecution has become a major problem, as in Uganda.[9] Yet in the midst of horrible atrocities, there have also been amazing conversions; even Muslim army officers have become Christians.[10] Undeniably, interreligious relations often in contexts of the spread of Islam and Christianity in general and the growth of Pentecostalism in particular at times accompanied by increasing occurrences of reli-

---

[2] Joyce Booze, 'Africa, North, and the Middle East', in Stanley M. Burgess and Eduard M. Van Der Maas (eds.), *NIDPCM* (Grand Rapids: Zondervan, 2002), p. 8.

[3] Robert F. Cook, *Half a Century of Divine Leading and 37 Years of Apostolic Achievements in South India* (Cleveland, TN: Church of God Foreign Missions Department, 1955).

[4] Margaret Gaines, *Small Enough to Stop the Violence* (Cleveland, TN: Cherohala Press, 2011).

[5] Booze, 'Africa, North, and the Middle East', pp. 8-11.

[6] Wonsuk Ma, 'Philippines', in *NIDPCM*, p. 203.

[7] David J. Garrard, 'Guinea, Republic of', in *NIDPCM*, p. 113.

[8] Paul Lewis, 'Indonesia', in *NIDPCM*, p. 127.

[9] David J. Garrard, 'Uganda', in *NIDPCM*, p. 273.

[10] Garrard, 'Uganda', pp. 275-76.

gion related violence is currently one of the key interests of Christian theology.[11]

Most of the time, Pentecostal encounters with other religions have occurred primarily in overtly evangelistic settings. However, Pentecostal missiologist David Kent Irwin, founder of the Center for Ministry to Muslims, learned that building real and lasting relationships through understanding and communication is more effective.[12] Similarly, David Garrard recommends building bridges and establishing friendships in an atmosphere of the Holy Spirit's power as a more effective avenue in religiously plural contexts.[13] Increasingly apparent is that evangelistic proclamation alone is inadequate for Pentecostal mission among other faiths.

At times, there have been strangely syncretistic (irresponsible mixing of religious beliefs and practices) Pentecostal-type groups arising out of an intersection between two or even three religious traditions. For example, the Original Gospel Movement in Japan mixes Pentecostal Christianity with strong Zionist-Judaic elements and Japanese folk religions, including an emphasis on Japanese mythology.[14] In other cases, as in Brazil, religious contextualization stressing commonalities in Pentecostalism and indigenous religions regarding belief in the spirit world may actually be part of Pentecostalism's local appeal.[15] Julie Ma argues that Pentecostalism's similarities with animism (belief in various spiritual beings, good or bad, whose power can affect humans) are not only critical to explaining its success in the majority world but should be an intentional point in its mission strategy.[16] Sociologically, the world Pentecostal movement blends diverse social, racial, economic, and national groups together with diverse religious and intellectual traditions.[17]

[11] David F. Ford, ed., with Rachel Muers, *The Modern Theologians: An Introduction to Christian Theology Since 1918* (Malden, MA: Blackwell Publishing, 2005), p. 12.

[12] David K. Irwin, *What Christians Should Need to Know About Muslims*, (Springfield, MO: Center for Ministry to Muslims, 1987).

[13] Garrard, 'Guinea', p. 115.

[14] David Hymes, 'Japan', in *NIDPCM*, p. 149.

[15] Everett A. Wilson, 'Brazil', in *NIDPCM*, pp. 38-39.

[16] Julie C. Ma, 'Animism and Pentecostalism: A Case Study', in *NIDPCM*, pp. 317-18.

[17] Jerry W. Shepperd, 'Sociology of World Pentecostalism', in *NICPCM*, p. 1084.

Accordingly, Pentecostal encounters with non-Christian religions tend to be characterized by complexity.

To be clear, there are radical fringe groups among the religions that are by definition disruptive to society and prone to violence against those they consider their enemies.[18] These terrorists represent real threats that cannot be dismissed or dealt with through simple dialogue or the usual channels of diplomacy. Clearly, naiveté regarding the spiteful propensities of evildoers can be not only counterproductive but actually destructive (Mt. 7.6). Yet at times radical evangelistic strategies, exclusivist and inflexible attitudes, and demonization of other religions by Pentecostal groups have contributed not only to misunderstanding and tension but also to violence and bloodshed. From Ghana, Cephas Omenyo traces recent intensification of violent hostilities (often resulting in persecution and death) between Christians and Muslims in Ghana and Nigeria to an upsurge of Pentecostal and Charismatic churches demonizing Muslims and emphasizing deliverance practices.[19] Omenyo's example is not an exception. Pentecostal theologian of religions Amos Yong suggests demonization of religious others, with dire consequences, is a pressing and prevalent problem among Renewal (read Pentecostal-type) groups.[20] In a worst case scenario, demonization of religious others by purported Pentecostals in positions of political and military power has resulted in the widespread massacre of indigenous peoples in Guatemala.[21]

Pentecostal encounters with Hinduism can also be problematic. As British theologian Kirsteen Kim explains, recent violent conflict between Hindus and Christians in Orissa, India, already tense because of economic and political factors, apparently with at least some level of mutual culpability, have been exacerbated by the incautious entry of Pentecostal groups employing aggressive conver-

[18] E.g. see Bobby Ghosh, 'The Rise of the Salifis', *Time* 180.15 (October 8, 2012), pp. 47-51.
[19] Cephas Omenyo, 'Renewal, Christian Mission, and Encounter with the Other', in Amos Yong and Clifton Clarke (eds.) *Global Renewal, Religious Pluralism, and the Great Commission: Towards a Renewal Theology of Mission and Interreligious Encounter* (Lexington, KY: Emeth Press, 2011), esp. pp. 152-53.
[20] Amos Yong, 'From Demonization to Kin-domization: The Witness of the Spirit and the Renewal of Mission in a Pluralistic World', in Yong and Clarke (eds.), *Global Renewal*, pp. 158-60.
[21] Yong, 'From Demonization to Kin-domization', p. 158.

sion tactics.[22] In this context, the stereotypical myth of Hindu tolerance is being exposed but also the failure of Christian pluralism, in
emphasizing the wider work of the Spirit at the expense of the
Great Commission and divorcing Christology and pneumatology,
for meeting the needs of local Dalit Christians is evident.[23] Kim
suggests 'a mission theology of the Holy Spirit which both affirms
religious plurality and is also obedient to the Great Commission' is
necessary.[24] She thus proposes that Pentecostalism may offer a
unique pneumatological contribution to contemporary Christian
theology of religions.[25]

Pentecostals can sometimes be found on opposite ends of the
spectrum regarding the same interreligious incident. For example, in
the United States, Dove Outreach World Church, a small inde-
pendent congregation with professed Pentecostal-Charismatic lean-
ings, greatly intensified tensions not only between America and the
Islamic world but between Christians and Muslims with their threat
to host an 'International Burn a Koran Day'. However, I responded
with an argument condemning the offensive act as unchristian and
inconsistent with Pentecostal faith and values.[26] Further, Raymond
Culpepper, Presiding Bishop (General Overseer) of the Church of
God (Cleveland, TN), a Classical Pentecostal denomination, issued
a statement against the burning as contradictory to the Spirit of the
gospel of Jesus Christ, and the Church of God joined a group of
Pentecostal organizations in placing a public advertisement to the
same effect in local news media.[27] George Wood, General Superin-
tendant of the Assemblies of God, another large Classical Pentecostal denomination, warned against the burning of the Quran on the
grounds that it sends the wrong message to the world's Muslims

---

[22] Kirsteen Kim, 'Theologies of Religious Pluralism', in Yong and Clarke
(eds.), *Global Renewal*, pp. 117-18.
[23] Kim, 'Theologies of Religious Pluralism', p. 118.
[24] Kim, 'Theologies of Religious Pluralism', p. 118.
[25] Kim, 'Theologies of Religious Pluralism', pp. 128-30 (p. 128).
[26] Tony Richie, 'Pentecostals on Publically Burning the Quran', Faith News
Network (September 8, 2010), www.faithnews.cc/2010/09/08/pentecostals-on-
publically-burning-the-quran.
[27] 'Church takes Stand on Book Burning', *Faith News Network* (September 10,
2010), www.faithnews.cc/2010/09/10/church-takes-stand-on-book-burning.

and causes Christians to come across like crusaders from the Middle Ages.[28]

Obviously, Pentecostal interaction with other religions around the world is not new. Neither is it simple; rather, it is characterized by great complexity. If for no other reason, the complexities of Pentecostal encounters with other religions point to a need for developing an intentional and articulate Pentecostal theology of religions. Only thus will Pentecostal Christians have much-needed consistent and coherent guidance for living and ministering in a world of multiple religious faiths. (In addition to addressing pragmatic needs, there are also theological and spiritual issues at stake. See my attempt to define the discipline of theology of religions on pages 11-12 below).

A Positive Model

Perhaps as much or more than anyone else, Walter J. Hollenweger, the Swiss historian and analyst of Pentecostalism, has helped make the broader Christian world and Pentecostals be more aware of and informed about each other.[29] Certainly Hollenweger's *The Pentecostals* has become an uncontested classic resource on the Pentecostal movement.[30] More recently Hollenweger has pushed the envelope regarding Pentecostals and other religions.[31] Specifically, he draws on the Acts 10 account of the encounter between the Christian apostle, Peter, and the Roman centurion, Cornelius, to suggest insights for Pentecostal theology of religions and interreligious interaction.[32] Hollenweger asserts that the encounter of Peter and Cornelius demonstrates a form of mutual conversion. The gospel is objective and enables both evangelist and evangelized to learn of

---

[28] 'Evangelical Leaders Pan Qu'ran Burn Plan', *Christianity Today* (July, 30, 2010), http://www.christianitytoday.com/ct/2010/julyweb-only/40.51.0.html.

[29] Allan Anderson, *An Introduction to Global Pentecostalism: Global Charismatic Christianity* (Cambridge: Cambridge University Press, 2004), p. 245.

[30] Walter J. Hollenweger, *The Pentecostals* (Peabody: Hendrickson, 1988, first published in English by SCM Press Ltd. London, 1972).

[31] E.g. Hollenweger, 'Evangelism: A Non-Colonial Model', *JPT* 7 (1995), pp. 107-28.

[32] Hollenweger, 'Critical Issues for Pentecostals', in Allan Anderson and Walter J. Hollenweger (eds.), *Pentecostals after a Century: A Movement in Transition* (JPTSup 15; Sheffield: Sheffield Academic Press, 1999), pp. 176-91.

Christ together. Thus the example of Peter and Cornelius becomes paradigmatic for dialogical and situational encounter between Christians and those of non-Christian religions.[33]

Even before Hollenweger, evangelical scholar Norman Anderson plumbed the example of Peter and Cornelius for purposes of interreligious dialogue.[34] Anderson offered several valuable observations. First, he noted that both Peter and Cornelius came away with benefits from the encounter. Second, he suggested that good dialogue can prepare the way for evangelism, or be a part of it. Third, he explained that dialogue carries an element of risk but is worth it when carried out in confidence of the lordship of Jesus Christ and in the power of the Holy Spirit. All three points are consistent with a Pentecostal sense of God's presence in the world.

The subtitle of the present book, *Encountering Cornelius Today,* draws inspiration from the example of Peter and Cornelius in Acts 10. It is particularly appropriate for Pentecostal theology of religions.[35] First, it enjoys a long association rooted in Pentecostal history, identity, spirituality, and theology. Second, it is consonant with Pentecostal experiences in global encounters with other religions today. Third, its biblical foundation in a context of a critical text for Pentecostals on Spirit baptism is quite strong. Fourth, it illustrates to Pentecostals the Holy Spirit's moving and working in unexpected places among surprising peoples. And, fifth, it exhibits faithfulness to Christian evangelism and mission as understood by Pentecostals.[36]

It might be added that there is a certain ambiguity about Cornelius that seems apropos for individuals involved in interreligious encounter today as well. Pentecostal New Testament scholar French Arrington describes Cornelius as 'a godly man' of prayer and generosity who had not been baptized or circumcised and was

---

[33] Hollenweger, 'Critical Issues', pp. 178, 183-88, and 190-91.

[34] Sir Norman Anderson, *Christianity and the World Religions: The Challenge of Pluralism* (Downers Grove, IL: InterVarsity Press, 1984), pp. 188-91.

[35] Tony Richie, 'Revamping Pentecostal Evangelism: Appropriating Walter J. Hollenweger's Radical Proposal', *IRM* 96.382/383 (July/October 2007), pp. 343-54.

[36] Richie, 'Revamping Pentecostal Evangelism', pp. 345-51.

thus still considered 'a pagan and unclean'.[37] Arrington notes that the encounter between Peter and Cornelius is characterized by direct 'divine guidance and empowerment'.[38] Yet he argues that understanding Cornelius and those who gathered at his house as repenting and believing upon hearing the gospel preached by Peter and subsequently being baptized in the Holy Spirit 'maintains a distinction between the indwelling of the Holy Spirit and the baptism of the Spirit'.[39]

Accordingly, Pentecostals may well view the encounter of Peter and Cornelius as exemplifying and modeling contemporary interreligious encounter without forfeiting their traditional interpretation of key Book of Acts passages (viz. chapters 2, 8, 9, 10, and 19) as paradigmatic of Spirit baptism subsequent to conversion. Significantly, God was at work among people of a non-Christian religion through angels, visions, and the ministry of the Holy Spirit in a preparatory mode prior to the Church's explicit involvement. This incident thus provides a biblical window through which Pentecostals can look into contemporary theology of religions.

The title of this book, *Toward a Pentecostal Theology of Religions,* can supply clues as to the nature of this text. It suggests positive movement in the direction of a clear goal without presuming final arrival at the destination. It also identifies an unapologetically Pentecostal perspective.[40] However, that does not mean that this work is merely confessional, or proclaiming its own convictions without dialogue with others. Quite the converse, it does interact with others in explicit and intentional ways. For a few instances, it interacts occasionally and with more or less depth and frequency with great Continental theologians such as Karl Barth or Emil Brunner and United Kingdom theologians such as Lesslie Newbigin as well as

---

[37] French L. Arrington, *The Spirit-Anointed Church: A Study of the Acts of the Apostles* (Cleveland, TN: Pathway Press, 2008), p. 177.

[38] Arrington, *The Spirit-Anointed Church,* p. 178.

[39] Arrington, *The Spirit-Anointed Church,* p. 185.

[40] In this text 'Pentecostal' references diverse Christian groups who trace their historical origins to the global revival occurring around the turn of the twentieth century that included a restoration of pneumatological and charismatic experience involving, among other things, emphases on Spirit baptism subsequent to conversion and contemporary operation of spiritual gifts, including glossolalia, divine healing, and so on. See Tony Richie, *Speaking by the Spirit: A Pentecostal Model for Interreligious Dialogue* (Lexington, KY: Emeth Press, 2011), pp. 297-311.

great American theologians such as Reinhold Niebuhr. Most of all, it carries on an extended conversation (see below) with Jürgen Moltmann, one of the greatest contemporary theologians in the world. The influence of eighteenth-century British evangelist and theologian John Wesley and subsequent Wesleyanism on Pentecostal theology as a rule will be evident throughout as well. Nevertheless, this work noticeably focuses on Pentecostal theology and theologians, too numerous to mention here but usually identified within the text, with representatives from all over the globe, including the so-called two-thirds world. Yet I readily acknowledge my own North American orientation, specifically the southeastern United States, and do not doubt that it will be evident in what follows, perhaps in more ways than I myself might imagine.

Also, this text is not polemical. It does not debate all the fine points of different perspectives in proving or demonstrating a certain position vis-à-vis another. It does not aim to convince or defend respecting this or that particular school of thought. Neither does it pretend to be entirely objective or neutral in all its claims. This text does, of course, support its proposals with biblical and theological justification. As the last statement indicates, it is put forth primarily as a theology text; but, it at times employs insights from or makes applications regarding other disciplines, such as, for example, missiology (doctrine of the mission of the Church) or pastoral ministry.[41] Yet as a constructive and systematic theology text it does endeavor to remain congruent with the discipline's general approach to theological studies.

A Few Assumptions and Presuppositions

As a theology text, this book does not address, at least not directly or in depth, some of the traditional issues which with which Pentecostal theologians have been generally concerned as part of the movement's existential apologetic task. It does not focus on the Godhead (Trinitarian-Oneness debate), the full gospel (Jesus as savior, sanctifier, Spirit baptizer, healer, and soon coming king), or the

---

[41] In the spirit of J.C. Thomas, 'Pentecostal Theology in the Twenty-First Century', *Pneuma* 20.1 (1998), pp. 3-19.

relationship between regeneration, sanctification, and Spirit baptism, or between water baptism and Spirit baptism, or on speaking in tongues, divine healing, the gifted congregation, or on events surrounding Christ's second coming.[42] However, as the author of this text, I am not incognizant of or in any way contra-disposed regarding these issues and the contexts giving rise to their attention among Pentecostals. Quite the contrary, this background and its implications are assumed. Rather, there is an effort to focus on approaching the topic of Christian theology of religions as a Pentecostal adherent in a Pentecostal mode. (Key issues involved in this approach are enunciated in the next chapter.)

The task of Christian theology, very simply, may be thought of in several ways, including as providing a clear and comprehensive presentation of Christian doctrine, or translating Christian thought into the language of contemporary culture, or addressing important issues that arise for the Christian faith.[43] Often there is overlap. Nonetheless, this text might be best described as focusing on the third. Plainly put, the present book thinks and talks from a Pentecostal perspective about a variety of issues regarding the co-existence of multiple religious faiths and its immense implications for today's Christians. As David Ford rightly observes in his monumental work on contemporary theology and theologians, the complexity of the world today is such that it has become difficult to do Christian theology with integrity without addressing the reality of other religions.[44] It has been persuasively argued that 'the credibility of Christianity' for this generation is on the line in its response to religious plurality.[45]

Now it is time for a word about methodological presuppositions. Two themes inform the approach of this book. First, *continuity* with the classical Pentecostal tradition is a fundamental value. Second, *creativity* in addressing contemporary contexts of religious plurality is a motivating vision. In other words, this text consciously

---

[42] See Frank D. Macchia, 'Theology, Pentecostal', in *NIDPCM,* esp. pp. 1125-40.

[43] Daniel L. Migliore, *Faith Seeking Understanding: An Introduction to Christian Theology* (Grand Rapids: Eerdmans, 1991, 2004), p. 1.

[44] Ford, *The Modern Theologians*, pp. 13-14.

[45] Gavin D'Costa, 'Theology of Religions', in Ford (ed.), *The Modern Theologians*, p. 638.

endeavors to be faithful to the heritage of Pentecostalism while striving to meet a critical need in the wider world today regarding Christian understanding of other religions. In the words of the late Clark Pinnock, 'We are being called to strive for the dynamic equilibrium of continuity and creativity that characterizes great theology'.[46] Therefore, this text aims throughout at that kind of bi-lateral focus.

Accordingly, *Toward a Pentecostal Theology of Religions: Encountering Cornelius Today* assumes that it is possible, and desirable, to hold traditional Pentecostal Christian beliefs while wrestling honestly and humbly with the reality of non-Christian religions in the world today. Therefore, nothing herein is intended to be or should be construed to be in contradiction with, say, the Church of God 'Declaration of Faith', or, the Assemblies of God 'Statement of Fundamental Truths', or, the International Pentecostal Holiness 'Articles of Faith'. That being said, this text confronts straightforwardly the reality of non-Christian religions in the world and calls for a substantive Pentecostal response that probably pushes the boundaries for many of the uninitiated. Readers are encouraged and challenged to keep the latter thrust under the umbrella of the former commitment – as do I.

Addressing a few questions is appropriate at this point. As Ford says, 'the need for high quality public discourse within and between the religions as well as about them' has become increasingly obvious to almost all reputable Christian theologians today.[47] Yet just what does that mean? What is Christian theology of religions? What difference, if any, does it make to speak specifically of *Pentecostal* theology of religions? And, why should Pentecostals do theology of religions at all? Some understanding of the answers to these questions is necessary before proceeding to the main body of this work.

Most simply, as Veli-Matti Kärkkäinen explains, Christian theology of religions is that discipline which 'attempts to account theologically for the meaning and value of other religions', adding that 'Christian theology of religions attempts to think theologically about what it means for Christians to live with people of other

---

[46] Clark Pinnock, 'A Pilgrim on the Way', *Christianity Today* 42.2 (Feb 9, 1998) http://www.christianitytoday.com/ct/1998/february9/8t2043.html.
[47] Ford, *The Modern Theologians,* p. 14.

faiths and about the relationship of Christianity to other religions'.[48] Put another way, Daniel Migliore explains that 'Christian theology of religions has the distinctive theological task of asking about the place of the plurality of the world religions within the purposes of God made known in Jesus Christ'.[49] There are of course other definitions or descriptions of what is at stake in doing Christian theology of religions. However, these are helpful in providing clear and concise summaries. An assumption of the present text is that the Sovereign Lord's decision to allow other religions to continue to coexist has theological significance worth discovering.

Furthermore, as Migliore adds, 'A crucial aspect of this task is to clarify how it is possible to maintain the conviction that Jesus Christ is Lord and Savior of the world and at the same time to honor the integrity and value of other religions'.[50] In accomplishing that task, he suggests that Christian theology of religions should be guided by two principles that guard against abstraction on the one hand and relativism on the other hand. These principles involve, first, recognizing that *'there are real and not merely surface differences among the world religions'*, therefore making it essential to *'avoid abstract definitions of an essence common to all religion'*; and secondly, maintaining *'a particular faith perspective'* which will *'necessarily involve critical judgment'*.[51] There are of course other principles that might be proposed. However, these two do take seriously the particularity and universality of God's saving grace, and the polarities involved therein, and therefore provide helpful parameters for doing theology of religions.

Pentecostal theology of religions may be thought of as approaching this task in a particular pneumatological mode, that is, with an experience of and orientation toward the Holy Spirit specifically in mind.[52] In this day of oft times forceful and sometimes violent interfaith conflict (viz. post-911 religion-related terrorism), Pentecostal Christians, along with other Christians, have a moral

---

[48] Veli-Matti Kärkkäinen, *Trinity and Religious Pluralism: The Doctrine of the Trinity in Christian Theology of Religions* (Burlington, VT: Ashgate, 2004), p. 2.

[49] Migliore, *Faith Seeking Understanding*, p. 301.

[50] Migliore, *Faith Seeking Understanding*, p. 301.

[51] Migliore, *Faith Seeking Understanding*, pp. 304-306 (emphasis original).

[52] Amos Yong, *Discerning the Spirit(s), A Pentecostal-Charismatic Contribution to Christian Theology of Religions* (JPTSup 20; Sheffield, England: Sheffield Academic Press, 2000), pp. 29-31.

and spiritual obligation, according to the biblical and theological underpinnings of their faith and practice, to assess the existence of non-Christian religions and its implications for life and faith in this world.[53] Violence aside, authentic Pentecostal identity, as well as the prominent place of Pentecostalism in the world today, requires Pentecostals to articulate responsibly their theology of religions.[54]

Following this brief Introduction, Chapter 1 identifies and discusses key issues for Pentecostal theology of religions. What about the person and work of Christ (Christology), the relation of evangelism and interreligious dialogue (ecclesiology and missiology), or the salvation of the unevangelized (soteriology)? How does a distinctively Pentecostal approach to the Holy Spirit (pneumatology) and last things (eschatology) fit in with a Pentecostal theology of religions? Can the Holy Scriptures be a positive resource for Pentecostal theology of religions? These and other related issues are explored and developed. A trajectory for theological consistency in the remaining body of the work is also established.

Chapter 2 surveys the context of Pentecostal theology of religions in an effort to place Pentecostals in the overall discipline. Is there a consensus on categories or typologies? Where do Pentecostals fit in with their views of religious others? Does traditional Pentecostal theology serve as a resource for contemporary theology of religions? If so, then how? Again, these and several other themes are addressed in an effort not only to understand but also to undergird the discipline. This chapter is foundational for understanding the discipline of theology of religions from a Pentecostal perspective. It helps place important early Pentecostal leaders such as Charles Fox Parham and Bishop J.H. King at the fount of a stream of Pentecostal theology of religions.

Chapter 3 identifies developments and directions in contemporary Pentecostal theology of religions. Who are the leading thinkers? What are their particular contributions? Who are their significant partners? This chapter really gives an overall survey and evaluation of the main contours of Pentecostal theology of religions as it stands today through a look at the work of Clark Pinnock, J. Rod-

[53] Richie, *Speaking by the Spirit*, pp. 29-30.
[54] Yong, *Discerning*, p. 206.

man Williams, Veli-Matti Kärkkäinen, and Amos Yong, as well as others.

Chapter 4 outlines a constructive approach to doing Pentecostal theology of religions that issues forth into the practice of interreligious dialogue. Why should Pentecostals desire to be involved in interreligious dialogue? Even if they do so desire, how can they participate in a manner faithful to their own beliefs and practices? What is an appropriate model for Pentecostal dialogue? This chapter draws primarily upon my own previous work in the discipline. It suggests that Pentecostals can best do dialogue in a manner that is intentionally informed by the traditional practice of Pentecostal testimony as a model.

Chapter 5 endeavors to move forward in conversation with key dialogue partners. It selects two leading Pentecostals in the field of theology of religions for a continuing conversation: Veli-Matti Kärkkäinen and Amos Yong. Each of these has in some way interacted directly with my own work in theology of religions. This section will analyze and respond to these intersections of ideas in such a way as to propose progressive development for the discipline as a whole. The focus will be on, first, the next step forward for Pentecostal theology of religions, with a constructive theological proposal regarding the current (and long running) crisis in the Middle East, particularly its interreligious dynamics, and improving international Christian–Muslim relations, and second, on a theological vision of Christian witness in a pluralistic society that is in equal parts both robust and responsible.

Chapter 6 once again endeavors to move forward in conversation with key dialogue partners. However, it selects a non-Pentecostal in the field of theology of religions for a continuing conversation: Jürgen Moltmann. A leading contemporary theologian, Moltmann has made a significant impact on Pentecostal thought and practice, including theology of religions. However, Pentecostals have not carried on sustained engagement of his theology of religions; therefore, a small move in that direction is here attempted. As the next chapter (7) indicates, Moltmann has also interacted with my own work in that discipline and thus his interaction with me will form the basis for further discussion on my part. This section will focus on how Pentecostal theology of religions helpfully informs the universal–particular theological conundrum in constructive ways. However, the conversation with Moltmann in these two conversational chapters is not offered in the vein of critical or in-depth analysis so much as interactive theological reflections from a Pentecostal viewpoint.

Finally, the Conclusion briefly offers some specific discussion about issues lying ahead for Pentecostal theology of religions and for Pentecostal participation in interreligious dialogue. Sometimes earlier themes are interwoven and applied with this objective in mind. It does not claim to be a complete sampling but only representative possibilities. Yet it proposes some possibilities on the shape of dialogue with religious others from the perspective of Pentecostal theology. This conclusion focuses on some potential joint theological endeavors, qualifies the nature of the task of dialogue, and affirms the influence of freedom of religion and separation of Church and State in dealing with the reality of religious pluralism in contemporary society.

Before moving on to Chapter 1, the pressing importance of articulating a Christian theology of religions from a Pentecostal perspective ought to be underscored. Of course, if for no other reason than theological consistency and completeness, Pentecostal theologians, especially systematic and/or constructive theologians who by definition seek to apply to contemporary topics the theological teaching of the Bible and of the historic Christian faith, ought to address the relevant issues of the day. Along this line, Yong suggests that one of two 'essential conversations' for Christians in general and Pentecostals in particular is 'the dialogue between the Christian faith and the world's religious traditions'.[55] Why is it so important and urgent that Pentecostal theologians give attention to theology of religions? Among other things, globalization has contributed to the unprecedented co-existence in close proximity of peoples of cultural diversity and religious plurality.[56] Preparing Pentecostal believers to live and serve in this context requires an articulate response from Pentecostal theology.

---

[55] Yong, 'Academic Glossolalia? Pentecostal Scholarship, Multi-disciplinarity, and the Science–Religion Conversation', *JPT* 14.1 (October 2005), p. 65.
[56] Richie, *Speaking by the Spirit,* p. 11.

Admittedly, there are existing texts on theology of religions by, if not always for, Pentecostals.[57] Then some are by and for Pentecostals.[58] What is missing is an introductory text for Pentecostal theology of religions.[59] Filling a lacuna in this area is a purpose of the present volume. Accordingly, this is primarily an introductory and preliminary text on Pentecostal theology of religions. It endeavors to acquaint teachers and students, clergy and laity with basic ideas and directions in the developing discipline of Christian theology of religions from a Pentecostal perspective. At certain junctures it briefly points to more sophisticated implications. Especially toward the latter portions of the book there is some sustained theological discussion of a bit more advanced nature. Even here, however, the conversation is kept fairly straightforward. The language of this text is necessarily academic but undue technicalities are avoided where possible or clarified where necessary. Attentive readers can expect to finish with a firm grasp of the salient features of the field.

Brief Explanations

Finally, it will perhaps be helpful to define a few key terms in advance even though there is often further clarification later. 'Religious pluralism' has become a loaded term but actually has layers of meaning. Technically, 'pluralism' in relation to religions is commonly used in three distinct senses.[60] In a general sense pluralism describes the simple fact that multiple religions do exist in the world today. Every candid observer believes in religious pluralism in this broad sense. More specifically, religious pluralism can refer to a political system that acknowledges and allows diverse religious beliefs and practices within its purview. Democratic governments are

---

[57] E.g. Kärkkäinen, *Trinity and Religious Pluralism*.

[58] Yong's *Discerning the Spirit(s)* is the classic in the field. Also see Amos Yong, *Beyond the Impasse: Toward a Pneumatological Theology of Religions* (Grand Rapids: Baker, 2003); and *Hospitality and the Other: Pentecost, Christian Practices, and the Neighbor* (Mary Knoll, NY: Orbis, 2008). Most recently is Richie, *Speaking by the Spirit*.

[59] Veli-Matti Kärkkäinen's excellent *An Introduction to the Theology of Religions: Biblical, Historical, & Contemporary Perspectives* (Downers Grove, IL: InterVarsity Press, 2003), includes short sections on Charismatic and Pentecostal theologies of religions but is primarily an ecumenical overview.

[60] Ninian Smart, 'Pluralism', in D.W. Musser and J.L. Price (eds.), *New Handbook of Christian Theology*, (Nashville: Abingdon, 1992), pp. 360-64.

pragmatically pluralist in this sense. In the third and most specific
sense of the term, and which is a focus of this study, pluralism references any ideology affirming the more or less equal validity and
verity of all or almost all religions. Pentecostal Christians reject this
latter ideological version of religious pluralism as unbiblical and untenable.[61] Such religious pluralism is by definition radically relativist
and seriously reductionist; therefore, it is totally unacceptable in
terms of lack of commitments to divine revelation and absolute
truth (e.g. Jn 14.6; Acts 4.12).

The current text, true to its Pentecostal orientation, rejects the
ideology or philosophy of religious pluralism. It presents a firm and
viable alternative of understanding and responding to the realistic
fact of religious pluralism without succumbing to the relativistic
philosophy of religious pluralism. In sum, articulating a sound, that
is, a reasonable and defensible, biblical and theological alternative to
the fallacy of philosophical pluralism is a central task of this book.
Additionally, this work affirms freedom of religion, that is, the legal
and moral right of people to choose and practice their religion,
within appropriate ethical boundaries, or freely and voluntarily to
convert to another religion. It distinguishes religious freedom from
religious pluralism as it defines the former as 'the right for citizens
to practice the religion of their choice without interference', without
defending the view that all religions are equally valid.[62] With Ravi
Zacharias, the popular Christian apologist, it agrees that everyone
has a right to his or her belief without insisting that everything everyone believes is right.[63] Particularly, it renounces the use of any
kind of force or violence as a means of propagating or suppressing
any religion or its adherents.[64] Indeed, the model and mandate regarding co-existence with religious others may be expressed best in
the remarkable statement of a Hebrew prophet to a new convert

---

[61] See Richie, *Speaking by the Spirit,* Chapter 1, esp. pp. 22-29.
[62] See David K. Clark, 'Religious Pluralism and Christian Exclusivism', in
Francis J. Beckwith, William Lane Craig, and J.P. Moreland (eds.), *To Everyone an
Answer: A Case for the Christian Worldview: Essays in Honor of Norman L. Geisler,*
(Downers Grove, IL: InterVarsity Press, 2004), p. 292.
[63] Ravi Zacharias, 'Eastern Thought: The Chimera of Pantheism', in Beckwith, Craig, and Moreland (eds.), *To Everyone an Answer,* p. 311.
[64] Clark, 'Religious Pluralism and Christian Exclusivism', pp. 298-99.

regarding his continuing relationship with a pagan king: 'Go in peace' (2 Kgs 5.19).[65]

Overlapping interests of religious freedom and religious plural-ism characterize the United States, the immediate setting of this writing. Not only Christians, but also Jews were persecuted for their faith in the 'Old World' and some came to the 'New World' strug-gling for survival and hoping for freedom.[66] Early America was characterized by unprecedented religious diversity, although ac-companied by struggles with the confusion brought on by such un-accustomed freedom.[67] After years of debate, the fledgling nation decided in favor of freedom of religion amidst a diversity of reli-gions.[68] An ongoing tradition of defending religious freedom and defining religious pluralism has since become a lasting legacy of America's system of government.[69] With few exceptions, many con-temporary Americans express strong commitment to their religion and to the religious freedom of others.[70] Nevertheless, unfortunate-ly some groups, such as Native Americans and Asians of Buddhist, Confucian, or Taoist backgrounds, and even Jews, and African Americans were often considered outsiders at least partly because of their faith.[71] In principle, the American doctrine of freedom of religion applies to all faiths, but in practice it has at times been diffi-cult to apply evenly.

Two other important terms in theology of religions are some-times popularly confused with the pejorative of pluralism. One is 'universalism'. The other is 'inclusivism'. Universalism can be relat-ed to pluralism but should be distinguished from 'universality', which it is not. Inclusivism is actually an alternative to pluralism.

[65] Zacharias, 'Eastern Thought', p. 319.

[66] Jon Butler, 'Worlds Old and New', in Jon Butler, Grant Wacker, and Ran-dall Balmer (eds.), *Religion in American Life: A Short History* (Oxford/New York: Oxford University Press, 2008), p. 13.

[67] Jon Butler, 'The Flowering of Religious Diversity', in Butler, Wacker, and Balmer (eds.), *Religion in American Life,* pp. 73, 88.

[68] Jon Butler, 'Religion and the American Revolution', in Butler, Wacker, and Balmer (eds.), *Religion in American Life,* pp. 145-49.

[69] Randall Balmer, 'In God We Trust', in Butler, Wacker, and Balmer (eds.), *Religion in American Life,* pp. 343, 355.

[70] Randall Balmer, 'Religion for the New Millennium', in Butler, Wacker, and Balmer (eds.), *Religion in American Life,* p. 426.

[71] Grant Wacker, 'Sojourners at Home', in Butler, Wacker, and Balmer (eds.), *Religion in American Life,* pp. 212-29.

Much more is said in subsequent chapters about the classic exclu-sivist–inclusivist–pluralist typology prevalent in Christian theology of religions. For now it should suffice to explain that Christian in-clusivism is something of a *via media* between relativistic pluralism and rigid exclusivity.[72] In any case, it is certainly not synonymous with pluralism.

As for universalism versus universality, these two are quite dis-tinct. Universalism, which argues everyone will ultimately be saved, certainly may be associated with religious pluralism. However, uni-versality argues that some will in fact finally reject Christ and there-fore be eternally judged and damned but that none will do so with-out authentic opportunity to accept him.[73] As Pentecostal theologi-an Keith Warrington rightly notes, the latter is not a move toward universalism or a weakening of Christianity's uniqueness but rather an enlargement of the lordship of Jesus Christ.[74] Universality is clearly not pluralist in its assumptions or implications.

One caveat should be kept in mind. Global Pentecostalism is a diverse and multifaceted movement. It is not homogeneous. This text does not presume to speak for all Pentecostals. It does endeav-or to present a representative approach in keeping with the general contours of the movement's traditional commitments, especially from a Classical Pentecostal perspective.[75]

Conclusion

With the preceding firmly in mind, it should be reasonably possible to approach this work and follow the thematic development of the subsequent chapters in an informed and unbiased manner. Chapter 1, therefore, begins by emphasizing some essential points that must be kept in mind in order for any Pentecostal theology of religions to address authentically and consistently the challenging topic of Christian theology of religions in a manner consistent with its own traditional theological identity

---

[72] Richie, *Speaking by the Spirit,* pp. 86-87.
[73] Anderson, *Christianity and the World Religions,* pp. 162-69.
[74] Keith Warrington, *Pentecostal Theology: A Theology of Encounter* (New York: T & T Clarke, 2008), pp. 40-44 (p. 44).
[75] See n. 12 above.

1

KEY ISSUES FOR A PENTECOSTAL THEOLOGY OF RELIGIONS

Introduction

When the New Testament church was struggling with how to relate appropriately to their Gentile constituents, they convened what has been called the 'Jerusalem Council' (Acts 15). Pivotal to their eventual decision was Peter's reminder to the assembly of his encounter with Cornelius (vv. 7-9). After much discussion, and some intense debate as well, they felt that the Holy Spirit had given them specific guidance at a critical juncture. They explained: 'For it seemed good to the Holy Spirit, and to us, to lay upon you no greater burden than these necessary things' (15.28 NKJV). Then they gave a list of some essential points for amicable fellowship between Jewish and Gentile Christians. In the same vein the following list is offered, emphasizing that 'these necessary things' are essential points of careful consideration in order for any Pentecostal theology of religions to make the grade.

The Christological Center

Pentecostal Christians are completely and uncompromisingly committed to the absolute and utter uniqueness of Jesus Christ. As Arrington explains, Jesus is at the heart – literally at the center – of who Pentecostals are, of what they believe, and what they do.[1] They believe Jesus preexisted from all eternity, that he is God incarnate,

---

[1] French L. Arrington, *Christian Doctrine: A Pentecostal Perspective* (Cleveland, TN: Pathway Press, 1992-94), II, pp. 25-26.

fully divine and fully human, that his sacrificial death provides atonement for sins, and that he rose bodily from the dead and is coming again.[2] In short, Jesus alone is Lord and Savior.

Yet the centrality of Jesus in Pentecostal theology is more than veneration for his sovereign person or appreciation for his saving work. David Nichols represents Pentecostal sentiment well when he says, 'The Lord Jesus Christ is the central figure of all Christian reality; therefore, the truths about Him are central to Christianity'.[3] Christology (doctrine of Christ) is at the core of all Christian theology. In one sense, this assertion indicates that any theological endeavor worthy of the label 'Christian' must relate rightly to Christology.

The all-determinative issue of Christianity is still how one answers the pair of questions posed by Jesus, 'Who do people say the Son of Man is?' and 'Who do you say that I am?' (Mt. 16.13, 15) As Kärkkäinen puts it, the continuing task of Christology throughout each generation is 'to interpret the meaning and significance of Jesus Christ for our own times in light of biblical and historical developments'.[4] And he rightly adds that 'no study comes closer to the core of Christian life and theology than Christology'.[5] Kärkkäinen is also likely correct in contending that of all the challenges facing Christian theology none 'can compete with the urgency and seriousness of theology of religions, namely, the relation of Christianity to other religions' – with focus on Jesus Christ at the center of this struggle.[6] However, this situation is not necessarily lamentable; although it truly is 'most scary', it also may be 'the most fruitful' for Christian theology and for the mission of the Church.[7] The crucial point is to speak to other religions and contexts from out of the biblical and historic tradition of Christian theology and Christology,

---

[2] Arrington, *Christian Doctrine*, II, pp. 25-116.

[3] David R. Nichols, 'The Lord Jesus Christ', in Stanley M. Horton (ed.), *Systematic Theology* (Springfield, MO: Gospel Publishing House, rev. edn, 1995), p. 291.

[4] Veli-Matti Kärkkäinen, *Christology: A Global Introduction* (Grand Rapids: Baker Academic, 2003), p. 9.

[5] Kärkkäinen, *Christology*, p. 10.

[6] Kärkkäinen, *Christology*, p. 287.

[7] Kärkkäinen, *Christology*, p. 288.

not 'by overthrowing its distinctively Christian heritage' or by 'uncritically adopting any kind of new framework'.[8]

Therefore, an adequate theology of religions will retain and reinforce the centrality of Jesus Christ. Accordingly, it absolutely cannot compromise the fundamental confession that 'Jesus is Lord' (Rom. 10.9; 1 Cor. 12.3). Consequently, Pentecostal theologians emphatically and uniformly reject the radical pluralism of John Hick, a philosopher/theologian who prefers to speak of Christ's incarnation as 'myth' or 'metaphor'.[9] Hick's denial of the necessity of Christ's saving work (or atonement) for everyone recognizes other saviors, such as Mohammed, Krishna, and Buddha for some but is ultimately non-Christian and must be rejected accordingly.[10] The consensus is that Christological deficiencies of religious pluralism clearly disqualify it as an authentically Christian theological proposal. Therefore, Pentecostal theology of religions is set over against, that is, in opposition to and refutation of, theologies of religions operating from a basis of pluralistic assumptions.

Of course, it is incumbent upon careful theologians to distinguish Jesus Christ as Lord and Savior from the religion of Christianity, or from any other religion for that matter, as a means of salvation. No religion saves. As Evangelical professor of philosophy and theology David Clark rightly argues, 'No religion leads to God … Only following Jesus, by the Holy Spirit's power, leads to God. And that's not religion'.[11] For Pentecostals, salvation is about relationship with Jesus Christ, not about religion, not even Christian religion. This distinction is important to the extent that it forces the focus to remain always on Jesus Christ as the premier alternative to religious pluralism or religious exclusivism – or religion of any kind. Not only must Pentecostal theology of religions avoid the obvious pitfalls of religious pluralism but it must also avoid the more subtle

---

[8] Kärkkäinen, *Christology*, p. 289.

[9] E.g. Kärkkäinen, *Trinity*, pp. 113-17; Yong, *Beyond the Impasse*, pp. 24, 109-10, 123; and Frank D. Macchia, *Baptized in the Spirit: A Global Pentecostal Theology* (Grand Rapids: Zondervan, 2006), pp. 182-90. Contra John Hick, *The Metaphor of God Incarnate: Christology in a Pluralistic Age* (Louisville, KY: Westminster John Knox, 1993).

[10] Roger E. Olson, *The Mosaic of Christian Belief: Twenty Centuries of Unity & Diversity* (Downers Grove, IL: InterVarsity Press, 2002), pp. 252-53.

[11] See David K. Clark, 'Religious Pluralism and Christian Exclusivism', in Beckwith, Graig, and Moreland (eds.), *To Everyone an Answer*, p. 304.

problems of religious exclusivism. The former diffuses the presence of Christ among a host of rivals. The latter displaces Christ with a sole religion named after him. Thus the famous German theologian, Dietrich Bonhoeffer, martyred by the Nazi regime, argued that Jesus Christ is the essence of a Christianity that cannot be reduced to a religion.[12]

In sum, Pentecostal theology of religions always insists on the uniqueness of Jesus Christ. He alone is Lord and Savior. Whatever understanding of non-Christian faiths and of their founders Pentecostals entertain must be set against the criterion of the incomparable stature of the Lord Jesus Christ (Jn 14.6; Acts 4.12).[13] Any theology of religions model that undermines a high Christology must be rejected as too low for Pentecostal appropriation.

A Pneumatological Basis

Pentecostals unabashedly affirm and defend the continuing validity of the Day of Pentecost for encounter with the Holy Spirit today (Acts 2.1-4). Warrington suggests 'That which is central to being a Pentecostal is the desire to encounter the Spirit'.[14] Another Pentecostal theologian, Terry Cross, explains that encountering God's Spirit is experiencing God's presence and power in personal and moral transformation in an atmosphere of 'radical openness'.[15] Of course, Pentecostals' experiencing the Holy Spirit includes Spirit-inspired energy and spontaneity in worship and the exercise of spiritual gifts such as speaking in tongues, interpretation of tongues, prophesying, healing, and others.[16]

---

[12] Dietrich Bonhoeffer, 'Jesus Christ and the Essence of Christianity', Lecture December 11, 1928, in Dietrich Bonhoeffer, *A Testament to Freedom: Essential Writings of Dietrich Bonhoeffer* (ed. Geffrey B. Kelly and E. Burton Nelson; NY: HarperCollins, 1990, 1995), pp. 50-53.

[13] Tony Richie, 'Much More than a Man among Men: The Supreme Significance of Jesus Christ', *COGE* 97.12 (December 2007), pp. 6-7.

[14] Warrington, *Encounter,* p. 130.

[15] Terry L. Cross, *Answering the Call in the Spirit: Pentecostal Reflections on a Theology of Vocation, Work and Life* (Cleveland, TN: Lee University Press, 2007), pp. 14-16, 107.

[16] Veli-Matti Kärkkäinen, *Pneumatology: The Holy Spirit in Ecumenical, International, and Contextual Perspective* (Grand Rapids: Baker, 2002), pp. 89-92.

Additionally, pneumatology (doctrine of the Holy Spirit) is an important theologizing principle for Pentecostals. Macchia argues that the distinctive nature of Pentecostal theology is inherent in its approach to Spirit baptism and therefore shapes the process of doing theology.[17] To put it another way, Pentecostal theologian Steve Land describes Pentecostal pneumatological spirituality as doing and living theology.[18] Pentecostal pneumatology is not simply a few extra add-ons about Spirit baptism and spiritual gifts inserted arbitrarily somewhere into the systematic study of theology; rather, it is foundational to all of Christian life and thought. Consequently, a valid Pentecostal theology of religions must be faithful to its unique pneumatological orientation.

In fact, for theology to be fully *Christian* it must cohere with 'the Christian concept of a trinitarian God – the Father, Son, and Holy Spirit', which of course requires appropriate attention to pneumatology.[19] Accordingly, Christian theology of religions must account for its pneumatological implications. A robust pneumatology includes attention to implications of the Spirit's work in 'creation and re-creation', that is, in the world as the natural created order and in the Church as the new creation in Christ.[20] Theologizing about the Spirit's work in the world beyond the Church implies attention to, among other things, the ontological reality of other religions. Of course, as Steve Land rightly notes, to speak of 'the universal character' of Pentecostal presence does not mean that people can access the Spirit whenever they want for whatever purposes they want.[21]

---

[17] Macchia, *Spirit Baptism,* pp. 11-18.

[18] Steven J. Land, *Pentecostal Spirituality: A Passion for the Kingdom* (JPTSup 1; Sheffield: Sheffield Academic Press, 1993), pp. 23-37.

[19] John R. Higgins, Michael L. Dunsing, and Frank D. Tallman, *An Introduction to Theology: A Classical Pentecostal Perspective* (Dubuque, Iowa: Kendall/Hunt, 1993), p. 123. For Pentecostals, this can be a complicated statement. A minority wing of Pentecostalism is Oneness or non-trinitarian in its theology. See David A. Reed, 'Oneness Pentecostalism', in *NIDPCM,* pp. 936-44. Reed concludes that 'OP is best described as a heterodox expression of Christianity whose relationship to the wider Christian community is at present ambivalent' (p. 944). For present purposes, judgment is not passed on the Christian (or Pentecostal) identity (or eternal destiny) of Oneness Pentecostals; however, it is frankly acknowledged that trinitarian theology is the historically orthodox Christian position.

[20] Arrington, *Christian Doctrine,* III, pp. 29-31.

[21] Related by Henry H. Knight III, *Is There a Future for God's Love: An Evangelical Theology* (Nashville: Abingdon Press, 2012), pp. 100-101 and 177 n. 25.

The Spirit is still sovereign (Jn 3.8). Nonetheless, Pentecostal Christianity must particularly explore and explain its own similarities to and differences from other Abrahamic or monotheistic religions such as Judaism and Islam.[22] That process inevitably involves doing theology of religions and requires explicit attention to pneumatology.

Critically important is underscoring the fact that Pentecostals' emphasis on the Holy Spirit in no way diminishes the Christological center of their faith because 'in the power of the Holy Spirit, the focus is on Jesus Christ and God'.[23] Cross explains that Pentecostal pneumatology does not displace Christology but rather provides a framework for testifying of the redemption that is in Christ.[24] Land probably puts it best for many Pentecostals when he says, 'Jesus Christ is the center and the Holy Spirit is the circumference'.[25] Christology and pneumatology seamlessly complement and complete each other. As Yves Congar succinctly expresses it, there is 'no pneumatology without Christology and no Christology without pneumatology'.[26] The Holy Spirit is always the Spirit of Christ, so there should never be a suggestion of rivalry or forced dichotomy between Jesus and his Spirit (Jn 15.26-27; 1 Pet. 1.11).[27]

Unfortunately, some who are apparently uncomfortable with pneumatology in general and with Pentecostals in particular falsely accuse Pentecostal pneumatological theology of religions of divorcing Christ and the Spirit or Christology and pneumatology; but, the charge is demonstrably false.[28] Fortunately, a number of non-

---

[22] Higgins, Dunsing, and Tallman, *An Introduction to Theology*, pp. 16-17.

[23] Richie, *Speaking by the Spirit*, p. 300.

[24] Terry L. Cross, 'A Proposal to Break the Ice': What Can Pentecostal Theology Offer Evangelical Theology?' *JPT* 11.2 (2002), p. 71.

[25] Land, *Pentecostal Spirituality*, p. 23.

[26] Yves Congar, *The Word and the Spirit* (trans. David Smith; San Francisco: Harper & Row, 1986), p. 1.

[27] Tony Richie, 'The Wide Reach of the Spirit: A Renewal Theology of Mission and Interreligious Encounter in Dialogue with Yves Congar', in Yong and Clarke (eds.), *Global Renewal*, pp. 52-54.

[28] James R.A. Merrick, 'The Spirit as Agent in False Religions? A Critique of Amos Yong's Pneumatological Theology of Religions with Reference to Current Trends', *Trinity Journal* 29.1 (Spring 2008), pp. 107-25; and Tony Richie, 'The Spirit of Truth as Guide into All Truth: A Response to James R.A. Merrick's "The Spirit as Agent in False Religions? A Critique of Amos Yong's Pneumatological Theology of Religions with Reference to Current Trends"', *Cyberjournal for*

Pentecostal theologians are recognizing that all too often 'the work of the Holy Spirit is neglected, or when it is included, it is not always related to the work of Christ'.[29] Conversely, an authentic Pentecostal theology of religions will accent the pneumatic for a fully and truly trinitarian vision.

An Ecclesiological Locus

For Pentecostals, no human institution or organization can begin to compare to the Church in terms of the importance of its place in God's eternal purpose for human beings. In fact, Pentecostals do not think of the Church so much as an organization as they do as an organism – a living body with Christ as its head (Eph. 1.22-23).[30] The Church as an institution is created by God and progressively formed throughout redemption history by saving grace in Christ.[31] At a profound level, the Church is a fellowship with the Triune God: God the Father (1 Jn 1.6), God the Son (1 Cor. 1.9), and God the Holy Spirit (2 Cor. 13.13). This divine 'fellowship', much deeper than close association or camaraderie, is *koinonia,* a reciprocal sharing together or mutual participation in the life of God by all believers, made possible by the redemption in Jesus Christ and given and sustained by the Holy Spirit.[32] God's Church is therefore distinctly set apart from all other religious institutions or organizations by its inherent identity.

Contrary to anecdotal stereotypes, as Pentecostal historian Dale Coulter has demonstrated, some early Pentecostal groups had a strong sense of the importance of ecclesiology (doctrine of the

Pentecostal-Charismatic Research 19 (January 2010), http://www.pctii.org/cyberj/cyberj19/ richie.html.

[29] Migliore, *Faith Seeking Understanding,* p. 316.

[30] William W. Menzies and Stanley M. Horton, *Bible Doctrines: A Pentecostal Perspective* (Springfield, MO: Gospel Publishing House, 1993, 1994), p. 175.

[31] Guy P. Duffield and Nathan M. Van Cleave, *Foundations of Pentecostal Theology* (Los Angeles: L.I.F.E. Bible College, 1983, 1987), pp. 417-20, and Arrington, *Christian Doctrine,* III, p. 166.

[32] French L. Arrington, 'Ecclesiology and the Great Commission', in Raymond Culpepper (ed.), *The Great Commission Connection* (Cleveland, TN: Pathway Press, 2011), pp. 107-109.

Church).[33] Indeed, Pentecostals believe inclusion in the Church's nature and destiny involves blessings that are 'spiritual, heavenly, and eternal'.[34] True, the Church is not thought of in salvific terms, that is, it is not in and of itself the dispenser or mediator of salvation – only Jesus can rightfully claim that role; however, it nurtures and sustains Christian faith and life through the crucial corporate dimension of Christian experience.[35] Furthermore, since the New Testament church was 'Pentecostal by nature', not in a sectarian sense but in that it was 'a fellowship led and empowered by the Holy Spirit', then the Church today is called to conform to that pattern as well.[36]

As Pentecostal New Testament scholar John Christopher Thomas notes, Pentecostal ecclesiology is best understood set in the context of a theology that shapes and informs it in significant ways, a theology commonly known as the 'full gospel'.[37] The full gospel involves five foundational motifs: Jesus as Savior, Sanctifier, Holy Spirit Baptizer, Healer, and Soon Coming King. The Church therefore may be seen as Redeemed Community, Holy Community, Empowered Community, Healing Community, and Eschatological Community with the 'accompanying sacramental signs' of Water Baptism, Footwashing, Glossolalia, Anointing with Oil, and the Lord's Supper, respectively.[38] Against this backdrop, dynamic charismatic spirituality is at the center of church life with emphases on experiencing God's presence in worship and empowerment for Christian living.[39]

Pentecostal theology distinguishes between the Church and the Kingdom of God.[40] The Church and the Kingdom are related but

---

[33] Dale Coulter, 'The Development of Ecclesiology in the Church of God (Cleveland, TN), A Forgotten Contribution?' *Pneuma* 29.1 (2007), pp. 59-85.

[34] E.S. Williams, *Systematic Theology: Volume 3* (Springfield, MO: Gospel Publishing House, 1953), p. 107.

[35] Michael L. Dusing, 'The New Testament Church', in Horton, *Systematic Theology*, p. 525.

[36] Arrington, 'Ecclesiology and the Great Commission', p. 111.

[37] John Christopher Thomas, 'Introduction', in John Christopher Thomas (ed.), *Toward a Pentecostal Ecclesiology: The Church and the Fivefold Gospel* (Cleveland, TN: CPT Press, 2010), p. 4.

[38] Thomas, 'Introduction', p. 4.

[39] Veli-Matti Kärkkäinen, *An Introduction to Ecclesiology: Ecumenical, Historical & Global Perspectives* (Downers Grove, IL: InterVarsity Press, 2002), pp. 70-71.

[40] Higgins, Dunsing, and Tallman, *An Introduction to Theology*, pp. 163-64.

not synonymous.[41] As Land says, the 'kingdom of God is larger than the church'.[42] This means that the Kingdom of God references a broader, more inclusive reality of God's reign throughout the ages and throughout the cosmos while the Church more narrowly references those who have been specifically spiritually reborn through faith in Jesus Christ.[43] Therefore, the Church is part of the Kingdom of God but the Kingdom of God is not limited to the Church.[44] Another way of saying it is that the Kingdom of God is 'the overarching reality' of which the Church is 'an expression'.[45] Accordingly, Pentecostals can affirm that in some sense 'God is at work outside of the Church as well as within and through it'.[46] Obviously, this observation calls for developing a responsible theology of religions.

The multiple and complex themes of ecclesiology, the Kingdom of God, and theology of religions can be integrated by understanding that 'the fulfillment of the kingdom of God has as its central locus the life of the church, but is not confined to it'.[47] According to Macchia, the Church as the locus of Christ and of the Spirit does not negate God's gracious and righteous work in the wider creation but rather extends and sustains it.[48] Therefore, Pentecostal theology of religions asserts intense activity and concentration of divine redemptive attention on the Church simultaneously with refusing to restrict or limit God. As Orlando Costas puts it, the Church is the penultimate goal but not the ultimate goal.[49] On the one hand, the Church must never be reduced to merely one among many religious institutions or organizations. It is uniquely the place where God's Spirit is at work through Christ in the world and for the world to God's glory and honor. On the other hand, the Church must never raise itself to a place usurping God's prerogative to work in God's

---

[41] Higgins, Dunsing, and Tallman, *An Introduction to Theology*, p. 163.
[42] Land, *Pentecostal Spirituality*, p. 224.
[43] Higgins, Dunsing, and Tallman, *An Introduction to Theology*, pp. 163-64.
[44] Higgins, Dunsing, and Tallman, *An Introduction to Theology*, p. 163.
[45] Raymond F. Culpepper, *The Great Commission: The Solution* ... (Cleveland, TN: Pathway Press, 2009), p. 37.
[46] Culpepper, *The Great Commission*, p. 38.
[47] Macchia, *Spirit Baptism*, p. 128.
[48] Macchia, *Spirit Baptism*, p. 175. See also pp. 188 and 196.
[49] Orlando Costas, *The Integrity of Mission: The Inner Life and Outreach of the Church* (New York: Harper and Row, 1979), pp. 56-57.

own creation according to God's own good pleasure and purpose to ultimately relate all things to Jesus Christ (Eph. 1.3-10). Finally, as Kärkkäinen well says, since the Church in the third millennium faces the challenges of relating to other faiths, 'ecclesiology can no longer accomplish its purposes in isolation from the rest of the world's religiosity'.[50] Christian systematic theology's obligation to account for the claims of other faiths places a special burden and responsibility upon its ecclesiology. Therefore, Pentecostal theology appropriately stresses the distinctive and continuing relevance of ecclesiology for its theology of religions.

A Missiological Setting

For Pentecostals, mission is the chief reason the Church exists. Ecclesiology and missiology are not only interrelated but inseparably linked. In fact, as Pentecostal missionary and educator Richard Waldrop observes, ecclesial mission is derivative of theology proper (doctrine of God) in that the Church's mission is reflective of the divine nature.[51] Thus it would probably be close to impossible to overstate the importance Pentecostals attach to the mission of the Church. Pentecostal missiologists Julie Ma and Wonsuk Ma affirm that ultimately mission belongs to God (*missio Dei*) and it describes God's plan to restore fallen creation, including humanity, through God's invitation to humans to participate in the working out of that divine purpose.[52] Pentecostal missions are driven, first, by a distinctive pneumatological orientation, and second, by a sense of eschatological urgency.[53] The latter has resulted in an emphasis on evangelism; the former is showing ability to incorporate other thrusts over time.[54] With this dynamic duo as motivators for mission, Pentecos-

---

[50] Kärkkäinen, *An Introduction to Ecclesiology*, p. 233.
[51] Richard E. Waldrop, 'The Triune God in Salvation History: Pentecostal Perspectives on Holistic Church Mission Today', in S.J. Land, R.D. Moore, and J.C. Thomas (eds.), *Passover, Pentecost, & Parousia: Studies in Celebration of the Life and Ministry of R. Hollis Gause* (JPTSup 35; Blandford Forum, UK: Deo, 2010), pp. 228-30.
[52] Julie C. Ma and Wonsuk Ma, *Mission in the Spirit: Towards a Pentecostal/Charismatic Missiology* (Regnum Studies in Mission; Eugene, OR: Wipf & Stock, 2010), p. 6. See also p. 286.
[53] Ma and Ma, *Mission in the Spirit*, p. 9.
[54] Ma and Ma, *Mission in the Spirit*, p. 9.

talism is equipped and prepared to embrace a broad range of missiological options without diminishing existing emphases.

Arrington insists that evangelistic witness continues to be the
Church's primary and foremost task.[55] Perhaps it is a small wonder
that Pentecostals are reputed to be the most aggressive and active
evangelists and missionaries ever.[56] Significantly, Pentecostals understand their evangelistic fervor and effectiveness to be a direct
result of their distinctive experience of Spirit baptism (cf. Acts
1.8).[57] Furthermore, Pentecostals believe that Christology and the
Great Commission (Mt. 28.18-20; Mk 16.15-18; Lk. 24.46-48; Jn
20.21) are closely connected.[58] Pentecostal New Testament scholar
John Christopher Thomas explains that the mandate of the Great
Commission 'finds its grounding, being, and sustenance' in Christology.[59] Accordingly, Pentecostal missiology is remarkably evangelistic, pneumatological, and Christological.

However, Pentecostals understand the mission of the Church to
include elements other than the task of evangelism. For example,
Higgins, Dusing, and Tallman enumerate four specific aspects of
the Church's mission: evangelization of the unsaved, worship of
God, edification of the saints, and social concern.[60] Interestingly,
they belabor the point that balance must be maintained among all
of these 'essential aspects' of mission.[61] Pentecostal educator Byron
Klaus combines their first and last aspects into a single category of
service to the world but otherwise emphasizes the essentiality of all
of them as well.[62] While on the surface Pentecostal missiology may
seem almost entirely evangelistic, a closer inspection suggests more
complexity and diversity. It is against this background that Pentecostal theology of religions lifts up a place for interreligious dialogue in ecclesial mission.

[55] Arrington, *Christian Doctrine*, III, pp. 197, 199.
[56] Grant L. McLung, Jr., 'Evangelism', in *NIDPCM*, pp. 617-20.
[57] Richie, *Speaking by the Spirit*, p. 102.
[58] John Christopher Thomas, 'According to John: Christology and the Great
Commission', in Culpepper (ed.), *Great Commission Connection*, pp. 53-76.
[59] Thomas, 'Christology and the Great Commission', p. 75.
[60] Higgins, Dusing, and Tallman, *An Introduction*, pp. 175-76.
[61] Higgins, Dusing, and Tallman, *An Introduction*, p. 177.
[62] Byron D. Klaus, 'The Mission of the Church', in Horton (ed.), *Systematic
Theology*, pp. 590-94.

Pentecostal scholar Shane Clifton and Roman Catholic Neil Ormerod argue that in today's context interreligious dialogue is one of the most pressing tasks for ecclesial mission.[63] They argue that the challenge of the Church is to decide on the role it will play, for good or for ill, in confronting conflict between the religions.[64] Additionally, they conclude that what is needed is 'a more thoroughgoing theology (or theologies) of religions that facilitates interreligious dialogue and understanding'.[65] Likewise, Julie and Wonsuk Ma suggest that Pentecostal missions carefully assess and address interreligious concerns.[66] Pentecostal theology of religions calls for ecumenical and interreligious dialogue as part of Christian mission.[67] Understanding the worldview of other religions can be critical for carrying out Christian mission, which requires study and dialogue as well.[68]

Important to note is that evangelism and dialogue are not mutually exclusive; rather, they function together as part of a holistic approach to ecclesial mission.[69] Arguably, Pentecostal mission is holistic by definition, interpretation, and application, for its ground and goal is *shalom* – God's wholeness for humanity.[70] Donald Miller and Ted Yamamori indicate that many contemporary Pentecostals engage the world through just such a broad-based Christian mission that includes, without minimization, evangelism and witness, but also embraces social aspects of ministry that, among other things, can include dialogue and cooperation with others.[71] Consequently, Pentecostal theology of religions does not limit the Church's mission but rather enlarges it. The mission of the Pentecostal movement continues to be evangelistic, pneumatological, and Christolog-

---

[63] Neil J. Ormerod and Shane Clifton, *Globalization and the Mission of the Church* (New York: T & T Clark, 2009), p. 141.

[64] Ormerod and Clifton, *Globalization and the Mission of the Church*, p. 177.

[65] Ormerod and Clifton, *Globalization and the Mission of the Church*, p. 178.

[66] Ma, *Mission in the Spirit*, pp. 97, 279, and 283.

[67] Richie, *Speaking by the Spirit*, pp. 102-103. Cf. Ma, *Mission in the Spirit*, p. 10.

[68] Ma, *Mission in the Spirit*, pp. 111-14.

[69] G. Howard Mellor, 'Evangelism and Religious Pluralism in the Wesleyan Tradition', in James C. Logan (ed.), *Theology and Evangelism in the Wesleyan Heritage* (Nashville: Kingswood Books, 1994), pp. 120-26.

[70] Waldrop, 'Holistic Church Mission Today', p. 331.

[71] Donald E. Miller and Tetsunao Yamamori, *Global Pentecostalism: The New Face of Christian Social Engagement* (Los Angeles: University of California Press, 2007), pp. 1-3.

ical while becoming more engaged and dialogical with other com-
munities. Yet nothing new is added. Rather, the challenge for the
Church is to adapt and apply its mission authentically to present
circumstances. As Klaus contends, 'each generation must attain a
fresh appreciation for the mission and purposes around which they
center their identity'.[72] This statement may be appreciatively applied
to Pentecostal theology of religions' missiological methodology.
Accordingly, a coherent and consistent Pentecostal theology of religions will thus stress a holistic missiology.

A Soteriological Focus

Pentecostal theology of religions emphatically affirms the distinctive nature and necessity of Christian salvation. One of the concerns that Pentecostal theology has with the ideology of religious
pluralism is its dangerous tendency to redefine Christian salvation
in terms acceptable to non-Christian religions.[73] Pentecostals believe salvation from sin and its consequences is essential, that it is
the provision of Christ's atonement personally experienced through
faith, and that it graciously imparts the gift of eternal life and includes present commitment to lived discipleship (Jn 3.16; Mt.
28.19).[74] And Christian salvation is always inextricably tied to Jesus
Christ as Savior (Jn 3.18; 20.31).[75] For Pentecostal theologian Hollis
Gause, terms such as repentance of sin, justification or forgiveness,
reconciliation, adoption and regeneration, assurance, sanctification,
and glorification describe literal experiences in the soteriological
journey.[76] In other words, the concept of salvation is not simply
some religious symbol; it is the actual experience of God's reconciling love in Christ (2 Cor. 5.17-6.2). Accordingly, it is appropriate to
describe salvation, as does Land, as 'a passion for God who is at

---

[72] Miller and Yamamori, *Global Pentecostalism,* p. 567.
[73] Paul Copan, 'Following a Unique Christ in a Pluralist Society', *Enrichment
Journal* (Fall 2008) http://enrichmentjournal.ag.org/200804/_040_Pluralistic.cfm.
[74] Arrington, *Christian Doctrine,* II, p. 159.
[75] See Larry Sterling, Jr., 'Our Only Hope in a Pluralistic World', *COGE* 97.12
(December 2007), pp. 8-9.
[76] R. Hollis Gause, *Living in the Spirit: The Way of Salvation* (Cleveland, TN:
Pathway Press, 1980). Cf. Duffield and Van Cleave, *Foundations of Pentecostal Theology,* pp. 206-60.

work in all things moving history into the consummation'.[77] There-fore, neither can Christian salvation be defined by non-Christian religions nor its essence altered to accommodate or placate them.

With philosopher and apologist Paul Copan, Pentecostals resist religious pluralists' efforts, under the disguise of tolerance, to rede-fine in non-biblical terms the truth of Christianity and the salvation it proclaims, including the universal need of conversion.[78] Pentecos-tals evangelistically proclaim the gospel of Jesus Christ to the world out of their conviction that conversion through faith in Christ is of ultimate salvific significance for the eternal destiny of every human being.[79] This perception of the ultimate and eternal significance of salvation explains why Pentecostal theology presents soteriology (doctrine of salvation) not as simply one doctrine among many but rather as interwoven with all the major doctrines of Christianity.[80] Put more picturesquely, Pentecostal theologian Daniel Pecota ar-gues that Christ's saving work is 'the central pillar' bearing the weight of 'God's redemptive temple', or 'the hub' around which all of divine revelation revolves.[81] Significantly, Menzies and Horton suggest that the eternal character of Christianity's doctrine of salva-tion gives it a distinctive place 'among the religions of the world'.[82] And Christian salvation involves conversion to Christ.[83]

One of the most controversial issues that confront any Christian theology of religions is the matter of the 'fate of the unevangelized', that is, those who do not hear the gospel 'through no fault of their

---

[77] Land, 'Pentecostal Spirituality', *JPT*, p. 33.

[78] Paul Copan, *True for You, But Not for Me: Overcoming Objections to Christian Faith* (Bloomington, MN: Bethany House, 2009), pp. 26-31.

[79] Stanley M. Horton, *What the Bible Says about the Holy Spirit* (Springfield, MO: Gospel Publishing House, 1992), pp. 135-37; and Arrington, *Christian Doctrine*, II, pp. 209-10.

[80] Higgins, Dunsing, and Tallman, *An Introduction to Theology*, pp. 97-98. For a dynamic integrative view of Pentecostal soteriology and spirituality, see Land, *Pentecostal Spirituality*, p. 46. Also, Edmund J. Rybarczyk, *Beyond Salvation: Eastern Orthodoxy and Classical Pentecostalism on Becoming Like Christ* (Waynesboro, GA: Pat-ernoster Press, 2004), suggests that Pentecostal views of salvation and spirituality may share much in common with Eastern Christianity.

[81] Daniel B. Pecota, 'The Saving Work of Christ', in Horton (ed.), *Systematic Theology*, pp. 325-73, esp. p. 325.

[82] Menzies and Horton, *Bible Doctrines*, p. 97.

[83] Menzies and Horton, *Bible Doctrines*, pp. 102-108.

own'.[84] The final fate of non-Christians who pass from this world without having specifically or authentically heard the gospel is a difficult but legitimate topic of discussion for theology of religions. Furthermore, the manner in which Pentecostals address this thorny theme has obvious and immense implications for self-identity and activity in the world and toward the world's religions. The contention of this text is that Pentecostal theology of religions must address the question of the salvation of devout non-Christians who have not received Christ but neither have they personally rejected Jesus in a manner consistent with Pentecostals' own innermost core convictions about Christian salvation.

Accordingly, Pentecostal theology of religions lifts up the distinctive nature and necessity of Christian salvation in an environment of wrestling sensitively with the reality of unevangelized peoples. It draws on the rich resources resident in Pentecostal theology and spirituality to address contemporary challenges confronting a fallen humanity in need of divine redemption that is provided only and solely in and of the Lord Jesus Christ. With Simon Peter, it asks, 'Lord, to whom shall we go?' and immediately answers with him as well, 'You have the words of eternal life. And we [ἡμεῖς is emphatic] have believed and have come to know that You are the Holy One of God' (Jn 6.68-69 NASB). And with Peter, it understands that, 'He is patient with you, not wanting anyone to perish, but everyone to come to repentance' (2 Pet. 3.9). Therefore, an adequate and acceptable approach to Pentecostal theology of religions will, with honesty and humility, remain firmly committed to the distinctive nature and necessity of Christian salvation as it explores the

---

[84] Something of the significance of this topic may be discovered by noting a spate of books covering it, e.g. Gregory A. Boyd and Paul R. Eddy, *Across the Spectrum: Understanding Issues in Evangelical Theology* (Grand Rapids: Baker Academic, 2002), ch. 12, 'The Destiny of the Unevangelized Debate', pp. 178-92; William V. Crockett and James G. Sigountos (eds.), *Through No Fault of their Own? The Fate of Those Who Have Never Heard* (Grand Rapids: Baker, 1991); Millard J. Erickson, *How Shall They Be Saved? The Destiny of Those Who Do Not Hear of Jesus* (Grand Rapids: Baker, 1996); Stanley N. Gundry *et al.* (eds.), *Four Views on Salvation in a Pluralistic World* (Grand Rapids: Zondervan, 1995); John Sanders, *No Other Name: An Investigation into the Destiny of the Unevangelized* (Grand Rapids: Eerdmans, 1992); and Gabriel Fackre, Ronald H. Nash, and John Sanders, *What About Those Who Have Never Heard: Three Views on the Destiny of the Unevangelized* (Downers Grove, IL: InterVarsity, 1995).

implications thereof for the unevangelized and devout devotees of other religions.

An Eschatological Lens

Pentecostals believe fervently in the literal return of Jesus Christ and the consummation of history according to God's eternal purpose for creation. Eschatology (doctrine of last things) is more than a key doctrinal category for Pentecostals. It is a driving force in their theology and spirituality as well as in their missiology. The entire Pentecostal worldview is shaped by a self-understanding that they are humble recipients of 'the last days' outpouring of the Holy Spirit (Acts 2.14-21 is paradigmatic). In other words, eschatology is a lens through which Pentecostals view reality. As William Faupel argues, eschatology was critical in the dramatic origination of the Pentecostal movement and remains essential for understanding its ongoing development.[85] Pentecostal theology of religions is complete without accounting for its eschatological aspects and their implications.

Steven Jack Land argues that Pentecostal identity, through a dynamic interrelatedness of Pentecostal theology, spirituality, and missiology, is expressed in eschatological passion for the Kingdom of God.[86] Pentecostal eschatology is premillennial and apocalyptic, stressing the literal and imminent return of Jesus Christ and the dramatic teleological consummation of human history in and through Christ, but also embracing the power and sovereignty of God as the Holy Spirit 'brings the life of the kingdom into the present' so that 'passivity and cultural pessimism are minimized as people are empowered for ministry'.[87] In Pentecostal eschatology there is constant interplay between living for the end with hope and serving in the present with power.[88] As Land says, 'the power of the kingdom to come is at work through the Holy Spirit to make all

---

[85] D. William Faupel, *The Everlasting Gospel: The Significance of Eschatology in the Development of Pentecostal Thought* (JPTSup 10; Sheffield: Sheffield Academic Press, 1996).

[86] Land, *Pentecostal Spirituality*.

[87] Land, *Pentecostal Spirituality*, p. 224.

[88] Land, *Pentecostal Spirituality*, pp. 61-64.

places and times serve the glory of God'.[89] For Pentecostals, revelation, history, and the Kingdom of God are closely interconnected.[90] In this now-not-yet eschatology, believers are already living in the energy of the inauguration of the Kingdom that is nevertheless not yet in its full and final form of consummation.[91] Finally, a passion for the Kingdom of God is ultimately in reality a passion for God.[92]

Pentecostal theology of religions must faithfully interpret and apply an inaugurated eschatology through a vision for personal and social transformation. As Pentecostal theologian Peter Althouse argues, Pentecostal eschatology should 'allow Pentecostals to engage the world in a socially responsible manner'.[93] Obviously, 'passive resignation in the face of world destruction is dangerous, both theologically and politically'.[94] Through its eschatology Pentecostal theology can move from 'isolation to inclusion, from separation to ecumenism and from otherworldly preoccupation to transformation'.[95] Accordingly, Pentecostal eschatology provides important impetus for Pentecostal theology of religions.

Along with many other Christians, Pentecostals desire to 'be blameless and holy in the presence of our God and Father when our Lord Jesus comes with all his holy ones' (1 Thess. 3.13 NIV). Among other things, this means acting wisely and responsibly toward neighbors of other faiths in the understanding that Christians will be accountable for cooperating with God's ultimate purpose regarding them – as Jesus taught in the Parable of the Good Samaritan (Lk. 10.30-37). Oft times acting responsibly toward religious others through living presently in light of the eschaton will involve doing evangelism in truthful love. At other times, it will require ministering compassionately and generously to physical needs during catastrophes or crises. On still other occasions, it will call forth some form of dialogue and/or cooperation carried out in sincere humility. In any case, heartfelt belief that Christ is coming again to

---

[89] Land, *Pentecostal Spirituality*, p. 93.
[90] Land, *Pentecostal Spirituality*, Chapter 2.
[91] Land, *Pentecostal Spirituality*, pp. 44, 46.
[92] Land, *Pentecostal Spirituality*, Chapter 4.
[93] Peter Althouse, *The Spirit of the Last Days: Pentecostal Eschatology in Conversation with Jürgen Moltmann* (JPTSup 25; New York: T & T Clarke, 2003), p. 196.
[94] Althouse, *Spirit of the Last Days*, p. 196.
[95] Althouse, *Spirit of the Last Days*, p. 197.

judge and redeem humanity according to God's holy purpose moti-
vates and empowers service in and to the world. Therefore, Pentecostal theologians of religions look at the world's religions through
an eschatological lens.

A Biblical Structure

Pentecostals are committed to the Bible as the inspired and authoritative Word of God. Every doctrine and practice must be evaluated
and endorsed in the light of the Scriptures – or else rejected as un-
reliable. Pentecostal historian Charles Conn noted that early Pentecostals reacted against an intellectual climate which placed the views
of rationalistic philosophers above faith in the Bible.[96] Centuries
earlier John Wesley famously said,

> I want to know one thing, the way to heaven; how to land safe
> on that happy shore. God Himself has condescended to teach
> the way; for this end He came from heaven. He hath written it
> down in a book. Give me that book! At any price give me the
> Book of God! Here is knowledge enough for me. Let me be *ho-
> mo unius libri.*[97]

'Let me be a man of one book!' This does not mean to read only
one book, even if that one book is the Bible. Rather, it indicates
that only the Bible should hold supreme sway over one's life. Contemporary Pentecostals concur. Thus Arrington asserts that just as
Pentecostals have been called 'people of the Spirit' even so they are
justly called 'people of the Book'.[98]

Pentecostal theology teaches that the Bible is inspired by the
Holy Spirit (2 Tim. 3.16).[99] Thus it is God's Word, 'completely
trustworthy for faith and conduct' and authoritative for Christian
life.[100] Other books, including religious books such as the *Analects*
of Confucius or the Islamic Koran have had (and do have) a level
of influence in the world but the Bible is incomparable and unparal-

---

[96] Charles W. Conn, *Like a Mighty Army: A History of the Church of God* (Cleveland, TN: Church of God Publishing House, 1955), p. xx.

[97] *CWJW* (Rio, WI: Ages Software, 2002), V, p. 62.

[98] Arrington, *Christian Doctrine*, I, p. 25.

[99] Arrington, *Christian Doctrine*, I, pp. 51-52.

[100] Arrington, *Christian Doctrine*, I, pp. 25-26, 30-31.

leled.[101] Pentecostals believe in divine revelation, that is, in God's personal self-disclosure.[102] Divine revelation is progressive, meaning it has unfolded more fully over time, and it includes general and special revelation.[103] General revelation refers to God's self-disclosure in creation and human conscience but is limited in its extent and value.[104] Special revelation refers to God's self-disclosure in history and occurs through providence, miracles, direct communications and manifestations, Christ, and the Bible.[105] As the record of God's deeds and words in history and of their significance, 'the Bible embodies God's revelation'.[106] As the author, preserver, and interpreter of the Scriptures, the Holy Spirit illumines and interprets them so that they may be understood and appropriated in faith.[107]

The topic of revelation is an area with particular relevance for Pentecostal theology of religions. A Pentecostal educator and missionary to India, John Higgins approaches examining the categories of God's revelation to humankind as a challenge for Christians to confront the hideous reality of human idolatry.[108] As Higgins asserts, 'the God of the Bible' is never confused with the idols of polytheistic paganism.[109] In this sense, divine revelation is quite exclusive: it only reveals one true God; all others are false.[110] That being said, Higgins notes that Scripture itself teaches that the true God nevertheless revealed God's self in some sense through general revelation in nature to the heathen of Lystra (Acts 14.15, 17) and Athens (Acts 17).[111] Yet pluralism ignores the fact that the world's religions contain 'serious distortions of God's true revelation'.[112] Significantly, although many world religions have their 'sacred scriptures', and although 'many of them may contain worthy moral teachings

---

[101] Arrington, *Christian Doctrine*, I, pp. 34-35.

[102] Higgins, Dunsing, and Tallman, *An Introduction to Theology*, pp. 34-35.

[103] Arrington, *Christian Doctrine*, I, pp. 38-40.

[104] Arrington, *Christian Doctrine*, I, pp. 40-44.

[105] Arrington, *Christian Doctrine*, I, pp. 44-49.

[106] Arrington, *Christian Doctrine*, I, p. 49.

[107] Arrington, *Christian Doctrine*, I, p. 73.

[108] John R. Higgins, 'God's Inspired Word', in Horton (ed.), *Systematic Theology*, p. 63.

[109] Higgins, 'God's Inspired Word', pp. 67-68.

[110] Higgins, 'God's Inspired Word', p. 68.

[111] Higgins, 'God's Inspired Word', pp. 70-71.

[112] Higgins, 'God's Inspired Word', p. 74.

… the Bible is uniquely and exclusively the word of God'.[113] As a former General Overseer of the Church of God (Cleveland, TN) has said, 'Beyond the text of every other world religion stands the Bible … no other book of any other religion compares to the divinely inspired Word of God'.[114]

Accordingly, any attempt at a theology of religions that underestimates the sacredness of Holy Scripture is reprehensible to Pentecostals and rejected out of hand.[115] As Pentecostal theologian of religions Amos Yong has rightly argued, the main challenge for a particular version of theology of religions is 'to pass muster biblically'.[116] Accordingly, Pentecostal theology of religions must be structured biblically, that is, it must be biblical in its orientations and in its assertions.

Theological Consistency

The preceding sections highlight specific theological categories judged necessary for a legitimate Pentecostal theology of religions. This section makes a more extensive claim with broader implications. In short, Pentecostalism is clearly part of a particular historic theological stream and therefore its theology of religions should reflect this identity for purposes of consistency. Classical Pentecostalism is in many ways an offspring of Wesleyan-Arminian theology via the American Holiness movement.[117] Specifically, John Wesley's emphasis on sanctification as a deeper experience beyond justification and on the agency of the Holy Spirit in the Christian life not only resulted in the founding of Methodism and contributed to the Holiness Movement but eventually 'became a major factor in the rise of Pentecostalism'.[118] While different contemporary Pentecostal

---

[113] Higgins, 'God's Inspired Word', pp. 83-84.
[114] Paul L. Walker, *Is Christianity the Only Way?* (Cleveland, TN: Pathway Press, 1975), p. 149.
[115] Richie, *Speaking by the Spirit*, p. 27.
[116] Amos Yong, *Beyond the Impasse*, p. 106.
[117] H.V. Synan, 'Classical Pentecostalism', in *NICPCM*, p. 553. Cf. C.E. Jones, 'Holiness Movement', in *NICPCM*, pp. 726-28; and Howard A. Snyder, 'Wesleyanism, Wesleyan Theology', in William A. Dyrness and Veli-Matti Kärkkäinen (eds.), *GDT* (Downers Grove, IL: InterVarsity Press, 2008), esp. p. 931.
[118] Snyder, 'Wesleyanism', p. 936.

organizations may continue to claim this heritage to varying degrees, and while global Pentecostals are certainly diverse and distinctive in their own identities, nevertheless the significance of this historical trajectory is nearly universally acknowledged. This affirmation in no wise lessens Pentecostal indebtedness to or interaction with other theological streams in the broader Christian tradition. On the contrary, as will be seen, it tends to open up such possibilities; but, as will also be seen, it does so from a particular perspective.

The Wesleyan doctrinal tradition is broad and deep. Its emphases include themes of God as holy love, the primacy of Scripture, the prior agency of God's grace, the image of God and salvation as the restoration of God's image, the gospel for the poor, the wisdom of God in creation, the renewal of the Church, and the restoration of all creation.[119] John Wesley's chief distinctive was Christian perfection, or 'the ongoing work of the Holy Spirit in the lives of believers whereby they are enabled to love God with all their hearts, souls and minds, and their neighbors as themselves'.[120] The contemporary relevance of Wesley's theology includes implications of his doctrine of prevenient grace for missiology, his pneumatology in light of contemporary Pentecostal and Charismatic movements, therapeutic view of salvation (as healing from the disease of sin), and applications of his doctrine of creation to environmental ethics.[121]

Pentecostal professor of religion and history John Sims identifies the understanding of conversion, doctrines of sanctification, divine healing, and the premillennial second coming of Jesus as Wesleyan-Arminian-Holiness themes that particularly impacted the development of the Pentecostal Movement.[122] Pentecostals follow Wesley in affirming the understanding of seventeenth-century Dutch Reformed theologian Jacobus Arminius of divine sovereignty and human freedom by reconciling these apparent polarities through viewing election as contingent upon divine foreknowledge of human

---

[119] Snyder, 'Wesleyanism', pp. 932-35.
[120] Snyder, 'Wesleyanism', p. 935.
[121] Snyder, 'Wesleyanism', p. 936.
[122] John A. Sims, *Our Pentecostal Heritage: Reclaiming the Priority of the Holy Spirit* (Cleveland, TN: Pathway Press, 1995), p. 63.

free choice contra John Calvin's logic of divine decrees and eternal predestination.[123] Therefore, with Wesley Pentecostals focus on faith in Christ and the atonement.[124] However, this focus is not simplistic. Most Pentecostals would agree that 'God by the death of Christ carries out an action that is bewilderingly vast and manysided [*sic*], an action which has cosmic and eternal effects'.[125] Obviously, the Wesleyan-Arminian tradition constitutes an overall approach to doing Christian theology that has interlinking (and interlocking) components vital for the development of a coherent system of thought and practice.

Wesleyan-Pentecostal theology turns on the pivot of grace. Wesley stressed the unqualified necessity of grace for salvation.[126] His 'optimism of grace' viewed justifying and sanctifying grace as more than a match for sin's penalty and its power.[127] Wesleyan scholar Howard Snyder notes that for Wesley 'Creation is suffused with grace as an unconditional benefit of the atonement'.[128] 'Nowhere', he adds, 'is God's grace absent, though people can and do close their hearts to God's grace'.[129] Accordingly, even before conversion, 'preventing' (from the Latin *praevenire*, that which comes before or anticipates), or prevenient, grace is given to all human beings.[130] Prevenient grace is 'the gracious, loving influence of God always working to draw all people to himself'.[131] In sum, it signifies that 'in Christ by the Holy Spirit God has gone ahead of every person, mitigating the effects of sin to the extent that people can be awakened and respond to God's initiative'.[132] Preceding grace is not saving grace. Prevenient grace is initial, not terminal. By definition, it expects that which is fuller to follow. Therefore, it is anticipatory and

---

[123] Sims, *Our Pentecostal Heritage*, p. 69.
[124] Sims, *Our Pentecostal Heritage*, p. 69.
[125] Vernon C. Grounds, 'Atonement', in Everett F. Harrison (ed.), *Baker's Dictionary of Theology* (Grand Rapids: Baker, 1960, 1987), p. 76.
[126] Snyder, 'Wesleyanism', p. 933. Cf. *Wesley's Works*, II, p. 500. Snyder's Wesley references are to *The Bicentennial Edition of the Works of John Wesley* (ed. Frank Baker *et al.*; Nashville: Abingdon Press, 1984-[35 volumes projected]).
[127] Snyder, 'Wesleyanism', p. 933.
[128] Snyder, 'Wesleyanism', p. 933.
[129] Snyder, 'Wesleyanism', p. 933.
[130] John Wesley, 'Sermon 85, "On Working Out Our Own Salvation"', *Wesley's Works*, III, p. 4.
[131] Snyder, 'Wesleyanism', p. 933.
[132] Snyder, 'Wesleyanism', p. 933.

preparatory. At some point, in this life or the next, those who respond positively to prevenient grace acknowledge Jesus Christ alone as Savior and Lord.[133]

Scripture abounds with stirring portraits of prevenient grace. The Lord is the life-giving fountain and the one whose light gives light to see light (Ps. 36.9; cf. Jn 1.4, 9). Humanity as a whole is lost in the wilderness of sin but finds grace through the Lord's drawing them in love to himself (Jer. 31.3; cf. Jn 6.44). The Lord God is as a shepherd seeking his lost sheep, bringing back the strays, healing and strengthening them (Ezek. 34.16; cf. Jn 10.1-18). God is a tender parent stooping to restore rebellious children who do not realize that it has been God that has been teaching, healing, leading, and feeding them all along (Hos. 11.1-4; cf. Lk. 15.11-32).[134] The atoning death of Jesus Christ on the cross enables the drawing unto himself of all people (Jn 12.32; cf. Ps. 69.18). God's goodness and kindness leads wayward sinners into repentance unto salvation (Rom. 2.4; cf. Tit. 3.4). The grace of God has appeared to all humanity in bringing salvation to them (Tit. 2.11; cf. Eph. 2.1-10). In short, God does a deep inward work enabling fallen and frail humans to respond positively in doing the divine will (Phil. 2.12-13; cf. 2 Chron. 29.36; 30.12). Therefore, biblically speaking, God is graciously working in every human being by his Holy Spirit preparing their hearts for his Son. That is prevenient grace. The goal of God's gracious action is that all may repent of sin and receive

---

[133] Thus Clark H. Pinnock, *Flame of Love: A Theology of the Holy Spirit* (Downers Grove, IL: InterVarsity Press, 1994), preferred to speak of some as 'pre-Christian' rather than 'non-Christian', p. 179.

[134] A succinct summary of the work of prevenient grace occurs in *Jamieson, Fausset, and Brown Commentary* (Electronic Database. Copyright © 1997, 2003, 2005, 2006 by Biblesoft, Inc.), on the text of Jer. 24.7 and 24.9:

> True repentance and conversion are not man's work, but the gift of God's grace preventing us; that is, going before us in the first instance, and 'giving us an heart to know the Lord' (Jer 24:7), and to become His people, anterior to any good-will or effort on our part. When God thus works with prevenient grace, the sinner returns to the Lord, not partially and outwardly, but 'with the whole heart'. Pardon is an act of grace, not the reward of our good-will or good works; yet it is invariably accompanied by repentance, and produces the fruits of love.

See *JFB* comments on Mal. 1.14 for specific application of doctrine of prevenient grace regarding reverential awareness of the Lord by the 'heathen'.

Christ Jesus as Savior and Lord (Col. 2.6; cf. Jn 1.11. See also 1
Tim. 2.4 and 2 Pet. 3.9).

The doctrine of prevenient grace is intertwined with pneumatology. As Land well says, 'By the Spirit the creative intention of the
Father and the redeeming passion of the Son are communicated to
all creation in a prevenient grace which is the source of all that is
good and true and beautiful'.[135] Speaking more specifically, that is,
soteriologically, Sims points out that Arminians, like Wesley and
like Pentecostals, believe that 'God, through one means or another,
extends his prevenient grace to all and that all who respond favorably to this grace can be saved'.[136] The only way to be justified is
through Jesus Christ alone; responding favorably to prevenient
grace leads to ever fuller offers of grace so that saving grace in
Christ can be received eventually.[137] Those who do not hear the
gospel in this life will be judged by their faithfulness to the grace
they have received. They are comparable to the patriarchs of old
who 'were justified by their faith in anticipation of Christ'.[138] God
grants every human being sufficient grace to respond and prepare
for eternity.[139] As Wesleyan scholar Henry Knight succinctly puts it,
'the Spirit is at work in all persons in the form of prevenient grace'
and therefore not only Christians have salvation – at least in the
sense of 'life with God after death'; although, 'Christian salvation in
its primary sense of new life in Christ' is 'necessarily different' than
anything in other religions.[140] In short, the doctrine of prevenient
grace explicates how the Holy Spirit works in all human beings
while emphasizing the uniqueness of Jesus Christ and necessity of
Christian salvation.

For all the notable pneumatological elements of the Wesleyan-
Pentecostal theology of prevenient grace, it is established on Christological basis. As Wesleyan-Arminian theologian Mildred Bangs
Wynkoop notes, John Wesley's emphasis was not on free will but
on free grace and for him 'Grace is Christocentric – an outpouring

---

[135] Land, 'Pentecostal Spirituality', *JPT,* p. 32.
[136] Sims, *Our Pentecostal Heritage,* p. 70.
[137] Sims, *Our Pentecostal Heritage,* p. 70.
[138] Sims, *Our Pentecostal Heritage,* p. 70.
[139] Cf. *Wesley's Works,* VI, p. 512 and VI, p. 206.
[140] Henry H. Knight III, *A Future for Truth: Evangelical Theology in a Postmodern World* (Nashville: Abingdon Press, 1997), p. 194.

of God's personal nature through Christ'.[141] Specifically, as Wesleyan theologian Thomas Langford puts it, 'Prevenient grace is an affect of the atonement of Jesus Christ'.[142] Accordingly, the 'grace of
God in Christ creates a new possibility for human life, and to every
human life God is antecedently and enablingly present'.[143] Theodore
Runyon observes that for Wesley certain benefits of the atonement
of Jesus Christ reach beyond those who are aware of the history of
the Incarnation – that is, to the unevangelized or those who have
not heard the gospel.[144]

Yet neither Wesley nor Wesleyans – and certainly not Pentecostals – adhere to universalism (belief that everyone will be eventually
and inevitably saved). Quite to the contrary, it is deemed essential
for each individual personally to accept by faith the benefits of the
atonement in order to enjoy Christian salvation.[145] Tragically, some
opt against grace. Judgment is the consequence. Nevertheless, the
atoning work of Christ is the objective basis upon which the universal offer of salvation can be subjectively received.[146] The general
and unconditional benefits of the atonement enable all to respond
to prevenient grace for individually receiving justifying grace upon
condition of faith in Jesus Christ and his atoning death and resurrection unto life. Thus Wesleyan-Pentecostal soteriology is established on Christology, accomplished by grace, and oriented to the
Holy Spirit. This theological model invites Christians to view non-
Christians, including those of non-Christian religions, as preliminary
participants in God's grace while proclaiming to everyone the necessity of faith in Jesus Christ for Christian salvation. Wesley came
to this perspective through studying the Scriptures (e.g. Pss. 19.1-4;

---

[141] Mildred Bangs Wynkoop, *Foundations of Wesleyan-Arminian Theology* (Kansas
City: Beacon Hill Press, 1967), p. 97.
[142] Thomas A. Langford, *Practical Divinity: Theology in the Wesleyan Tradition*
(Nashville: Abingdon Press, 1993), p. 34.
[143] Langford, *Practical Divinity*, p. 34.
[144] Theodore Runyon, *The New Creation; John Wesley's Theology Today* (Nashville:
Abingdon Press, 1998), p. 35. Cf. *Wesley's Works*, X, p. 178.
[145] R. Larry Shelton, 'Initial Salvation: The Redemptive Grace of God in
Christ', in Charles W. Carter (ed.), *A Contemporary Wesleyan Theology Volumes 1 & 2*
(Grand Rapids: Francis Asbury Press, 1983), I, pp. 490, 492, 503.
[146] Colin W. Williams, *John Wesley's Theology Today: A Study of the Wesleyan Tradition in the Light of Current Theological Debate* (Nashville: Abingdon Press, 1969,
1990), pp. 88-89; and Kenneth J. Collins, *The Theology of John Wesley: Holy Love and
the Shape of Grace* (Nashville: Abingdon Press, 2007), pp. 107-108.

145.9; Jn 1.9; Acts 10.35; Rom. 1.19-21; 2.12-16; Gal. 4.1-6), the writings of the Church Fathers (e.g. Justin Martyr, Clement of Alexandria), and theological interaction with others (e.g. Arminius, John Fletcher).[147]

Pentecostal scholar French Arrington's comments on Rom. 5.12-21 clarify Pauline atonement theology in regards to universality and individuality, and therefore shed light on implications for theology of religions. Arrington helpfully elucidates the Pauline assumption of human solidarity, both with Adam in sin and with Christ in salvation, and its implications for personal responsibility.[148] Paul's contrast of the age of Adam and the age of Christ illustrate that just as Adam's sin affected the whole human race, including those who did not know Adam, even so Christ's atonement affects the whole human race, even those who do not know Christ, without destroying personal responsibility.[149] Rather, 'the superior effects of Christ's saving work' are demonstrated in the surpassing grace and salvation wrought in him.[150] Nevertheless, the importance of personally responding to grace is still undergirded.[151] Another Pentecostal biblical scholar, Hollis Gause, commenting on Romans 5.12-21, also affirms corporate solidarity and personal responsibility as well as profound implications for Christology, anthropology (doctrine of humanity), hamartiology (doctrine of sin), and soteriology.[152] Accordingly, a theology of Christ's atonement affirming both the universal and unconditional and the individual and conditional benefits of Jesus Christ's saving death and rising again to life, including the importance of prevenient grace and its applications to non-Christians, correspond well to the insights of Pentecostal biblical scholarship.

In sum, Wesleyan-Arminian theology and Methodist spirituality has an inherent 'wideness of embrace' that is conducive to ecumen-

---

[147] Tony Richie, 'Mr. Wesley and Mohammed: A Contemporary Inquiry Concerning Islam', *ATJ* 58.2 (Fall 2003), pp. 86-90.

[148] French L. Arrington, *The Greatest Letter Ever Written: A Study of the Book of Romans* (Cleveland, TN: Pathway Press, 2012), pp. 149-51.

[149] Arrington, *Greatest Letter Ever Written*, pp. 152-55.

[150] Arrington, *Greatest Letter Ever Written*, pp. 156-61.

[151] Arrington, *Greatest Letter Ever Written*, pp. 157-58.

[152] R. Hollis Gause, *The Preaching of Paul: A Study of Romans* (Cleveland, TN: Pathway Press, 1986), pp. 67-72.

ical involvement both in the narrow sense of intra-Christian relations and in the broad sense of interreligious dialogue.[153] This theological framework provides Pentecostals with helpful categories for
developing and articulating a consistent theology of religions. Pentecostalism is of course a distinctive tradition which inevitably contributes to the development of these categorical precedents with
unique nuances. Nevertheless, Pentecostal theology of religions advances most effectively when it moves forward in a manner that is
consciously consistent with its own Wesleyan-Arminian-Holiness
historical, spiritual, and theological roots.

Conclusion

The concern of Chapter 1 has been to set forth some 'necessary
things' that are required if a Pentecostal theology of religions is to
make the grade according to Pentecostal faith and values. The selected items discussed serve as a backdrop for the following discussion, even when not referenced specifically. They may be considered as points on a compass, guiding the Pentecostal theology of
religions project in the right direction and toward the right destination. Therefore, doing Pentecostal theology of religions is not an
exercise in unrestrained speculation. Quite to the contrary, there are
clear guidelines for its successful advancement. Now it is time for
the next two chapters to trace a general outline of what has transpired in the discipline.

---

[153] Gillian Kingston, 'Methodist Spirituality', in Philip Scheldrake (ed.), *The New Westminster Dictionary of Christian Spirituality* (Louisville, KY: Westminster John Knox Press, 2005), p. 439.

2

CONTEXT OF PENTECOSTAL THEOLOGY OF RELIGIONS

Introduction

As has been noted, the interreligious encounter of Peter the Jewish Christian apostle with Cornelius the Roman centurion of pagan background (Acts 10) is being loosely resourced to frame this conversation about Pentecostal theology of religions. Following that event, Peter related the details of the Cornelius encounter back to his Jewish Christian colleagues in Jerusalem (Acts 11).[1] In a sense, he surveyed the events which transpired and suggested some implications. Paul and Barnabas followed a similar pattern in reporting to the Jerusalem Council what had been said and done through their ministries among the Gentiles (Acts 15.13). Only when they had finished hearing a full description of all the facts did James, in his presiding role, render the formal decision extending Jewish and Gentile relations within the New Testament church (vv. 13-21) that was adopted and enacted by the consensus of the council (vv. 22-30). In a similar vein, this chapter will survey the developing discipline of Pentecostal theology of religions in order to enable sound judgment and responsible enactment.

---

[1] It is normally understood that the 'Jerusalem Council' in Acts 15 dealt with *intra*-Christian concerns, not *inter*religious concerns. However, with the interreligious elements of the Peter-Cornelius encounter looming large in the background, not to mention the diversities of religious cultures behind the differences between Jewish and Gentile Christians, the Jerusalem Council nonetheless serves as a helpful heuristic device for the present discussion.

Early Stages of a Developing Discipline

As a distinct discipline, theology of religions is a relatively new endeavor.[2] Of course, Christianity has from earliest times had to deal theologically and practically with the concrete reality of other religions. However, that task was not usually done as part of a systematic and sustained process. In recent decades that has changed. Increasing communication and transportation abilities in today's world have facilitated ongoing and in-depth cultural cross-fertilization thus contributing to interreligious exchanges reaching heretofore unprecedented levels. Accordingly, Christian theology of religions has arisen in response to this felt need. Kärkkäinen says that 'No doubt the existence of and communication among world religions is the most significant challenge and opportunity for the Christian church in the new millennium'.[3] That assessment quite obviously places theology of religions at the forefront of vital tasks for thoughtful Christians during the present age.

Major Figures and Leaders

Sir Norman Anderson and Bishop Stephen Neill certainly stand out as non-Pentecostal pioneers who have had significant impact on the discipline of Christian theology of religions and therefore have affected how it is currently being developed by Pentecostal theologians.[4] A British theologian, Anderson has particularly impacted the Evangelical movement.[5] Anderson distrusts religious syncretism and insists on the veritable historicity of Christ's incarnation, atonement, and resurrection.[6] He rejects any religion, including

---

[2] See Kärkkäinen, *Introduction to Theology of Religions,* pp. 20-22.

[3] Kärkkäinen, *Introduction to Theology of Religions,* p. 17.

[4] Others such as Jürgen Moltmann, Clark Pinnock, and Lesslie Newbigin will be dealt with subsequently at appropriate points in this text. However, even this group represents a selective sampling, though one with special relevance.

[5] Kärkkäinen, *Introduction to Theology of Religions,* p. 261. Evangelicalism is a loosely defined movement usually signifying distinctive commitments to a quadrilateral of conversionism, biblicism, crucicentrism, and activism. See David Bebbington, *Evangelicalism in Modern Britain: A History from the 1730s to the 1980s* (New York: Routledge, 2002). Although not synonymous, the Evangelical and Pentecostal movements have been closely aligned. See Vinson Synan, 'Evangelicalism', in *NIDPCM,* pp. 613-16.

[6] Sir Norman Anderson, *Christianity and World Religions: The Challenge of Pluralism* (Downers Grove, IL: InterVarsity Press, 1970, rev. edn, 1984), pp. 16-20.

Christianity, as salvific, affirming that Christ alone is Savior; but, only those who knowingly persist in rejecting Jesus will be damned.[7] Anderson suggests that God's Spirit may work in the hearts of those from other religions to show them their sinfulness and need of divine mercy and that God characteristically will show grace to those who respond positively.[8]

However, Anderson rejects relativistic religious pluralism out of hand, and severely criticizes liberal theology for negating the uniqueness of Christ.[9] Rather, he maintains that the claim of salvation through Jesus Christ alone and the possibility of salvation beyond the Judeo-Christian sphere are not incompatible (Acts 4.12).[10] In spite of some parallels in the world's religions, the essence of Christianity is *sui generis* – or of its own kind, unique in its character-istics – because it is derived from and dependent on Christ.[11] God may reveal God's self to some extent through other means but the historical event upon which Christianity is founded is unparalleled.[12] Anderson firmly believes that the Bible (e.g. Jn 10.8; 14.6; Mt. 11.27; 1 Jn 2.23; Acts 4.12) teaches it is only through Christ that anyone can come to a personal knowledge of God and experience salvation.[13]

Anderson argues that since pre-Christian Jews and Gentiles be-fore the incarnation experienced forgiveness and communion with God through the eternal Christ (Rom. 4.7; 3.25; Heb. 9.25), some non-Christians today may be considered as in a similar state.[14] That is, some who do not explicitly know Christ may nevertheless know Christ implicitly. However, two things are essential. First, although they are without the preached Word they must respond to whatever revelation they do have, such as dreams, visions, and direct com-munications, as well as nature and conscience. Second, as sinners they cannot depend on their own righteousness but only on God's mercy. Even with all of that, everyone still needs to hear and be-

---

[7] Anderson, *Christianity and World Religions*, pp. 30-34 (p. 31).
[8] Anderson, *Christianity and World Religions*, pp. 32 and 45-55.
[9] Anderson, *Christianity and World Religions*, pp. 34-35 and 46-51.
[10] Anderson, *Christianity and World Religions*, p. 110.
[11] Anderson, *Christianity and World Religions*, p. 137.
[12] Anderson, *Christianity and World Religions*, p. 138.
[13] Anderson, *Christianity and World Religions*, pp. 142-43.
[14] Anderson, *Christianity and World Religions*, pp. 143-45.

lieve the gospel.[15] Ultimately, Anderson suggests, Christians should not be dogmatic but humbly leave the soteriological fate of the unevangelized in the hands of a faithful Creator.[16]

Finally, Anderson describes several specific perspectives on the possible nature of non-Christian religions.[17] A non-Christian religion may be *preparatio evangelica,* a preparation for the gospel. In that case, it would have some elements that are good and true through general revelation but be mixed with much that is false. Another possibility is that a particular non-Christian religion may in fact be satanic or demonic in nature. In that case, it is overtly evil and inherently harmful. Finally, a non-Christian religion may be a result of human aspiration for God. In that case, to varying degrees it may have noble or base elements but still would fall far short of real religion. Anderson considers only Christianity to be an actual revealed religion. Thus it contains the highest truth. However, he warns against making any religion absolute.[18] Arguably, absolutizing any religion is at best probably blasphemous and at worst possibly idolatrous.[19]

Norman Anderson's theology of religions leads rather naturally into the practice of interreligious dialogue. He suggests that Christians may learn from other religions, but he always warns against religious syncretism, insisting that Christians must guard against that which is false and imperfect in the religions.[20] For Anderson, the example of Paul at Athens (Acts 17) indicates interreligious dialogue can be an important part of gospel proclamation.[21] If dialogue is to be mutually beneficial, a respectful attitude is necessary. However, religious believers do not need to pretend to be objective in their perspectives. The encounter of Peter and Cornelius in Acts 10

[15] Anderson, *Christianity and World Religions*, pp. 145-55.
[16] Anderson, *Christianity and World Religions*, p. 148.
[17] Anderson, *Christianity and World Religions*, pp. 169-74.
[18] Anderson, *Christianity and World Religions*, p. 175.
[19] Thus thinkers as different as Pentecostal historian and administrator Charles W. Conn, *Like a Mighty Army*, pp. 311-14 (esp. p. 312) and pp. 332-34, and Catholic pneumatologist Yves Congar, *I Believe in the Holy Spirit* (trans. David Smith, NY: Seabury, 1983), II, pp. 209-10, both strong churchmen, nonetheless agree against ecclesiolatry (excessive reverence for the Church making it central rather than Christ or God).
[20] Anderson, *Christianity and World Religions,* pp. 139-40.
[21] Anderson, *Christianity and World Religions,* pp. 184-88.

is a good example of mutual benefit through dialogue in which evangelism also became an integral part.[22] Interreligious dialogue involves vulnerability but is valuable when carried out in the confidence of Christ's lordship and in the power of the Holy Spirit.[23] In a real sense, dialogue may be more about relationship than religion.[24] Yet it is not always possible to distinguish clearly between evangelism and dialogue; they may overlap as Christians inevitably point to Christ in all they say or do whether directly or indirectly.[25] In dialogue, as in other forms of ecclesial mission, Christians participate in the vulnerability of the God of love who is creator and redeemer.[26]

A brief assessment of Norman Anderson's theology of religions is suggestive. First, it is an ardent attempt to integrate uncompromising commitment to traditional Christian theology, especially in the areas of Christology and soteriology, while providing space for affirming God's compassionate love and providential care for all human beings. Second, it is quite firm in its endeavor to guard against the relativistic errors of religious pluralism and the inconsistencies of religious syncretism while expressing approbation for all goodness and truth wherever they may be found as ultimately coming only from God. Third, it is unstinting in its support of Christian evangelism and proclamation when setting forth an expansive missiology that also embraces interreligious dialogue. Finally, Pentecostals especially might note that at its core is an implied emphasis on pneumatology through its assumption about the extraordinary works of the Spirit of Christ in the world beyond the boundaries of religious institutions.

Anglican Bishop Stephen Neill develops his approach to interreligious dialogue out of a theology of religions that is uncompromisingly evangelical in its commitments. Neill's work can be described as brilliant but complex and paradoxical.[27] For example, as Harold

---

[22] Anderson, *Christianity and World Religions*, pp. 188-91.
[23] Anderson, *Christianity and World Religions*, pp. 188-91.
[24] Anderson, *Christianity and World Religions*, pp. 191-92.
[25] Anderson, *Christianity and World Religions*, p. 192.
[26] Anderson, *Christianity and World Religions*, p. 192. For more on Norman Anderson, see Richie, *Speaking by the Spirit*, pp. 46-48.
[27] Harold Netland, *Encountering Religious Pluralism: The Challenge to Christian Faith & Mission* (Downers Grove, IL: InterVarsity Press, 2001), p. 47.

Netland notes, Neill often simultaneously affirms ecumenism (spiritual unity among different Christians) and orthodoxy (doctrinal conformity among different Christians), evangelism and dialogue, and a high Christology with honest respect for non-Christian religions.[28] Furthermore, Neill advises dialogue participants to endeavor to enter into the 'heart and spirit of another religion' but always 'without disloyalty' to one's own religious faith.[29] Neill sees objective detachment as idealistic and unrealistic, and so insists that the best dialogue partners are able to be firmly committed to their own traditions while assuming an attitude of temporary suspension of judgment toward another tradition.[30] He suggests meeting others confidently at their strongest without a need for self-assertion.[31] In this way, Neill thinks Christians engaging in dialogue with adherents of other religions will joyously celebrate discovering the richness and wideness of Jesus Christ in the world of religions.[32]

Neill models theology of religions and dialogue by taking his discussion to Jews, Muslims, Hindus, Buddhists, and others.[33] He attempts to assess religious others from the inside, often allowing their own writers to speak for them, and admits mistakes by Christians as well as giving credit to others where it is deemed due. In the process Neill expresses great appreciation for the beauty and symmetry often found in other religious faiths but always crisply defends a Christian view, albeit one clearly enhanced and transformed by the dialogue experience.[34] For Neill, interreligious dialogue is not merely academic but is a real life struggle carried on in friendship and mutual respect. Hard topics must be addressed but only in an attitude of sincerity and integrity that assiduously avoids aggressiveness and narrowness.[35] Always the constant goal of interreligious encounter and dialogue must be to lift up Jesus Christ through lovingly representing him to the world.[36]

---

[28] Netland, *Encountering Religious Pluralism*, p. 47.
[29] Stephen Neill, *Christianity and Other Faiths: Christian Dialogue with Other Religions* (New York: Oxford University Press, 1961, 1970), pp. 4-5.
[30] Neill, *Christianity and Other Faiths*, p. 18.
[31] Neill, *Christianity and Other Faiths*, p. 19.
[32] Neill, *Christianity and Other Faiths*, pp. 18-19 and 207.
[33] Neill, *Christianity and Other Faiths*, pp. 20, 40, 70, 99, 125, and *passim*.
[34] Neill, *Christianity and Other Faiths*, pp. 205-32.
[35] Neill, *Christianity and Other Faiths*, p. 29.
[36] Neill, *Christianity and Other Faiths*, pp. 69, 124.

Neill thinks Christian dialogue with religious others is guided by theological principles and must work to be aware of its own pre-suppositions because it has to tackle the hard questions honestly in order to enjoy the benefits of mutual enrichment.[37] However, in the process of exchanging information and experiencing transformation Christians must adhere to some 'basic convictions' that are non-negotiable if they are to remain recognizably Christian.[38] Therefore, Neill lists seven basic theological convictions that must guide all Christian involvement in interreligious dialogue:

> 1. There is only one God and Creator, from whom all things take their origin. 2. This God is a self-revealing God, and he himself is active in the knowledge that we have of him. 3. In Jesus the full meaning of the life of man, and the purpose of God for the universe, has been made known. In him the alienated world has been reconciled to God. 4. In Jesus Christians see the way in which they ought to live; his life is the norm to which they are unconditionally bound. 5. The Cross of Jesus shows that to follow his way will certainly result in suffering; this is neither to be resented nor to be evaded. 6. The Christian faith may learn much from other faiths; but is universal in its claims; in the end Christ must be acknowledged as Lord of all. 7. The death of the body is not the end. Christ has revealed the eternal dimension as the true home of man's spirit.[39]

For Neill, these points may be debated but not ceded. They are cardinal in their character. In other words, for him these basic theological presuppositions are the point at which Christians must draw a line in the sand over which they cannot cross – at least, not without disastrous consequences.

Nevertheless, for Neill the Christian approach to interreligious dialogue should be characterized by congeniality and humility.[40] Arrogance and aggression do not belong at the dialogue table. Yet Neill knows Christians can and must ask others if they have taken Christ and Christian history seriously. In fact, Christians can and

---

[37] Neill, *Christianity and Other Faiths*, pp. 207-34.
[38] Neill, *Christianity and Other Faiths*, pp. 231-32.
[39] Neill, *Christianity and Other Faiths*, pp. 231-32.
[40] Neill, *Christianity and Other Faiths*, pp. 232-33.

must ask themselves and others what Christ really means for them and for their life. The definitive question behind all discussion of Christ is, if these things be so, then 'What manner of men [or women] ought ye to be?' (cf. 1 Thess. 1.5; 2 Pet. 3.11).[41]

In sum, Neill's theology of religions and interreligious dialogue, like that of Anderson, is committed to maintaining the tension between a high Christology and distinctive Christian soteriology with hopeful openness toward those of other faiths. However, Neill's theology is even more pronounced in its resolve that Christians will benefit from interreligious encounter and dialogue, at least when it is well done. And of course religious others will benefit also. His theology of religions, therefore, is chiefly characterized by themes of mutual appreciation and transformation in a context of uncompromising Christian commitment. In this line of reasoning, Christians literally become better Christians through transformative encounters with religious others. Presumably, others become better representatives of their respective faiths as well. Accordingly, interreligious encounter and dialogue is especially central to Neill's theological system as the crucial means whereby transformative information and personal relationship building occurs.

Concepts and Categories

As with any technical discipline, Christian theology of religions has developed a certain level of sophistication and specialization of which it is helpful to have a fundamental understanding in order to follow well its substantial ideas and supporting arguments. Before examining in greater detail the complexities of Christian theology of religions, it is well to note, though perhaps a bit of an oversimplification, that behind most of the work of Christian theology of religions is an attempt to address the relationship between two decisive issues: God's universal love and concern for all souls (Jn 3.16; 1 Jn 4.9; 1 Tim. 2.4) and the sole provision of salvation in Jesus Christ alone (Acts 4.12; Jn 14.6).[42] As Kärkkäinen says, 'How one puts these two axioms together and accounts for the built-in tension be-

[41] Neill, *Christianity and Other Faiths*, pp. 232-34 (p. 234). For more on Stephen Neill, see Richie, *Speaking by the Spirit*, pp. 92-94.
[42] Kärkkäinen, *Introduction to Theology of Religions*, pp. 26-27.

tween them largely accounts for one's theology of religions'.[43] There are of course several ways of dealing with these basic ideas.

Perhaps the most important clarification has to do with the typology with which theology of religions is approached. The act of distributing into classes or categories of the same type, that is, with shared characteristics or traits, in its turn affects the subsequent study of any topic under analysis. Yet typologies are often immensely helpful as heuristic devices or interpretative aids. Therefore, it is important to understand the benefits and limits of a particular typology, such as the typologies of theologies of religions, while employing it. More is said about this aspect subsequently. For the present, the major typologies need to be identified and briefly defined.

Undoubtedly, the typology most frequently used in Christian theology of religions is the now classic exclusivist-inclusivist-pluralist model.[44] Exclusivism insists that only a particular religion has revelation or possesses the truth with all others being false or possibly demonic. Inclusivism recognizes some goodness and truth in other religions but still asserts the priority of a specific faith. Pluralism asserts that all major religions point to the same ultimate reality and verity expressed differently in particular contexts.[45] This model places emphasis on soteriology. Hence Christian exclusivism has a closed attitude toward the salvation of the unevangelized or devout adherents of other faiths, Christian inclusivism is more optimistic regarding the redemptive reach of Christ, and pluralism more or less argues that salvation is experienced by means of all the religions.[46] Overall, inclusivism comes off as something of a *via media,* or middle way, between the extreme polarities of exclusivism and pluralism.[47]

Leading exclusivists have included Swiss Reformed theologian Karl Barth and Dutch Reformed missionary Hendrick Kraemer. Prominent inclusivists have included the Methodist reformer and

---

[43] Kärkkäinen, *Introduction to Theology of Religions,* pp. 26-27.
[44] For the definitive presentation of this paradigm see Alan Race, *Christianity and Religious Pluralism: Patterns in the Theology of Religions* (Maryknoll, NY: Orbis, 1983).
[45] Smart, 'Pluralism', pp. 360-64.
[46] Richie, *Speaking by the Spirit,* p. 52.
[47] Richie, *Speaking by the Spirit,* pp. 286-87.

revivalist John Wesley and the Anglican apologist C.S. Lewis. Notable pluralists include Protestant philosopher John Hick and Catholic theologian Paul Knitter.[48] Biblically speaking, exclusivists argue from texts stressing the uniqueness of Christ and Christian salvation (e.g. Jn 14.6; Acts 4.12); inclusivists hold these texts together with those stressing God's universal care and concern (e.g. Ps. 145.9; Jn 1.9); and pluralists tend to rely rather less on scriptural support than philosophical argumentation.

There are several variations on the exclusivist-inclusivist-pluralist paradigm. For instance, Boyd and Eddy list the no other name (restrictivist) view, God does all he can (universal opportunity) view, hope beyond the grave (postmortem evangelism) view, and God has not left himself without witness (inclusivist) view as a range of options popular among Evangelicals.[49] These are actually variations on only two types, the exclusivist and inclusivist positions, as pluralism is simply not an Evangelical option. They do, however, demonstrate something of the intricacies inherent in each of these categories.

Daniel Migliore is an example of a well-respected Protestant theologian who critiques the standard exclusivist-inclusivist-pluralist typology. He admits that it is attractive because of its simplicity but insists it has serious limitations.[50] Migliore identifies as a weakness its 'pigeonholing mentality that ignores the important overlap of positions and obscures significant differences among theologians placed in any of the three categories'.[51] Also, he argues that the complexities inherent in inclusivism cause it to come off as a less definable hopeless mediating position when in fact exclusivism and pluralism do not adequately address the polarities of 'the particularity and universality of God's grace'.[52] Accordingly, he proposes a revised and expanded typology that includes a total of seven more precise categories.[53]

Worth noting briefly is that Pentecostal theologians struggle with the standard typology. True enough, they often employ it. May Ling

---

[48] Richie, *Speaking by the Spirit*, pp. 11-12.
[49] Boyd and Eddy, *Across the Evangelical Spectrum*, pp. 178-92.
[50] Migliore, *Faith Seeking Understanding*, p. 306.
[51] Migliore, *Faith Seeking Understanding*, p. 306.
[52] Migliore, *Faith Seeking Understanding*, p. 307.
[53] Migliore, *Faith Seeking Understanding*, pp. 307-16.

Tan-Chow argues that Pentecostalism should transcend traditional exclusivism by drawing on its own rich resources of spirituality and theology for a more inclusive approach.[54] Kärkkäinen excludes pluralism as an option for Pentecostals in discussing inclusivism versus exclusivism.[55] However, Kärkkäinen also organizes his *An Introduction to the Theology of Religions* around an altogether different typological set, focusing instead on ecclesiocentrism, Christocentrism, theocentrism, and realitycentrism.[56] Yong questions the viability of the classic typology except as a heuristic device, suggesting it is inadequate for a well-rounded theology of religions.[57] Similarly, for me the exclusivist-inclusivist-pluralist paradigm is problematic because of its fixation on salvation to the exclusion of other issues and because of its intention more to provide Christian self-understanding than categories for understanding the religions.[58] Nevertheless, it is probably impossible to avoid the standard typology altogether. More likely, Pentecostals and other Christian theologians of religions will continue to use it while offering clarifications and reservations along the way.

In that vein, perhaps the best approach to date on the topic of Christian theology of religions typology is exemplified by Lesslie Newbigin. A pastor, a practicing missionary, and a prolific author on theological topics, Newbigin is well known for his work on missiology and theology of culture, especially with emphases on a pluralistic society. He outlines his position on the relation of Christianity to the world religions as

> exclusive in the sense that it affirms the unique truth of the revelation in Jesus Christ, but it is not exclusivist in the sense of denying the possibility of the salvation of the non-Christian. It is inclusivist in the sense that it refuses to limit the saving grace of God to the members of the Christian Church, but it rejects the inclusivism which regards the non-Christian religions as vehicles

---

[54] May Ling Tan-Chow, *Pentecostal Theology for the Twenty-First Century: Engaging with Multi-Faith Singapore* (Surrey, UK: Ashgate, 2007), pp. 22-23.

[55] Veli-Matti Kärkkäinen, 'A Response to Tony Richie's "Azusa-era Optimism: Bishop J.H. King's Pentecostal Theology of Religions as a Possible Paradigm for Today"', *JPT* 15.2 (April 2007), pp. 263-68.

[56] Kärkkäinen, *An Introduction to Theology of Religions*, pp. 25-26.

[57] Yong, *Discerning of Spirit(s)*, p. 34.

[58] Richie, *Speaking by the Spirit*, pp. 59-60.

of salvation. It is pluralist in the sense of acknowledging the gracious work of God in the lives of all human beings, but it rejects a pluralism which denies the uniqueness and decisiveness of what God has done in Jesus Christ.[59]

One might say Newbigin proposes an 'in which way what?' approach to Christian typology in theology of religions. In other words, one may be simultaneously exclusivist, inclusivist, and pluralist in different senses. Rather than rejecting outright the classic typology, Newbigin expands it to be more accurate and holistic. Thus Newbigin provides Pentecostals with an approach to interpreting the classic typology in a more holistic way.

Survey of Early Pentecostal Contributions

Some of the dynamics behind the newly developing discipline of Christian theology of religions were noted above. However, it is important to note that Pentecostal theology of religions is not merely a pragmatic response to a critical need of the time – as important and pressing as that aspect may be in its place for its origination and formulation. Yong suggests several reasons that Pentecostals should engage in theology of religions. He lists the international roots and global presence of the Pentecostal movement, a need to attend to urgent missiological issues, such as syncretism, relations between gospel and culture, and the balance of proclamation with social justice. Significantly, he concludes with a simple responsibility to articulate authentic Pentecostal identity in the world.[60] So then, while the current global situation of diverse religious traditions co-existing in close proximity has brought the need for theology of religions into sharper focus, arguably Pentecostalism's own theological and spiritual identity serves as its chief justification for pursuing its distinctive approach to the discipline.[61]

---

[59] Lesslie Newbigin, *The Gospel in a Pluralist Society* (Grand Rapids: Eerdmans, 1989), p. 182.

[60] Yong, *Discerning the Spirit(s)*, p. 206.

[61] Tony Richie, 'The Unity of the Spirit: Are Pentecostals Inherently Ecumenists and Inclusivists?' *JEPTA* 26 (2006), pp. 21-35.

Charles Fox Parham

Two notable early Pentecostals who stand out for their nascent theologies of religions are Charles Fox Parham and Bishop J.H. King.[62] Parham (1873-1929), an enigmatic and idiosyncratic figure often surrounded by swirling controversy, was nevertheless a key leader and perhaps even in some sense a founder in the modern Classical Pentecostal movement.[63] Significantly, Parham opined at length about non-Christian religions.[64] In short, Parham advocated what might be called an 'eschatological inclusivism' in that he combined commitment to the uniqueness and necessity of Jesus Christ as Lord and Savior with openness to a possibility of divine redemption in non-Christian religions that would be brought to completion in the eschaton by Christ.[65]

More specifically, Parham's non-institutional ecclesiology enabled him to argue that all who sincerely believe in God are in a kind of general or secondary sense a part of the Church rather than only followers of Jesus.[66] Parham's typical eschatological emphasis combined with his reflections on other religions eventuated in a system of thought suggesting a number of observations for theology of religions. First, he suggested that the 'heathen' (devout adherents of non-Christian religions) who never had the Jewish law would be judged apart from that condemnatory code.[67] Second, he had a close friendship with a Jewish rabbi that may have contributed to his making a suggestion that Jews and Christians have separate religions in the present age but will be united as one in the eschaton

---

[62] Some other early Pentecostals are also interesting in this regard. See A.A. Boddy, *To Kairwan the Holy: Scenes in Mohammedan Africa* (London: Kegan Paul, Trench & Co., 1885); G.F. Taylor, *The Rainbow* (Franklin Springs, GA: Advocate Press, 1924); and George L. Britt, *When Dust Shall Sing: The World Crisis in the Light of Bible Prophecy* (Cleveland, TN: Pathway Press, 1958).

[63] Tony Richie, 'Eschatological Inclusivism: Early Pentecostal Theology of Religions in Charles Fox Parham', *JEPTA* 27.2 (2007), pp. 138-52, esp. pp. 138-39.

[64] Parham's thoughts on theology of religions are mostly ad hoc and homiletic in nature, rather than systematic theological reflections, but are nevertheless suggestive. See Charles F. Parham, *The Sermons of Charles F. Parham* (New York: Garland, 1985), a collection of earlier and separate publications by Parham published as *A Voice Crying in the Wilderness* (1902) and *The Everlasting Gospel* (1919).

[65] Richie, 'Eschatological Inclusivism', p. 139.

[66] Richie, 'Eschatological Inclusivism', p. 140.

[67] Parham, *A Voice Crying in the Wilderness,* p. 85.

(i.e. the millennium).[68] He saw the 'heathen' as being part of Christ's 'inheritance' in the eschaton (cf. Ps. 2.7-12), with clear soteriological intimations.

Parham could sometimes be quite subtle. He suggested that Mohammed was 'a true prophet of a false religion'[69] in an apparent attempt to recognize some authenticity in roots of Islam without a blanket affirmation of the overall system. However, he was not hesitant in offering stern assessments when he considered it necessary, as in his unequivocal condemnation of cultic and occult religions.[70]

Parham suggested that in the eschatological 'Judgment Age' Christians will indeed be awarded special glory but those who have done good works still may be rewarded with eternal life and restoration to a kind of Edenic existence (referencing Matthew 25 and Rev. 20.11-15).[71] Significantly, Parham argued specifically against an exclusive view of redemption, insisting that God's 'promised Savior' must be for all humanity, although stopping short of universalism.[72] His doctrine of 'the general blood of the atonement of Jesus Christ' allowed him to affirm that many would enjoy the benefits of Christ in a general or secondary sense from full believers who specifically follow Jesus and thus receive the primary benefits of Christ's atoning work.[73] Accordingly, in the final state there would be three classes of people: those fully redeemed and sharing in Christ's special glory, those generally redeemed and blessed with life on earth, and those eternally judged (annihilated).[74] Prior to the es-

---

[68] Parham, *A Voice Crying in the Wilderness,* pp. 103-104.

[69] Parham, *A Voice Crying in the Wilderness,* pp. 121-22.

[70] Parham, *A Voice Crying in the Wilderness,* pp. 122-23.

[71] Parham, *A Voice Crying in the Wilderness,* p. 137.

[72] Parham, *A Voice Crying in the Wilderness,* p. 138. Universalist teaching can be presented quite apart from theology of religions *per se.* Universalism has no direct or necessary relation either to exclusivism, inclusivism, or pluralism. Yet it may (or may not) be adopted and incorporated into any of these models. One assumes that universalism appears least compatible with exclusivism and most compatible with pluralism. However, this is not a hard and fast rule. E.g. an exclusivist like Karl Barth might be adamantly opposed to anything revelatory or salvific in the world religions and yet argue that the extent of Christ's reconciliatory work implies universal salvation. See David L. Mueller, *Karl Barth: Makers of the Modern Theological Mind* (Waco, TX: Word Books, 1976), pp. 89-90 and 109-10.

[73] Parham, *Everlasting Gospel,* pp. 50-51.

[74] Parham, *Everlasting Gospel,* pp. 51-52, 92-95, and 98-100.

chaton, the Holy Spirit works progressively in all different classes of people in preparing them for eternity.[75]

In brief, Charles Parham's nascent theology of religions was characterized by several key elements, including a universal cosmology, an elevated Christology, dynamic pneumatology, what might anachronistically be labeled an inclusive soteriology, and, of course emphatically, an apocalyptic eschatology.[76] As I have said of Parham's thought at this point,

> All things and every creature exist in accordance with God's ultimate plan. Jesus Christ is the full and final representation of God's revelation. The Holy Spirit works with and in all along ever advancing stages of divine experience. All who do not intentionally, completely, and finally rebel against God will share in some measure of salvation. The dramatic conflagration and consummation of history and prophecy will eventually and inevitably accomplish God's intentions for eternity.[77]

Thus Charles Parham exemplifies an admittedly flamboyant but nonetheless remarkable example of an early Pentecostal theology of religions. Bishop King was of an entirely different temperament and style but also exemplifies early Pentecostal theology of religions in even more remarkable fashion.

Bishop J.H. King

Joseph Hillary King (1869-1946) was an important early Pentecostal who helped found and lead one of the oldest and strongest classical Pentecostal denominations.[78] Well-educated and widely traveled, especially for a Pentecostal in his period, King addressed theology of religions fairly frequently and with comparative depth in his var-

---

[75] Parham, *Everlasting Gospel,* pp. 54-57, 63-69, 74-76, and 101-10.
[76] Richie, 'An Inclusive Eschatology', p. 143.
[77] Richie, 'An Inclusive Eschatology', pp. 143-44. For a discussion of the likely minimal influence of Parham's British Israelitism on his theology of religions, see pp. 144-45.
[78] Tony Richie, 'Azusa-era Optimism: Bishop J.H. King's Pentecostal Theology of Religions as a Possible Paradigm for Today', in Veli-Matti Kärkkäinen (ed.), *The Spirit in the World: Emerging Pentecostal Theologies in Global Contexts* (Grand Rapids: Eerdmans, 2009), p. 227.

ious writings.[79] King's international travels brought him into direct contact with other religions. His reflections reveal a wide range of responses. On the one hand, his candid assessments of Buddhism, indigenous Chinese religions, Islam, and Hinduism could be sharp and stinging, basically charging them with various levels of idolatry, superstition, and demonic influence.[80] However, King was nothing if not fair, castigating some Christians whom he suspected were 'the real heathen after all' because of unchristian behavior.[81] Further-more, he criticized the Jews of Jesus' day for being narrow-minded and rejecting him.[82]

On the other hand, King decried any religious prejudice and consistently called for religious tolerance.[83] Further, he gave specific examples of God at work in religious others. He believed that the Creator God led a Hindu priest in educating his daughter in ad-vance of conversion, intervened in a Mongolian heathen's search for spiritual peace, and granted visions and angelic visitations to practicing heathen in preparation for the gospel.[84] King admitted that the Jews play a providential role in the world in spreading the knowledge of God.[85] He was so impressed with a particular raja that he refused to call him 'a heathen in the common meaning of the term'.[86] But King consistently lifted up the uniqueness and necessity of Jesus Christ and of his sacrificial death and resurrection.[87]

The biblical and theological basis of King's theology begins with an incessant orientation to Christology.[88] He emphasizes both the historical, temporal Christ of the incarnation and the universal, eternal Christ. Thereby he roots redemption in the Christ event

---

[79] Of course, King was not a systematic theologian. He tended to address top-ics as they came before him for consideration due to his duties as an administra-tor and a preacher. Nevertheless, he did engage in theological studies and his writings reveal careful reflection and consistent emphases regarding what is today called Christian theology of religions.

[80] J.H. King, *Yet Speaketh* (Franklin Springs, GA: Advocate Press, 1949), pp. 155-60, 222, 166-70, 179-84.

[81] King, *Yet Speaketh*, pp. 199-200.

[82] King, *Yet Speaketh*, pp. 142-44.

[83] King, *Yet Speaketh*, pp. 169, 171.

[84] King, *Yet Speaketh*, pp. 185, 204, and 123.

[85] King, *Yet Speaketh*, pp. 229-30.

[86] King, *Yet Speaketh*, pp. 212-13.

[87] King, *Yet Speaketh*, pp. 244, 257.

[88] The following summarizes Richie, 'Azusa-era Optimism', pp. 230-34.

without limiting Christ to time and space. King's doctrine of the general atonement argues that as the counterpart to the fall God's response to sin through the atoning work of Christ has first uncon-ditional universal effects taking away original sin and then condi-tional particular aspects dealing with individual sin (referencing 1 Pet. 1.20; Rev. 13.8). Thus infants and heathen are to an extent beneficiaries of Christ's sacrifice apart from or at least prior to ex-plicit knowledge of Christ but without diminishing the importance of Christian conversion (referencing, for example, Jn 1.9; Rom. 1.19-20; 2.14-15).[89]

King argued for the reality and efficacy of general revelation as a preparatory stage for the necessary special revelation.[90] Although limited, general revelation cannot be discounted in its significance for those who do not have the Scriptures. The Holy Spirit works along a kind of revelatory continuum in which those who have the Scriptures and are regenerate and Spirit-filled are thus enabled to move progressively beyond natural light for deeper and more direct illumination. Christology, atonement, revelation, and religious expe-rience come together in King's theology of religions. King says,

> The Atonement is parallel to the Fall. The fall is universal. Sin touches every living being. No one has escaped. Wherever man is found, sin is found. Wherever sin is found, there is some vague idea that there is some power that can remove it, or that there is some way to escape from its consequence. The atone-ment covers all the ground of sin. Millions know nothing of it, historically. Yet everyone one is mysteriously touched by the atonement in that aspect of it which is unconditionally applied. There may be those who have the essential Christ that know nothing of the historic Christ. They may have pressed, in heart, up through the mist of heathenism, and prayed to the God that made heaven and earth, and in that way touched the Christ and

---

[89] Another notable early Pentecostal theologian and church leader, E.S. Wil-liams, *Systematic Theology: Volume 2* (Springfield, MO: Gospel Publishing House, 1991 [1953]), pp. 143, 145, from a different denomination, the Assemblies of God, espoused a similar view.

[90] Richie, 'Azusa-era Optimism', pp. 230-34.

found peace. We do not know this to be true, but we infer the same from certain statements it the Word.[91]

Thus, for King, some may experience Christ beyond their level of specific intellectual knowledge of Christianity. This experience was precipitated by God's role as Creator, consistent with an individual's personal desire and longing for peace, ultimately satisfied only in Christ, and implicated in biblical teaching, although not a point about which to be dogmatic.

Finally, King tied his theology of religions, and in actuality all of his theology, to a progressive and dynamic pneumatology.[92] For him, all that is in Christ, and all God's work in humanity, is carried out by the active and ongoing agency of the Holy Spirit. Thus, 'Everything divine in us is directly related to the Holy Spirit', and 'Every work of grace' must be wrought by the Spirit because apart from the Spirit 'there is nothing left'.[93] Accordingly, although less directly and more implicitly, King's theology of religions is pneumatological in nature while having a clear Christological center. When King talks about God at work in the hearts of non-Christians, he assumes it is the Holy Spirit in action.

Regarding King's theology of religions, a couple of further points are especially pertinent. First, although King always maintained the unique and superior nature of Christianity, he distinguished between institutional or ecclesial Christianity and what he termed 'the religion of Christ'.[94] The religion of Christ signifies the pre-incarnation, hidden work of God in all of humanity that is nevertheless utterly dependent upon Christ and the universal agency of his Spirit. Thus it transcends chronological and ecclesiastical boundaries but is no less rooted in the person and work of Christ. Accordingly, Christianity, especially in the sense of the religion of Christ, is the only true religion; but, it is not to be confused or conflated with institutional or ecclesial Christianity. Ostensibly, the lat-

---

[91] J.H. King, *From Passover to Pentecost* (Franklin Springs, GA: Advocate Press, 4th edn, 1976), p. 101. Significantly, *From Passover to Pentecost* represents King's most sustained and systematic theological work.

[92] Richie, 'Azusa-era Optimism', pp. 230-34.

[93] J.H. King, *Christ – God's Love Gift: Selected Writings of J.H. King* (Franklin Springs, GA: Advocate Press, 1969), I, p. 136.

[94] J.H. King, 'Today', *The Pentecostal Holiness Advocate* 9.31 (December 3, 1925), pp. 1, 8. Cf. Richie, 'Azusa-era Optimism', pp. 235-36.

ter would include the former but the former would not be limited to the latter. This interpretative insight is completely consistent with King's emphatic Christological orientation integrating universal and eternal with particular and historical categories.[95]

Secondly, King's theology of religions is not an abstract speculative process but is biblically based and theologically grounded. His approach to the book of Jonah is suggestive in this regard.[96] For King the narrative of the Hebrew prophet's interaction with the pagan people of Nineveh represents God's redemptive willingness and soteriological openness beyond established religious boundaries (i.e. the Judeo-Christian religions). He is clear about the implications of this sometimes startling story for contemporary theology. The Lord 'not only taught Jonah a lesson to enlarge his view of mercy and compassion, but was using him in a way to reveal great truths that should belong to future generations' regarding divine preference in forbearance rather than punishment toward those considered by many as beyond reach. In a sense, therefore, the book of Jonah narrates a divine challenge to Jews (and Christians) for greater openness toward those of other faiths.

By way of brief evaluation, early Classical Pentecostal theology of religions as represented by Charles Parham and J.H. King suggest close intersections at a point that would today be called exclusive and inclusive categories. Pluralism is out altogether. All religions are not equal; conversely, some religions have very destructive elements. Rather, early Pentecostal theology of religions maintains a high Christology and distinctive soteriology with pneumatological suggestions of openness to the Spirit's working in or among religious others. Further, the distinctive nature and mission of the Church are maintained with recognition of a more expansive scope of redemptive activity. Finally, its authoritative support is Scripture and its teleological imprint is essentially eschatological.

Although serious theological reflection is evident at times, the ad hoc occasional nature of early Pentecostal theology of religions is

---

[95] Chapter Five includes more on this in conversation with Jürgen Moltmann.

[96] J.H. King, 'Jonah's Gourd', *The Pentecostal Holiness Advocate* 20.29 (Nov. 19, 1936), pp. 1-2. Cf. Richie, 'Azusa-era Optimism', pp. 236-38. Although a short homily, King's exposition of Jonah in 1936 taken with previous statements beginning as early as 1911 and continuing through 1925 suggest a consistent and coherent pattern for a hopeful theology of religions.

often apparent as well. It should be remembered that these cogita-
tions occur prior to the advent of the formal discipline of Christian
theology of religions as well as at a primitive (though fertile) stage
in the development of Pentecostal theology itself. All the more remarkable perhaps is the bold freshness of these comparatively basic
investigations. Consequently, a contemporary Pentecostal theology
of religions benefits greatly from these early insights but now finds
it necessary to advance to a more sophisticated and systematic ar-
ticulation regarding its contribution to the discipline.

Conclusion

Chapter 2 has looked at some contextual background for contemporary Pentecostal theology of religions as a distinctive discipline. It
has set forth some of the basic terms and categories for Christian
theology of religions and pointed out a few major figures and leaders. It has particularly surveyed some early Pentecostal contributions to theology of religions. Not surprisingly, given the richness
and diversity of the Pentecostal movement, it appears that Pentecostal theology, in spite of its comparative or relative youthfulness,
appears well poised to make a distinctive and valuable contribution
to the discipline of Christian theology of religions. The next chapter
will examine more contemporary Pentecostal approaches to the
discipline by a few of its leading proponents.

3

CONTEMPORARY PENTECOSTAL THEOLOGY OF RELIGIONS

Introduction

Peter's encounter with Cornelius (Acts 10) became a recurring topic in the New Testament church (Acts 11; 15.6-11). At the Jerusalem Council Peter's testimony precipitated Paul and Barnabas' report of what had been said and done through their ministries among the Gentiles (Acts 15.13). When they had finished hearing a full description of all the facts James rendered the formal decision extending Jewish and Gentile relations within the New Testament church (vv. 13-21) as it was adopted and enacted by the consensus of the council (vv. 22-30). This chapter continues the survey of the last chapter on the developing discipline of Pentecostal theology of religions with a focus on a significant partner and contemporary Pentecostal contributors.

Significant Charismatic Partners

Several streams of thought have exerted convergent influence on Pentecostal theological development in many ways, including on its theology of religions.[1] Perhaps the most direct and sustained non-Pentecostal influence on Pentecostal theology of religions has come from Clark Pinnock.[2] A charismatic Baptist, Pinnock has worked

---

[1] Richie, *Speaking by the Spirit*, p. 53.
[2] E.g. Clark H. Pinnock, *Flame of Love: A Theology of the Holy Spirit* (Downers Grove, IL: InterVarsity Press, 1994), is popular among Pentecostals and has a major treatment of theology of religions in Chapter 6. See also his *A Wideness in*

closely with Pentecostals in such areas as hermeneutics (science of biblical interpretation), pneumatology, and ecclesiology.[3] Pinnock's theology of religions is characterized by dialectic diversity. He affirms the uniqueness and necessity of Christ's incarnation and of God's revelation in Christ; yet, he refuses to restrict the reach of the Holy Spirit to those who have specifically heard the gospel through the Church's proclamation – even though he supports its evangelistic mission.[4] In a context of commitment to a high Christology Pinnock turns to pneumatology in his theology of religions. For Pinnock, Jesus Christ represents divine particularity and the Holy Spirit represents divine universality (although not in an absolute sense).[5] In other words, Jesus Christ is the concrete historical manifestation efficaciously accomplishing the goal of God's powerful redemptive love while the Holy Spirit transcends the limits of time and space in extending the benefits of God's powerful redemptive love.

In unpacking his pneumatological turn, Pinnock plumbs John Wesley's doctrine of prevenient grace (literally, grace that goes before, or preceding grace, i.e. pre-conversion grace) to suggest that God's Spirit is graciously at work in the religions of the world revealing God and preparing the way for salvation.[6] He notes that prevenient grace for Wesley signified 'the universal, gracious operations of the Spirit' and infers that it thus may be fruitful in the world and its religions.[7] Pinnock argues that for Wesley prevenient grace/the universal working of the Spirit 'eased the problem of the fate of the unevangelized' and 'enabled him' to say that people would be judged by their response to 'the light that they have'.[8] Consequently, pneumatology, soteriology, and theology of religions can jell together as legitimate parts of a coherent whole.

Significantly, for Pinnock non-Christian religions are not vehicles of salvation; but, neither is the Spirit restricted to the Church.

God's Mercy: The Finality of Jesus Christ in a World of Religions (Grand Rapids: Zondervan, 1992).

[3] Richie, *Speaking by the Spirit,* pp. 56, 73.

[4] Pinnock, *Flame of Love,* pp. 14, 21, 105, and 118, 213.

[5] Pinnock, *Flame of Love,* pp. 188, 194-95, and 197.

[6] Pinnock, *Flame of Love,* pp. 61, 63.

[7] Pinnock, *Flame of Love,* pp. 199. See also p. 200.

[8] Pinnock, *Flame of Love,* p. 199. For more on Wesley's own theology of religions, see Tony Richie, 'Mr. Wesley and Mohammed: A Contemporary Inquiry Concerning Islam', *ATJ* 58.2 (Fall 2003), pp. 79-99.

Thus some devout adherents of other religions may be thought of as 'pre-Christians'.[9] Nevertheless, the lack of knowledge regarding God's reconciling love in Christ is an undeniable deficit in the religions not to be downplayed.[10] Accordingly, the Spirit empowers the followers of Jesus as a community (the Church) which is in fact 'the vehicle of God's saving activity' in the world.[11] Pinnock describes the Church as the Spirit-anointed herald of God's Kingdom, a relational and social trinitarian reflection, oriented to mission, a fellowship of the Spirit, with a continuing charismatic structure that still has an institutional dimension.[12] This pneumatological ecclesiology represents the expansive and integrative aspects of a theology that is able, among other things, to reach out to the religions simultaneous with reaffirming an ecclesiology that retains the Church's distinctive identity and nature.

In short, Pinnock is concerned to demonstrate God's global reach in salvation, that is, God's compassionate concern for the salvation of the people of all nations.[13] Yet Pinnock firmly defends God's gracious revelation in Christ as definitive and final.[14] He reevaluates the biblical record on non-Christian religions, and suggests contemporary religions have a dynamic (non-static) quality and that God's purpose is to bring in the Kingdom (i.e. not a religion).[15] Thus Pinnock views the religions as potentially capable of being impacted or even transformed by Christ. For Pinnock, eschatology, or the working out of God's redemptive purpose over time in history toward God's ultimate goal, allows for a generous view of salvation.[16]

Pinnock sees his theology of religions as a bold attempt to counteract religious pluralism in a manner faithful to 'the finality of Jesus Christ and the global mission of the church'.[17] He insists that he

---

[9] Pinnock, *Flame of Love*, p. 179.
[10] Pinnock, *Flame of Love*, p. 206.
[11] Pinnock, *Flame of Love*, p. 115.
[12] Clark H. Pinnock, 'The Church in the Power of the Spirit: The Promise of Pentecostal Ecclesiology', *JPT* 14.2 (April 2006), pp. 147-65.
[13] Pinnock, *Wideness in God's Mercy*, p. 13 (Chapter 1).
[14] Pinnock, *Wideness in God's Mercy*, p. 13 (Chapter 2).
[15] Pinnock, *Wideness in God's Mercy*, p. 14 (Chapters 3-4).
[16] Pinnock, *Wideness in God's Mercy*, p. 14 (Chapter 5).
[17] Pinnock, *Wideness in God's Mercy*, p. 181.

adheres faithfully to 'the central doctrines of classical theology'.[18] Pinnock is convinced the way to meet the 'challenge of many religions' is 'with a biblically grounded and theologically sound argument' that 'does not sacrifice any important Christian convictions' and yet 'gives some fresh answers and angles of vision'.[19] In this sense, it might be observed that Pinnock's theology of religions prefers to combat radically relativistic religious pluralism not merely negatively by attacking its inadequacies but positively by presenting a more efficient and favorable alternative that is faithful to the historic Christian theological tradition.

Additionally, Pinnock deplores the soteriological negativity, or 'all-too-common pessimism of salvation', that has been the default mode of what he sees as defective theological systems.[20] Contrariwise, he celebrates the 'inexhaustibility of the Scriptures' in addressing hard topics in theology of religions and is inspired by the 'fresh relevance and power' of the theological renewal that ensues.[21] Therefore, Pinnock's approach to theology of religions can be described as optimistic rather than pessimistic, dynamic rather than static, and biblical rather than speculative.

Pinnock's theology of religions clearly falls within the complex of what is called the inclusive types. That is, he maintains a high Christology and distinctive Christian soteriology in a context of hopeful openness to religious others. His theology of religions is also distinctively pneumatological. It relies heavily on the presence and work of the Holy Spirit in accounting for extra-ecclesial redemptive activity. Yet Pinnock's theology of religions is ecclesiologically and missiologically grounded. The distinctive identity and nature of the Church and its mission are retained. Furthermore, it endeavors to be biblically and theologically sound. With these and other similar characteristics in mind, it is notable that Pinnock's work has exerted significant influence on contemporary Pentecostal theologies of religions.[22]

---

[18] Pinnock, *Wideness in God's Mercy*, p. 181.
[19] Pinnock, *Wideness in God's Mercy*, p. 181.
[20] Pinnock, *Wideness in God's Mercy*, p. 182.
[21] Pinnock, *Wideness in God's Mercy*, p. 183.
[22] E.g. many of the theologians reviewed in the rest of this chapter frequently reference Pinnock in their work.

Another Charismatic theologian who wrestled with the reality of non-Christian religions, although to a much lesser extent than did Pinnock, was J. Rodman Williams, most noted for producing the first systematic theology from a Charismatic Renewal perspective. Williams clearly prioritized the evangelistic mission of the Church.[23] However, he also understood the mission of the Church as expressed in the Great Commission (Mt. 28.19-20) to include ministering to physical and social needs.[24] As for the salvation of the unevangelized, Williams suggests that 'God's mercy in Christ' may be extended 'to some who do not outwardly know him'.[25] He maintains, on the one hand, the nonnegotiable necessity of Jesus Christ and the critical importance of evangelism, and, on the other hand, an openness to the possibility of a width in God's mercy for the unreached (per Jn 1.9; 3.21; 14.6; Acts 4.12; 1 Tim. 2.5).

Williams is careful to confirm that his hopeful position does not 'lessen the urgency of proclaiming Christ Himself as the only hope of salvation'.[26] Yet he is insistent that 'to state bluntly that the countless numbers of people who have never heard the gospel verbally are all consigned to hell seems to go beyond the New Testament message'.[27] Again, he clearly rejects universalism, always maintaining that 'God's grace *in Christ*' is the effectual cause of salvation and 'the urgency of proclaiming the gospel' because 'not only are there many far from the light but some who are doing "what is true" are all the more eager to come to the light of Christ when they hear the gospel'.[28]

There is a clear concern above for unevangelized individuals in Williams rather than for world religions as such. Nevertheless, he acknowledges the common commitment to monotheism shared by Judaism, Christianity, and Islam.[29] Humankind as a whole, however, has suffered from idolatry.[30] Williams emphasizes the importance of

[23] J. Rodman Williams, *Renewal Theology: Systematic Theology from a Charismatic Perspective,* three volumes in one (Grand Rapids: Zondervan, 1996), III, pp. 133-36.
[24] Williams, *Renewal Theology,* III, p. 135.
[25] Williams, *Renewal Theology,* III, p. 476.
[26] Williams, *Renewal Theology,* III, p. 476 n. 126.
[27] Williams, *Renewal Theology,* III, p. 476 n 126.
[28] Williams, *Renewal Theology,* III, p. 476 n 126 (emphasis original).
[29] Williams, *Renewal Theology,* I, p. 84.
[30] Williams, *Renewal Theology,* I, p. 246 and I, p. 253.

knowledge of the gospel and a response of faith, but also affirms that God's will is revealed inwardly to every person.[31] For him, the teaching of Rom. 2.14-15 'that some may be excused' supports the conclusion that 'God will surely honor any genuine witness to truth'.[32] Yet humanity's own pursuit of God as expressed in the religions of the world is ineffective and unsuccessful.[33]

The theology of religions of Rodman Williams is cautious, even guarded, but nevertheless hopeful and open to redemptive possibilities. Significantly, it is Williams' attempt to be biblically consistent and theologically congruent that brings him to a kind of guarded optimism. In any case, for him the narrow negativity of a closed system is indefensible. At the very least, Christian theology holds out hope for a greater breadth and depth in God's gracious revelatory and redemptive work in Christ than has perhaps sometimes been presumed.

Although not as influential in the specific discipline of Christian theology of religions as Clark Pinnock, Rodman Williams supplies an important example of doing theology of religions by fleshing out implications of the overall theological endeavor at relevant points. It may therefore be noted that, first, doing Christian theology today requires attention to theology of religions, even for 'non-specialists'. That has, of course, always been the case; but, it has become increasingly evident that the theological enterprise cannot be adequately accomplished apart from some amount of direct attention to theology of religions. There are simply too many intersections between the topics of theology of religions and the major categories of systematic theology to ignore and still claim anything like a satisfactory result.

Second, and perhaps negatively, it may be noted from a comparison of Williams' efforts with Pinnock's that the classic categories of theology do point to hopeful theology of religions but are incomplete, even hesitant or timid, without a turn to pneumatology. Only through explicating the implications of the presence and activity of the Spirit of God and of Christ in the whole world does an adequate and confident theology of religions emerge. Therefore, it

---

[31] Williams, *Renewal Theology*, II, p. 29 and III, p. 459.
[32] Williams, *Renewal Theology*, I, pp. 239-40.
[33] Williams, *Renewal Theology*, I, p. 266.

is all the more notable that each of the following Pentecostal theologians of religions emphasizes, in one way or another, to a greater or lesser extent, a robust trinitarian theology accenting a balanced pneumatological theology of religions.

Contemporary Pentecostal Contributors

There are several contemporary Pentecostal theologians who contribute to Pentecostal theology of religions as a plank in the structure of their overall theological work. For example, Frank Macchia has taken the time to offer a serious critique of religious pluralism, particularly of the radical philosophy of John Hick, especially his weak Christology.[34] Perhaps most importantly, at least for Pentecostal theology, Macchia argues that Christ's role as Spirit Baptizer establishes his divine identity (only God can give God's Spirit) and thereby the uniqueness of the Christian message.[35] Nevertheless, the tongues of Pentecost embrace and exhibit cultural and religious diversity so as to inform contemporary theology of religions in remarkable ways that sustain the identity and mission of the Church while suggesting that those of other religions are in some sense 'fellow travelers'.[36] Macchia's theology of religions, therefore, is explicitly Pentecostal through his purposeful appropriation of the categories of Spirit baptism and of Pentecost, respectful and appreciative of adherents of other religions, and to an extent cast in an antipluralist polemical mode.

Steven Studebaker is another Pentecostal theologian who, though he does not focus on theology of religions per se, nevertheless includes a significant treatment of the topic in his theological enterprise. Studebaker laments negative theologies of religions as out of step with the biblical narrative of the Spirit of Pentecost.[37] He argues, 'From creation to Pentecost, the mission of the Spirit of God is not only to breathe life into all human beings but also to draw them into the fellowship of the trinitarian God', insisting 'that

---

[34] Macchia, *Baptized in the Spirit,* pp. 182-90.
[35] Macchia, *Baptized in the Spirit,* pp. 184-87.
[36] Macchia, *Baptized in the Spirit,* p. 188.
[37] Steven M. Studebaker, 'Christian Mission and the Religions as Participation in the Spirit of Pentecost', in Yong and Clarke (eds.), *Global Renewal,* p. 71.

mission is universal and perennial'.[38] The Spirit of Pentecost offers rich resources for both Christian theology of religions and for the mission of the Church through providing continuity and connectivity between creation, redemption, the Incarnation, Pentecost, and the eschaton, and thereby inviting all into the possibility of 'progressive and partial participation' in the Spirit of Pentecost.[39] Like Macchia, Studebaker's theology of religions is an explicitly Pentecostal approach; however, he stresses the all-encompassing work of the Spirit in arriving at possibly even more far-reaching assertions regarding the Spirit's redemptive working in the world of religions.

Other examples could be given. In his survey of contemporary Pentecostal theology Keith Warrington notes that more Pentecostal theologians are beginning to call for dialogue with those of other religions.[40] Warrington suggests that consistently with Pentecostal history and tradition some Pentecostal theologians are opening up to possibilities of the working of the Spirit of Christ beyond the Church.[41] He further proposes that this approach enlarges Christology and pneumatology without weakening ecclesiology or soteriology.[42] Arguably, there is a trend among some Pentecostal theologians toward a hopeful and pneumatological approach to Christian theology of religions.

Of course, Pentecostals such as missiologist Robert Gallagher are concerned, and rightly so, about any theology of religions, no matter how purportedly pneumatological in nature, which appears to undermine a high Christology or the urgency of Christian mission in order to offer some politically correct attempt at placating non-Christian religions.[43] Nevertheless, as will be seen, the present consensus of Pentecostal theologians working most directly in the discipline of theology of religions, as well as some other Pentecostal theologians, and of this work as well, is that a theology of religions faithful to traditional Pentecostal faith and values is not necessarily antagonistic to themes of openness and optimism (hope) regarding

---

[38] Studebaker, 'Christian Mission and the Religions', p. 71.

[39] Studebaker, 'Christian Mission and the Religions', pp. 86-87.

[40] Warrington, *Pentecostal Theology*, p. 40.

[41] Warrington, *Pentecostal Theology*, pp. 40-44.

[42] Warrington, *Pentecostal Theology*, p. 44.

[43] Robert L. Gallagher, 'The Holy Spirit in the World: In Non-Christians, in Creation, and Other Religions', *AJPS* 9.1 (2006), pp. 17-33.

the working of the Spirit of Christ in the wider world, so long as foundational principles and presuppositions (e.g. as enumerated in Chapter 1 of this work) of historic Pentecostal theology are properly respected and appropriated.

The author of nearly a dozen books, and the co-author/editor of several more, as well as more than a hundred articles in scholarly venues, Veli-Matti Kärkkäinen is one of the world's most prolific Pentecostal theologians. This Finnish theologian has written major monographs on theology proper (doctrine of God/Trinity), Christology, pneumatology, ecclesiology, soteriology, missiology, and so on. He has devoted two books solely to the topic of theology of religions. *An Introduction to the Theology of Religions: Biblical, Historical, and Contemporary Perspectives* is his extensive overview of the discipline covering every major confessional tradition and their respective contributors to Christian theology of religions from biblical times to the present era. It is vast in its scope and includes a couple of Pentecostal and Charismatic thinkers like Clark Pinnock and Amos Yong. It is not constructive in intent, but concludes with some important pointers on the way forward for Christian theology of religions in general, primarily an expression of hopefulness regarding the discipline itself.

Kärkkäinen's *The Trinity and Religious Pluralism: The Doctrine of the Trinity in Christian Theology of Religions* takes the doctrine of the Trinity as the distinguishing characteristic of Christian theology in general and then applies that concept to Christian theology of religions in particular. It surveys the major international and ecumenical contributors and their particular contributions to theology of religions utilizing a trinitarian framework. Finally, Kärkkäinen addresses future challenges and areas needing development and provides a case study of interreligious relations through the example of the Roman Catholic Church and Islam. Kärkkäinen concludes with an argument for and brief explication of the doctrine of the Trinity as the most reliable and fertile resource for developing and articulating a Christian theology of religions.

Neither Kärkkäinen's *An Introduction to the Theology of Religions* nor his *The Trinity and Religious Pluralism* is written primarily with Pentecostals in mind. The books are much broader, more ecumenical. Of course, they are written by Kärkkäinen as a Pentecostal theologian. As such, these and other writings by Kärkkäinen have major significance for Pentecostal theology of religions. Kärkkäinen's theology of religions might be best described as an ecumenical approach from a Pentecostal perspective.

Kärkkäinen's theology of religions is clear and concise. As might be expected, Kärkkäinen is extremely critical of the ideology of religious pluralism. He notes that 'While pluralism is not the sole problem of theology of religions, it is currently the most impending one'.[44] For him, the thought of leading pluralist John Hick, who posits some sort of generic 'Ultimate Reality' in the place of a personal God, is shapeless and vague, and has 'left behind the particular God of the Bible'.[45] He argues that Hick, and thereby pluralism, is contradictory and absolutist in its efforts to force all religions into a common mold.[46] Kärkkäinen thinks Hick's pluralism fails epistemologically (how humans know what they know), because it assumes an unknowable abstract Reality, and linguistically, because it cannot bridge the impersonal and personal aspects of their so-called Ultimate Reality within the limits of human language.[47]

Kärkkäinen particularly objects to Hick's pluralist attack on the Christian doctrine of the Trinity and on Christology. He refutes the claim of Hick that these teachings are not in New Testament, and charges Hick with arguing from a basis widely discredited by scholarly consensus.[48] More importantly, perhaps, Kärkkäinen adroitly exposes a pluralist attempt to revise the doctrine of the Trinity and Christology in order to make it fit its own assumptions and the assertions arising from them.[49] Furthermore, Hick's pluralist theology takes a functionalist approach to doctrine that attempts to bypass the question of truth.[50] Finally, the rejection by Hick's pluralism of the Trinity and historic Christology results from his discomfiture with the paradoxical nature of transcendent mystery in relation to the divine – although Hick himself sometimes appeals to the same paradoxical category in support of his own views.[51] In short, ac-

---

[44] Kärkkäinen, *Introduction to Theology of Religions,* p. 354.
[45] Kärkkäinen, *Introduction to Theology of Religions,* pp. 25, 171.
[46] Kärkkäinen, *Introduction to Theology of Religions,* pp. 292-93.
[47] Kärkkäinen, *Introduction to Theology of Religions,* pp. 350-51.
[48] Kärkkäinen, *Trinity and Religious Pluralism,* pp. 113-14.
[49] Kärkkäinen, *Introduction to Theology of Religions,* p. 114.
[50] Kärkkäinen, *Introduction to Theology of Religions,* pp. 114-15.
[51] Kärkkäinen, *Introduction to Theology of Religions,* p. 115.

cording to Kärkkäinen, Hick has truncated Christology and desert-
ed the classical Christian doctrine of God as triune.[52]
  Basically, Kärkkäinen argues that trinitarian theology serves as a
critique of 'normative' religious pluralism.[53] Religion is essentially
the search for ultimate truth.[54] However, the triune God of the Bible is unique.[55] High Christology is critical to the doctrine of the
Trinity.[56] Furthermore, the Church points beyond itself to the eschatological Kingdom and the Triune God's presence in the world
in the harmony and unity of diverse peoples.[57] Of particular import
is the manner in which the doctrine of the Trinity specifically informs Kärkkäinen's theology of religions. In the doctrine of the
Trinity communion, unity, and difference come together in the divine being.[58] The Trinity extends communion, through self-
revelation, to the other, to those who are different, and this provides the paradigm for human relationships as well, including interreligious engagement, with respect for tolerance but without denial
of the challenges of differences.[59]
  What Kärkkäinen reaches for in his trinitarian theology of religions is a pneumatological theology of religions that is nevertheless
Christocentric and ecclesiologically faithful.[60] Thus, in spite of his
stinging critique of Hick and religious pluralism, Kärkkäinen's theology of religions is primarily formulated in a positive mode. The
Spirit of Christ reaches beyond the Church into the Kingdom and
into the world while abiding in unique relationship with Christ's
Church. Non-Christian religions are not salvific but neither is the
presence of the Triune God in their midst inconceivable. Accord-

---

[52] Kärkkäinen, *Introduction to Theology of Religions*, pp. 116-17.
[53] Kärkkäinen, *Introduction to Theology of Religions*, p. 165.
[54] Kärkkäinen, *Introduction to Theology of Religions*, p. 166.
[55] Kärkkäinen, *Introduction to Theology of Religions*, p. 169.
[56] Kärkkäinen, *Introduction to Theology of Religions*, p. 171.
[57] Kärkkäinen, *Introduction to Theology of Religions*, p. 175.
[58] Kärkkäinen, *Introduction to Theology of Religions*, pp. 176-78.
[59] Kärkkäinen, *Introduction to Theology of Religions*, pp. 179-80.
[60] Kärkkäinen, 'Toward a Pneumatological Theology of Religions: A Pentecostal-Charismatic Inquiry', *IRM* 91.361 (2202), pp. 187-98.

ingly, interreligious engagement and dialogue are both desirable and possible out of the context of a trinitarian theology of religions.[61]

Thus the theology of religions of Veli-Matti Kärkkäinen leads rather naturally into interreligious engagement and dialogue. For him, the knowledge of God is not confined but has 'universal intention' that is to be in some sense 'shared by all'.[62] This acknowledgement provides a basis for a process in which Christians can share their faith with others 'in the spirit of a confident, yet humble witness'.[63] Kärkkäinen suggests that although the purpose of dialogue is not only to present information but also persuasion, 'it must be done in ways that honor the Other and give him or her the right to make up his or her own mind'.[64] There need be no claim that interreligious dialogue is an entirely neutral experience because participants know everyone already has convictions about ultimate questions. Otherwise, so-called dialogue would only be 'two or more monologues'.[65] Although the approach and the tone differ, different aspects of Christian mission can and do inform the dialogue of Christians with others. The possibility of the Spirit's presence among those of other religions 'ties the church to dialogue' because wherever God's presence is found 'it bears some relation to the church'.[66] Of course, discernment through dialogue in the process of discovery is critically important.[67]

Kärkkäinen admits that there are many issues he does not address. Major among them would be the question of the salvation of the unevangelized. However, he explains that he has focused on what he considers 'the one major divide theologically … the one between the pluralists and the rest'.[68] As noted previously, for him 'While pluralism is not the sole problem of theology of religions, it

---

[61] Kärkkäinen, 'How to Speak of the Spirit among the Religions: Trinitarian "Rules" for a Pneumatological Theology of Religions', *International Bulletin Missionary Research* 30.3 (2006), pp. 121-27.

[62] Kärkkäinen, *Trinity and Religious Pluralism*, p. 180.

[63] Kärkkäinen, *Trinity and Religious Pluralism*, p. 180.

[64] Kärkkäinen, *Trinity and Religious Pluralism*, p. 181.

[65] Kärkkäinen, *Trinity and Religious Pluralism*, p. 181.

[66] Veli-Matti Kärkkäinen, 'The Uniqueness of Christ and the Trinitarian Faith', in S.W. Chung (ed.), *Christ the One and Only: A Global Affirmation of the Uniqueness of Jesus Christ* (Grand Rapids: Baker Academic, 2005), p. 128.

[67] Kärkkäinen, 'The Uniqueness of Christ', p. 128.

[68] Kärkkäinen, *Trinity and Religious Pluralism*, p. 182.

is currently the most impending one'.[69] Thus the ideology of religious pluralism stands out against all other lesser problems confronting Christian theology of religions as the paramount concern.

Kärkkäinen offers several questions for the future. First, '[W]hat exactly is the relationship between the Spirit and Jesus Christ in the outward works of the triune God in the world?' Second, 'Is a distinctively "pneumatological" theology of religions needed as complementing the older, now much rejected "Christological" or should we only aim at a trinitarian one?' Third, 'Are there various forms of trinitarian theologies of religions that are biblical and theologically sound?' And finally, 'If so, what are the essential criteria for their soundness (other than those discussed above)?'[70] Pursuing answers to these questions could quite easily lead to charting the course of Christian theology of religions for at least the near future.

A few brief observations about Kärkkäinen's theology of religions are in order. First, it is quite obviously driven by a primary concern for the problem of the ideology of religious pluralism. Kärkkäinen definitely sees radical religious pluralism as a significant threat to classical historic Christianity that must be confronted vigorously. Second, it draws on the definitive essence of Christianity, the doctrine of the Trinity, in presenting not only a defense of Christianity and a critique of pluralism but also in developing a response to the issues of religious pluralism through a trinitarian theology of religions. Here Kärkkäinen is ingeniously counting on the genius of Christian theology to rise to the occasion for a multiplicity of interconnected concerns. Third, its broad basis, the doctrine of the Trinity, shared by the vast majority of Christian traditions, should be appealing to a wide audience but also, because of its innate complexities, may make it capable of vastly diverse interpretations and applications. As a Pentecostal and ecumenical theologian, Kärkkäinen has offered an approach to Christian theology of religions which is simultaneously inviting and intimidating.

Amos Yong is undoubtedly the leading Pentecostal theologian of religions in the world today. Yong was born in Malaysia and immigrated to the United States as a child. He has published scholarly monographs on interreligious dialogue and comparative theology,

---

[69] Kärkkäinen, *Introduction to Theology of Religions,* p. 354.
[70] Kärkkäinen, *Trinity and Religious Pluralism,* p. 182.

global Pentecostal theology, theology of disability, political theology, dialogue between science and religion, theology of economics, and a theology of love as well as a book on a trinitarian theological method and hermeneutic. He has also co-authored or co-edited several more books as well as writing several dozens of articles in scholarly venues. His major works on theology of religions include: *Discerning the Spirit(s), A Pentecostal-Charismatic Contribution to the Christian Theology of Religions; Beyond the Impasse: Toward a Pneumatological Theology of Religions;* and *Hospitality and the Other: Pentecost, Christian Practices, and the Neighbor.* Yong also co-edited (with Clifton Clarke) *Global Renewal, Religious Pluralism, and The Great Commission: Towards a Renewal Theology of Mission and Interreligious Encounter.* Most recently, he has published *Pneumatology and the Christian-Buddhist Dialogue: Does the Spirit Blow through the Middle Way?*[71] In addition, many of his works on other themes include sections with more or less treatment of theology of religions and interreligious encounter and dialogue.

As might be noticed even from a chronological reading of the titles of Yong's theology of religions publications there is a discernible trajectory from establishing a pneumatological orientation for a Christian theology of religions, toward the practice of Christian mission in contexts of interreligious encounter, to a full-fledged comparative theology project. Overall, Yong's work tends to be biblically informed, theologically articulate, intellectually abstract, and praxis oriented. Also, it is Pentecostal in an intentional way, especially in its use of pneumatological categories, but reaches out to a larger audience as well. Finally, an adept systematic and constructive theologian, Yong has strong interdisciplinary instincts. The following provides a brief overview of some of the most salient features of his considerable body of work at it relates directly to Pentecostal theology of religions.

Yong's driving desire in his theology of religions work is to formulate a distinctively Pentecostal theology of religions.[72] He proposes that the Pentecostal experience produces a unique 'pneuma-

---

[71] Yong, *Discerning the Spirit(s)*; idem, *Beyond the Impasse*; idem, *Hospitality and the Other*; Yong and Clarke (eds.), *Global Renewal*; and Amos Yong, *Pneumatology and the Christian-Buddhist Dialogue: Does the Spirit Blow through the Middle Way?* (Leiden and Boston: Brill, 2012).

[72] See Yong, *Discerning the Spirit(s)*, especially Chapter 6.

tological imagination', or a way of thinking and theologizing informed by an experience of and orientation toward the Holy Spirit, suggesting possibilities of the Spirit's presence and influence in the world and in the world's religions.[73] Yong therefore develops a 'foundational pneumatology' as a framework to support 'not only a pneumatological interpretation of the religions but also a general understanding of divine presence and activity'.[74]

Yong's theology of religions is best described as 'pneumatological' since it is chiefly characterized by an accent on the agency and universality of the Holy Spirit. In other words, Yong's pneumatological theology of religions suggests that the Holy Spirit is present and active in some sense throughout the world, even beyond the Church and with potential implications for alethiology (study of truth/nature of truth) and soteriology. Therefore, whatever truth or grace is present in the religions, or at least among their adherents, if any, would be traceable to the influence of the Spirit of Christ, howbeit perhaps unknown as such in a particular religious culture at the time.

Yong is not naïve or gullible regarding the world or its religions and therefore emphasizes a need for discernment because there are many 'spirits' (good and evil) in the world. For Yong, Christian discernment in the Pentecostal-Charismatic tradition includes both divine gifting and human discretion.[75] Criteria for discerning the Holy Spirit from other spirits includes the fruit of the Spirit, ethical conduct, and signs of the coming Kingdom.[76] He suggests that, within this theological framework, 'the pneumatological imagination derived from the outpouring of the Spirit' enables a relatively impartial, sympathetic, yet critical engagement with the religions.[77] Yong's recognition of multiple spirits, good and evil, gives his work a distinctive Pentecostal dynamic, and his emphasis on discernment helps guard its Christian character.

Carefully interrelating Christology and pneumatology is a special (and serious) challenge in any pneumatological theology of reli-

---

[73] Yong, *Discerning the Spirit(s)*, pp. 29-31 and Chapter 4.
[74] Yong, *Discerning the Spirit(s)*, pp. 98 and 122-32.
[75] Yong, *Discerning the Spirit(s)*, p. 249.
[76] Yong, *Discerning the Spirit(s)*, pp. 243-55.
[77] Amos Yong, *The Spirit Poured Out on All Flesh: Pentecostalism and the Possibility of Global Theology* (Grand Rapids: Baker, 2005), p. 254.

gions. However, Yong's pneumatology does not stand apart from his Christology. John 3.8 compares the mystery of the Spirit to the moving of the wind. For Yong, the implications of this text suggest the fruit and gifts of the Spirit may appear among other religious cultures and traditions.[78] Yet Yong understands the Holy Spirit as 'both universal and particular, both the Spirit of God and the Spirit of Jesus the Christ'.[79] Accordingly, by definition there cannot be any disjunction between Christ and the Spirit – distinction yes, but disjunction no. Thus, Kärkkäinen rightly observes that Yong enlarges the theology of religions' framework through pneumatology but does not unloose pneumatology from Christology.[80] In other words, although Amos Yong obviously stresses the Spirit's presence in the world and its religions that emphasis alone does not sacrifice the uniqueness or necessity of Jesus Christ.

Still, Yong does suggest that Christians may begin conversations (i.e. dialogue) with adherents of non-Christian religions without first talking explicitly about Jesus Christ. Yong proposes that the Holy Spirit's universal presence and activity provides a substantive starting point for interreligious understanding, helping overcome problems arising from starting instead with the greatest point of difference, the person of Christ.[81] However, he also indicates that the nature of the Trinity means that Christians cannot speak of the Holy Spirit without speaking of the Father and the Son, and that Christians cannot but speak in terms of Christ.[82] This conundrum seems a bit difficult to reconcile unless it is remembered that much of it is mostly a matter of methodology.[83] Although complex, to be borne in mind here is that this is a discussion of a possible starting point in dialogue not about minimizing Christology or maximizing pneumatology (although critics might argue that this could be an implied result).

---

[78] Amos Yong, '"Not Knowing Where the Wind Blows…": On Envisioning a Pentecostal-Charismatic Theology of Religions', *JPT* 14 (April 1999), pp. 81-112. Cf. Yong, *Spirit Poured Out*, pp. 24, 71, and 200.

[79] Yong, *Beyond the Impasse*, p. 21.

[80] Kärkkäinen, *An Introduction to the Theology of Religions*, pp. 279-80.

[81] Yong, *Beyond the Impasse*, pp. 36, 47.

[82] Yong, *Beyond the Impasse*, pp. 42, 47.

[83] Cf. Yong, *Discerning the Spirit(s)*, pp. 140-41.

Like Kärkkäinen, Yong's theology of religions leads naturally to an affirmation of the importance of interreligious dialogue in a context of Christian mission.[84] For him, the goal of dialogue is not to establish generic agreement or to ignore real differences between religions; rather, it serves the righteousness, peace, and truth inherently characteristic of God's Kingdom. Dialogue helps make possible 'the kind of self-criticism that leads to the mutual and, ultimately, eschatological transformation of religious traditions, including the Christian faith'.[85] This means that meaningful dialogue should be both 'a journey of critical self-discovery' and 'a faithful Christian discernment of the other'.[86] Therefore, interreligious dialogue at its best is an authentic encounter with untold possibilities. Furthermore, the eschatological component of theology of religions and interreligious dialogue implies penultimate historic process and ultimate providential realization of the divine purpose for all.

Commitment to interreligious dialogue nonetheless affirms the unique nature of Christian salvation and reaffirms the evangelizing vocation of the Church. Yong does not suggest that Pentecostals 'should desist in their evangelistic activities'.[87] The needs of dialogue do not trump the necessities of evangelism. Rather, interreligious dialogue is broad enough to encompass a wide range of activities that can be held in balance, including service, organized debates, open forums, and so on.[88] Evangelistic witness, dialogue, and social activism are all legitimate elements of broadminded ecclesial mission.[89] Yong insists that Pentecostal theology of religions should 'invigorate the proclamation of the Christian gospel even as it recognizes the eschatological horizon of the Holy Spirit's presence and activity'.[90]

Evangelism continues to be important because of the unique nature of Christ and of Christian salvation. For Yong, 'The perennial problem for Christian theology of religions has been how the affirmation of the divine presence in the universe of human religious-

---

[84] Yong, *Discerning the Spirit(s)*, p.313.
[85] Yong, *Discerning the Spirit(s)*, p. 313.
[86] Yong, *Discerning the Spirit(s)*, p. 143.
[87] Yong, *Discerning the Spirit(s)*, p. 25.
[88] Yong, *Discerning the Spirit(s)*, p. 25.
[89] Yong, *Hospitality and the Other*, pp. 62-64.
[90] Yong, *Discerning the Spirit(s)*, p. 313.

ness can be compatible with the affirmation of salvation through the particular person of Jesus Christ'.[91] He suggests that the New Testament holds in tension two truths: the universality of God's loving purpose and the uniqueness of Christian salvation.[92] Yong affirms a historical theological tradition holding these distinctive poles together through distinguishing between Christological soteriology and ecclesial soteriology.[93] In other words, many Christians can and do affirm that Christ alone is Savior without necessarily asserting that the Church is the sole mediator of the salvation of Christ.

At this point, Yong's Christology and pneumatology come together. Yong argues that the 'whole christological question is, after all, whether or not Christ is *the* savior or just *a* savior'.[94] He answers with the definite article yet insists on 'a pneumatological account for the transformative character of human experience in general and the experience of ultimate salvation in particular'.[95] In other words, the doctrine of Christ as the Savior includes the agency of the Holy Spirit. Christ and the Spirit are co-equal and perichoretic (interpenetrating, mutually indwelling) persons of the Holy Trinity. Thus, the Holy Spirit works in the Church and beyond it as the Spirit of Christ without any contradiction. Therefore, Christology, pneumatology, ecclesiology, missiology, and soteriology may be thought of as seamless whole sustaining Christian theology of religions.

Finally, Yong's at times admittedly rather abstract theology of religions becomes quite pastoral and practical through his employment of the theme of biblical hospitality as a model for interreligious encounter and dialogue.[96] Through a biblical and theological study of hospitable beliefs and practices of Jesus and the post-Pentecost Church, Yong argues that contemporary practices need to extend hospitality beyond the boundaries of faith, nation, and ethnicity.[97] Hospitality relates and integrates Christian beliefs and

---

[91] Yong, *Discerning the Spirit(s)*, p. 35.
[92] Yong, *Discerning the Spirit(s)*, p. 35.
[93] Yong, *Discerning the Spirit(s)*, pp. 38-39.
[94] Yong, *Discerning the Spirit(s)*, p. 58 (emphasis original).
[95] Yong, *Discerning the Spirit(s)*, pp. 311-12.
[96] See Yong, *Hospitality and the Other*.
[97] Yong, *Hospitality and the Other*, pp. 131-39.

practices in such as way as to inform and enhance pastoral faith and life and practical Christian living involving interfaith encounters. Whether at a grassroots/congregational level or at an academic/theological level the hospitality motif provides a basis for gracious and generous interaction with a deeply human component.[98] As Yong says, 'Christians can and should respond with acts of interreligious hospitality'.[99]

A few general characteristics of Yong's over all theological work were listed briefly above. It remains to make a few summary remarks on his theology of religions, particularly in comparison to Kärkkäinen. First, Yong's work is more directly pneumatological and Kärkkäinen's is more intentionally trinitarian. On the one hand, this may be more of a superficial difference than initially apparent. Arguably, a restoration of pneumatology is an essential element in a robust trinitarian theology, of any kind, including theology of religions. However, on the other hand, drawing, as Kärkkäinen does, on trinitarian unity and diversity and communal and personal themes as a resource for a theology of human relationships with the other, including and especially, in this case, with the religious other, is something else than accenting a neglected pneumatological aspect, as Yong does, with its extensive implications. Nevertheless, the two distinctive approaches seem complementary rather than contradictory. Both Kärkkäinen's trinitarian theology of religions with a pneumatological component and Yong's pneumatological theology of religions within a trinitarian construct rely heavily on trinitarian and pneumatological categories, albeit with differing emphases, in formulating their theologies of religions.

Second, as noted above, Kärkkäinen approaches pluralism primarily as a problem. He nevertheless celebrates diversity and inclusivity but apparently the ideology of religious pluralism is for him an identifiably dangerous threat to Christianity. Yong rejects the ideology of pluralism as inconsistent with orthodox Christian theological commitments. However, for Yong religious pluralism ap-

---

[98] Hospitality may provide a category with even further implications for theology and praxis in Pentecostal theology of religions and interreligious coexistence. See Sang-Ehil Han (ed.), *Christian Hospitality and Neighborliness: A Wesleyan-Pentecostal Ministry Paradigm in the Multi-Faith Context* (Cleveland, TN: CPT Press, forthcoming).

[99] Yong, *Hospitality and the Other*, p. 65.

pears to present Christianity with more of an opportunity than a problem. For him, it poses a challenge, to be sure, but perhaps not so much of a threat as such. Again, there is more of a difference in emphasis between Kärkkäinen and Yong than anything else. In any case, both the negative and positive angles are needed, like two sides of the same coin. Religious pluralism is indeed a threat that Christian theology must confront but it also presents Christianity with an opportunity to grow. Arguably, the history of Christianity – against paganism, against heresies, against secularism – indicates that Christianity's remarkable resilience lies in part in its incredible ability to adapt to changing contexts without acquiescence of its essential ethos – indeed, while expanding and enhancing its own self-understanding along with its image before others in the world.

Finally, regardless of whether a Pentecostal theology of religions is primarily trinitarian with a pneumatological component or pneumatological in a trinitarian construct, or whether religious pluralism mostly presents Christians with a problem or an opportunity, the theologies of Kärkkäinen and Yong suggest that relating Christ and the Spirit to each other and to the Church and its mission, to the Kingdom, and to the world, especially the world's religions, in a manner faithfully consistent with biblical, historic Christianity simultaneously with a vision for an inclusive embrace of the other, is its chief challenge. Indeed, even the thorny issue of the salvation of the unevangelized may be thought of in these thematic terms. And of course by all accounts this theological endeavor is set in stark contrast to the ideology of religious pluralism and is certainly at the center of the struggle against religious relativism, and therefore, ultimately, at its worst, the actual anti-religiosity, it represents.

Conclusion

Chapter 3 has surveyed the theology of religions contributions of some significant partners from the Charismatic Renewal movement and also of some leading Pentecostal thinkers. Drawing on the tradition of the words of Peter, Paul, and Barnabas at the Jerusalem Council, in which the Cornelius encounter played such a pivotal role, it has been more of a reminder and a report than anything. However, it indicates that Pentecostal theology of religions is already developing in some profound ways through some obviously quite competent thinkers. The next chapter demonstrates an attempt to build on their resourceful work for creatively advancing Pentecostal theology of religions in a direction consonant with the Pentecostal movement's traditional core faith and values.

4

CONSTRUCTING A PENTECOSTAL THEOLOGY OF RELIGIONS

Introduction

Following the encounter between the Christian apostle, Peter, and the Roman centurion from a pagan background, Cornelius, Peter's testimony before church leaders about what transpired was critical for moving forward accordingly (Acts 11.1-18). With its great significance for the New Testament church again underscored at the Jerusalem Council (15.7-11), they realized that a specific approach was required to coordinate interaction between Jewish Christians and Gentile Christians. For this occasion the council constructed a letter detailing a recommended procedure for this process which was well received (15.22-35). Similarly, although of course in a different context, it is necessary for Pentecostals to have an explicit procedure guiding theology of religions and interreligious encounter and dialogue. This chapter briefly sketches such a proposal.[1] Again, testimony becomes critical for moving forward.

Recognizing an Urgent Need

One of the greatest and most urgent needs facing Christians today involves effectively dealing with the reality of unprecedented confrontational encounters between diverse faith groups and their devotees. The popular American pastor, theologian, ethicist, and politi-

---

[1] The following proposal draws, at times more or less directly, on Tony Richie, 'Translating Pentecostal Testimony into Interreligious Dialogue', *JPT* 20.1 (2011), pp. 155-83.

cal commentator, Reinhold Niebuhr, once observed that 'religious diversity remains potentially the most basic source of conflict'.[2] The September 11, 2001 attack by Islamic terrorists on the United States, and the unsatisfactory effectiveness of subsequent efforts to deal with religion-related violence through the usual political and military channels, illustrate the continuing relevance of Niebuhr's comment. And a host of scholars from diverse denominations and disciplines apparently agree. Lutheran Martin Marty, who specializes in religion in the public square, suggests interreligious rivalry, coupled with economic and political complexities, threatens the security and stability, even the survival, of contemporary society.[3] Harvard comparative religions scholar Diana Eck argues that relations between religions today are far too often characterized by fear and violence.[4] Catholic theologian and ecumenist Hans Küng insists that ongoing interreligious violence is a chief obstacle to peace among the nations.[5] Perhaps few would disagree that violence among the religions is undoubtedly one of the most pressing problems facing the world today.

Sociologist Mark Juergensmeyer suggests religion-related violence is a particularly disturbing and prevalent characteristic of contemporary society.[6] Historically, Juergensmeyer points out, faith has been used to provide moral justification for violence in all of the major religions – Jewish, Christian, Muslim, Hindu, Buddhist, Sikh, and so on.[7] However, religion-related violence is currently rising dramatically, probably as a resistant reaction to discomfiting challenges of modern globalization.[8] Often those who resort to religious violence, that is, religious terrorists, are attempting to defend or promote a narrow worldview they perceive to be under threat in

---

[2] Reinhold Niebuhr, *The Children of Light and The Children of Darkness: A Vindication of Democracy and A Critique of Its Traditional Defense* (New York: Charles Scribner's Sons, 1960), p. 125.

[3] Martin E. Marty, *When Faiths Collide* (Malden: Blackwell, 2005), pp. 1-14.

[4] Diana L. Eck, *A New Religious America: How A 'Christian Country' Has Become the World's Most Religiously Diverse Nation* (New York: HarperCollins, 2001), p. 295.

[5] Hans Küng, *Christianity and World Religions: Paths to Dialogue with Islam, Hinduism, and Buddhism* (New York: Doubleday, 1986), pp. 440-43.

[6] Mark Juergensmeyer, *Terror in the Mind of God: The Global Rise of Religious Violence* (Berkeley and Los Angeles: University of California Press, 2001), p. ix.

[7] Juergensmeyer, *Terror in the Mind of God*, pp. 19-118.

[8] Juergensmeyer, *Terror in the Mind of God*, pp. 4-10.

today's world.[9] Therefore, religious contributions to contemporary global violence, either as orchestrated terrorism or spontaneous outbreaks, and their underlying interreligious nature, must be addressed. In this regard, Juergensmeyer argues that the deepest and best resources of religion itself are one of the greatest instruments for overcoming interfaith conflict. In short, religion can be either 'a cause' or 'a cure' for the modern malady of violent interfaith conflict.[10]

Both a clinical psychologist and an authority on comparative religion, James William Jones argues that the psychology of violence suggests that ordinary human beings may react violently when overcome with feelings of humiliation or shame, especially when their existing worldview involves perceiving reality in stark black and white contrasts and invites the dehumanization and demonization of others.[11] Propensity to violent religious reaction may be particularly acute when extremely authoritarian religion (i.e. fundamentalism) is entrenched.[12] Jones indicates that religious leaders may either foster or counter the psychological factors contributing to violence depending on their own ideas and models.[13] He advises religious leaders to teach and model compassion and to train their followers to practice love and compassion as well.[14] However, a problem is that the religions have an inherently ambivalent nature that, under various circumstances, can be appropriated for either peaceful or combative purposes.[15] For example, Buddhism, which the West usually considers a peaceful, even pacifist, religion, in actuality has its own history of violence.[16]

Nor are Pentecostals without a share of the blame. According to historian and analyst of the global Pentecostal movement, Allan Anderson, the challenges of religious pluralism are exacerbated because Pentecostals have at times exhibited markedly antagonistic

---

[9] Juergensmeyer, *Terror in the Mind of God*, pp. 10-15.
[10] Juergensmeyer, *Terror in the Mind of God*, pp. 218-24.
[11] James William Jones, *Blood that Cries Out from the Earth: The Psychology of Religious Terrorism* (New York: Oxford University Press, 2008), pp. 142-70.
[12] Jones, *Blood that Cries Out*, p. 157.
[13] Jones, *Blood that Cries Out*, pp. 157-59.
[14] Jones, *Blood that Cries Out*, pp. 158-62.
[15] Jones, *Blood that Cries Out*, p. 10.
[16] Jones, *Blood that Cries Out*, p. 53.

attitudes and behavior on the interfaith front.[17] As noted in the introduction of this volume, Omenyo traces recent intensification of violent hostilities, often resulting in persecution and death, between Christians and Muslims in Ghana and Nigeria to an upsurge of Pentecostal and Charismatic churches that demonize Muslims.[18] Further, Yong reports that demonization of religious others and consequential violence is a much more prevalent problem among many Pentecostal groups than might have been previously imagined.[19] Other examples in various parts of the world could be added, but these illustrate that Pentecostals shoulder a share of the responsibility for violent conflict among the religions and in society.

Arguably, Pentecostals have a moral and spiritual obligation to work for mitigation of current conflicts. A key biblical text for Pentecostals, probably due to the movement's deep roots in the nineteenth-century Holiness Movement, has been Heb. 12.14: 'Make every effort to live in peace with all men and to be holy; without holiness no one will see the Lord' (NIV). The ancient and universal significance of this statement may be observed in Chrysostom's homily on this text in which he asserts, 'There are many things characteristic of Christianity: but more than all, and better than all, Love towards one another, and Peace'.[20] Pentecostal biblical scholar John Wesley Adams argues that this text connects the foundational importance of practical holiness in the Christian life with the pursuit of peace, although he primarily limits it to the Christian community.[21] However, his affirmation of the unique solidarity of Christian fellowship need not restrict the reach of peace. The biblical text itself utilizes the usually all-encompassing πάντων, which generally denotes ideas such as 'each, every, any, all, whole, every

---

[17] Anderson, *An Introduction*, p. 283.

[18] Omenyo, 'Renewal, Christian Mission, and Encounter with the Other', pp. 148-53 (esp. pp. 152-53).

[19] 'Amos Yong, 'From Demonization to Kin-domization: The Witness of the Spirit and the Renewal of Missions in a Pluralistic World', pp. 157-74, *Global Renewal*, pp. 158-60.

[20] John Chrysostom, Homily XXXI, *Nicene and Post-Nicene Fathers: 14* (Peabody, MA: Hendrickson, 1999), p. 506.

[21] John Wesley Adams, 'Hebrews', in French L. Arrington and Roger Stronstad (eds.), *FLBCNT* (Grand Rapids: Zondervan, 1999), pp. 1382-83.

kind'. Here πάντων has a clear universally inclusive thrust.[22] The pursuit of holy peace is not limited to Christians only. It includes Christians pursuing peace among the religions. An inherent Pentecostal value, pursuing peace as part of holy living, provides a basis for responding to the current crisis of interfaith conflict in a positive and proactive manner.

Consistency with the best of widely respected Christian theological tradition also points to the importance of undertaking peacemaking among the religions. For instance, Niebuhr outlines three distinct options as potential responses to situations of religion-related violence.[23] First is authoritarianism, or one religion dominates all others, and second is secularism, which relegates religions to irrelevance. He rejects both of these options as ineffective and offensive for deeply pious believers from any faith. The third option, a religious solution to a religious problem, is really the only one that is realistic and workable. This solution requires firm commitment to humility and charity, however. According to Niebuhr, if a religious resolution to interfaith conflict is not ardently sought out then by default one of the inferior ways will inevitably become prominent with counterproductive results.[24] In short, it falls to the religions, including Pentecostalism, to deal with interreligious issues, especially violence.

Accordingly, scholars from Pentecostal backgrounds, such as Gerald McDermott, are increasingly calling for engagement and dialogue with other religions.[25] Many solid Evangelical scholars,

---

[22] Unless there is a qualifying restriction in the text itself πάντων (in its various forms) should be taken in an encompassing sense. There is no such restrictive qualification in Heb. 12.14. The text of Rom. 5.12 is another example. There πάντας ἀνθρώπους clearly signifies that the entrance of sin into the world resulted in the sentence of death upon literally every human being. However, in Acts 21.28 πάντας πανταχῇ is an obvious exaggeration. Paul had not and could not have taught 'all men everywhere'; rather, it signifies that he went abroad teaching and all whom he taught, which nonetheless included all kinds of men (e.g. Jews and Gentiles), he taught the gospel (although not in the pejorative sense intended by his accusers).

[23] Niebuhr, *Children of Light and Children of Darkness*, pp. 126-38.

[24] Niebuhr, *Children of Light and Children of Darkness*, pp. 137-38.

[25] Gerald McDermott, *Can Evangelicals Learn from World Religions: Jesus, Revelation, & Religious Traditions* (Downers Grove: InterVarsity Press, 2000). Cf. Warrington, *Pentecostal Theology*, p. 40.

such as Asbury Theological Seminary president Timothy Tennent and Canadian theologian John Stackhouse, are part of this chorus.[26] Furthermore, John Wesley and subsequent Wesleyans have long supplied historical and theological precedents for Pentecostal heirs on engaging other religions.[27] In a word, a need to address contemporary interfaith conflict coupled with an acknowledgement that interreligious dialogue is an essential instrument for that process is becoming increasingly clear to many Christian theologians, including Pentecostals.

In short, when complex economic, political, and ethnic challenges to a religious worldview, especially including the encroachment and influence of other religions, is perceived as compromising or destroying cultural and religious identity, and when violently destructive reactions follow, it becomes an urgent need to address underlying interreligious dimensions for resolving conflict, rescuing human lives, and reestablishing the integrity of religious traditions. As stated above, an extremely important tool in that process is interreligious dialogue. To be clear, dialogue is not a panacea for any and all problems with more or less interreligious connotations.[28] That view is unforgivably naïve. Radical fringe groups irreversibly devoted to disruptive violence as an acceptable utilitarian policy for achieving their extreme political agendas cannot be satisfactorily dealt with through simple dialogue.[29] Gullibility regarding the destructive nature of these kinds of groups is not only self-defeating but outright dangerous.

Regarding the delimitations of dialogue, the cryptic proverb utilized by Jesus in Mt. 7.6 appears applicable: 'Do not give what is holy to dogs, and do not throw your pearls before swine, lest they trample them under their feet, and turn and tear you to pieces'

---

[26] Timothy Tennent, *Christianity at the Religious Roundtable: Evangelicalism in Conversation with Hinduism, Buddhism, and Islam* (Grand Rapids: Baker Academic, 2002). Also see John G. Stackhouse, Jr. (ed.), *No Other Gods Before Me? Evangelicals and the Challenge of World Religions* (Grand Rapids: Baker Academic, 2001).

[27] George H. Mellor, 'Evangelism and Religious Pluralism in the Wesleyan Tradition', in James C. Logan (ed.), *Theology and Evangelism in the Wesleyan Heritage* (Nashville: Kingswood Books, 1994), pp. 119-20. Cf. Theodore Runyon, *The New Creation: John Wesley's Theology Today* (Nashville: Abingdon, 1998), pp. 215-21. On Wesley himself see Tony Richie, 'Mr. Wesley and Mohammed', *ATJ*, pp. 79-99.

[28] Marty, *When Faiths Collide*, pp. 123, 143, 146.

[29] Marty, *When Faiths Collide*, pp. 96, 146.

(NASB). Augustine thought this graphic image instructs believers to use wise restraint when dealing with those who are violent and bitter or filled with hatred and contempt.[30] Mounce suggests that at the least it counsels discretion when dealing with those who seem unwilling or unable to accept Christian mission.[31] James Shelton, a Catholic Pentecostal Bible scholar, points out, among other things, that in the context of 'the previous prohibition against judging demonstrates that discernment between holy and profane, good and bad, is *not* to be prohibited'.[32] Chrysostom suggested that this enigmatic saying is a warning to beware of those who first 'feign gentleness' or friendliness; but, 'then after they have learnt, quite changing from one sort to another', they violently abuse Christians with what they have heard from them of the truth.[33] In any case, contemporary Christians, no matter how committed to dialogue, are well advised to be circumspect in their dealings with groups or individuals ideologically prone to the use of force and violence for an agenda of conquest. As Marty admits, interreligious dialogue is not an effective instrument for dealing with terrorists.[34]

Nevertheless, dialogue can be a crucial method for promoting cooperation and growth among moderate and legitimate faith groups with valid issues to discuss.[35] While the indiscriminately zealous certainly need the disturbing caution from Mt. 7.6, sincere Christians should guard against too readily setting neighbors down as dogs and swine as a cover for their own indifference or failure.[36] Well worth remembering is the Hebrew sage's observation that 'Death and life are in the power of the tongue, And those who love it will eat its fruit' (Prov. 18.21 NASB). Essentially, dialogue ordinarily involves mutual conversation between differing faith groups

---

[30] See Manlio Simonetti (ed.), *Matthew 1-13* (ACCS; Downers Grove, IL: InterVarsity Press, 2001), pp. 148-49.

[31] Robert H. Mounce, *Matthew* (NIBC; Peabody, MA: Hendrickson, 1985, 1991), p. 65.

[32] James B. Shelton, 'Matthew', in *FLBCNT,* p. 171 (emphasis original).

[33] John Chrysostom, Homily XXIII, *Nicene and Post-Nicene Fathers: 10* (Peabody, MA: Hendrickson, 1999), pp. 159-60.

[34] Marty, *When Faiths Collide*, pp. 196, 146.

[35] Angelo Maffeis and Lorelei F. Fuchs, *Ecumenical Dialogue* (Collegeville, MN: Unitas, 2005), p. 65.

[36] On Mt. 7.6: *Jamieson, Fausset, and Brown Commentary*, Electronic Database, Copyright © 1997, 2003, 2005, 2006; Biblesoft, Inc.

in pursuit of potential common ground and improved understanding. In recent decades, the significance of interfaith relations and of interfaith dialogue has increasingly attracted more attention among Christian churches.[37] With the remarkable growth and maturation of the Pentecostal movement comes a moral and spiritual responsibility, even obligation, for Pentecostals to respond actively to this urgent need.

However, Pentecostal participation in interreligious encounter and dialogue can only take place acceptably and successfully when carried out in a manner entirely consistent with Pentecostal beliefs and practice or faith and values. In other words, what is needed is an explicitly Pentecostal model for interreligious dialogue. A model for Pentecostal interreligious dialogue should meet certain theological and practical criteria. It must be adequate for effective practice in dialogue. It must arise out of authentic, already-existent Pentecostal belief and practice. And it must be capable of application and development in accordance with the current state of the discipline in Pentecostal theology. Accordingly, the next section of this chapter offers testimony as a model for interreligious dialogue in accordance with these stated criteria.[38]

Identifying a Ready Model

In its simplest form and in the sense perhaps most often understood by Pentecostals, a testimony is usually an oral presentation that tells others about one's faith. A particular testimony may explain why one is a Christian or relate experiences one has had as a Christian. Testimonies are often presented to other people to help them through situations or to demonstrate a point. They may be used to reinforce the truth of a matter. The practice of sharing testimonies has a longstanding pedigree in the Pentecostal movement. Official historian of the Church of God (Cleveland, TN), Charles Conn, observes that testimonies functioned in the earliest days of the Pentecostal revival as a part of congregational worship that like-

---

[37] Michael Kinnamon, 'Ecumenism', in D.W. Musser & J.L. Price (eds.), *New Handbook on Christian Theology* (Nashville: Abingdon, 1992), p. 145.
[38] For a fuller treatment of this approach to dialogue, see Richie, *Speaking by the Spirit*.

ly contributed to the revival's momentum.[39] Similarly, the Assemblies of God (internationally the largest Pentecostal denomination) historian Cecil M. Robeck reports that the globally renowned Azusa street mission and revival to which many contemporary Pentecostal groups trace their roots regarded testimony as a valuable practice infused with the Spirit's presence.[40] Mark Cartledge, a Charismatic practical theologian from the United Kingdom, suggests testimony occupies a place of central significance among contemporary Charismatics and Pentecostals as well.[41] Clearly, testimony is a specific practice familiar to Pentecostals in a broad way.

If testimony is to serve as a model for dialogue, then it must also be familiar to others with whom Pentecostals engage. Jean-Daniel Plüss is Chairperson of the European Pentecostal Charismatic Research Association in Zürich, Switzerland. Plüss explains that testimony is a universally prevalent practice among humans, occurring in juridical, religious, or social contexts.[42] Testimony may be 'expressed as a sign of something that exists' but more often 'in terms of a claim that something happened', and 'given by a person or a group of people in dialogue with others'.[43] Testimony relates to 'the understanding of one's faith', and why or how a particular experience or event is significant.[44] Of course, testimony requires interpretation, evaluation, and judgment as well as weighing against the character of the one who testifies; it is, therefore, significant both individually and socially.[45] In any case, testimony is a universal category that bodes well for a model of dialogue attempting to reach across religious cultures.

Christian philosopher Paul Ricoeur links testimony with attestation as exemplifying not 'I believe-that' but 'I believe-in'; or, in other words, it is 'a kind of belief' but not that of modernistic rational-

---

[39] Conn, *Like a Mighty Army*, pp. 23-24.

[40] Cecil M. Robeck, *The Azusa Street Mission & Revival: The Birth of the Global Pentecostal Movement* (Nashville: Nelson, 2006), pp. 2-4, 14, 16, and 46.

[41] See Mark J. Cartledge, *Testimony: Its Importance, Place, and Potential* (Cambridge: Grove, 2002).

[42] Jean-Daniel Plüss, 'Testimony', in Dyrness and Kärkkäinen (eds.), *GDT*, p. 877.

[43] Plüss, 'Testimony', p. 877. Note testimony's intrinsic connection with dialogue.

[44] Plüss, 'Testimony', p. 877.

[45] Plüss, 'Testimony', p. 877.

ism.[46] However, Plüss suggests Christian testimony stems from the biblical tradition of the community of faith's encounter with God in God's self-revelation as God 'is experienced and remembered'.[47] Christian testimony relates to its biblical roots and context but includes interpretation and awareness of both its religious and social significance.[48] For New Testament theologian Richard Bauckham, one may best understand the biblical gospels as eyewitness testimonies.[49] Bill Freeman presents Christian history as the Church's testimony to its experience of God.[50] Plüss suggests that the theological significance of testimonies lies in its ability to relate one's perception of God, point away from self to God, and avoid deceptiveness through a process of careful evaluation.[51] Furthermore, testimony 'engenders action' because 'What begins with a religious perception leads to praise and ultimately to ethical commitment'.[52]

Many Pentecostals see additional dimensions in testimony. Cartledge suggests that like speaking in tongues, prophecy, preaching, messages of wisdom and knowledge, testimony is a kind of Spirit-inspired speech.[53] For Duffield and Van Cleave, and for Arrington, testimony has a functional-practical role bearing witness to experiencing God and also participating in the process of experiencing God and its implications (as in divine healing or Spirit baptism).[54] For Cheryl Bridges Johns, testimony is transformational, occupying an important place in Pentecostal catechesis for spiritual formation.[55] For Jerome Boone, testimony has specific liturgical value

---

[46] Paul Ricoeur, *Oneself as Another* (trans. Kathleen Blamey; Chicago, IL: University of Chicago Press, 1992, 1994), p. 21.

[47] Plüss, 'Testimony', p. 877.

[48] Plüss, 'Testimony', pp. 877-79.

[49] Richard Bauckham, *Jesus and the Eyewitnesses: The Gospels as Eyewitness Testimony* (Grand Rapids: Eerdmans, 2006), pp. 1-11.

[50] Bill Freeman, *The Triune God in Experience (The Testimony of Church History)* (Spokane, WA: Ministry, 1992).

[51] Plüss, 'Testimony', p. 879.

[52] Plüss, 'Testimony', p. 879.

[53] Cartledge, *Encountering*, pp. 32, 58, 69, and 119.

[54] See Duffield and Van Cleave, *Foundations of Pentecostal Theology*, p. 402; and Arrington, *Encountering the Holy Spirit*, pp. 20-21 and 421-66. Cf. David Martin, *Tongues of Fire: The Explosion of Protestantism in Latin America* (Cambridge, MA: Wiley-Blackwell, 1993), p. 167.

[55] Cheryl Bridges Johns, *Pentecostal Formation: A Pedagogy among the Oppressed* (JPTSup 2; Sheffield, England: Sheffield Academic Press, 1993, 1998), pp. 126-27.

er suggests Pentecostal testimony can be an important part of strengthening identity formation.[72]

In sum, the context of Pentecostal testimony may be described as autobiographical, biblical, theological, pastoral, doxological, Christological, pneumatological, historical, and sociological. Pentecostal testimony is autobiographical and historical in that it relates actual experiences or events that occur in the teller's life. It is biblical and theological in that the framework of understanding and interpretation is the Christian faith as understood according to the biblical and theological tradition. To the extent that the autobiographical history and biblical and theological interpretation necessarily revolve around the Christ event, testimony is of course intrinsically Christological. In that Pentecostals believe the Holy Spirit inspires, enlivens, and energizes the testimonial process, it is certainly pneumatological. Finally, as testimony obviously involves the interaction of people in groups the sociological (and psychological) dimensions of the process are readily recognized. Pentecostal testimony is emphatically doxological in that its underlying gestalt and overarching goal is to publically give glory to God for God's ongoing mighty acts of love and goodness.

The purpose of the preceding description of Pentecostal testimony in this section is preparation for a discussion of how Pentecostal testimony informs and equips a distinctively Pentecostal approach to interreligious dialogue. Toward that end, the first section presented an urgent demand for interreligious dialogue, including Pentecostal participation, in the context of interfaith conflict and the resultant need for moral and spiritual action in the interests of societal stability and personal security.[73] The remainder of this chapter sets forth testimony as a theologically informed and praxis oriented instrument for interreligious dialogue faithful to biblical and traditional Pentecostal values and effective for a pressing need for immediate dialogical engagement with religious others.

---

[72] See Grant Wacker, *Heaven Below: Early Pentecostals and American Culture* (London: Harvard University Press, 2001), pp. 68-69.

[73] Of course there are many compelling reasons for interreligious dialogue. See Yong, *Discerning the Spirit(s)*, pp. 206-19, and Amos Yong and Tony Richie, 'Missiology and the Interreligious Encounter', in Allan Anderson, *et al.* (eds.), *Studying Global Pentecostalism: Theories and Methods* (Berkeley, CA: University of California Press, 2010), p. 245.

Pentecostals have been fond of quoting biblical texts such as Ps. 107.2 'Let the redeemed of the Lord say so' (KJV) and Rev. 12.11 'And they overcame him by the blood of the Lamb, and by the word of their testimony; and they loved not their lives unto the death' (KJV) as inspiration for their practice of testimony. And it is fitting for a people who emphasize the Spirit-filled life to be characterized by testifying in the Spirit to Jesus (Jn 15.26-27). Of course, Pentecostals have long realized that these texts have broader implications as well.[74] Now they may also realize that their beloved practice of testifying to the Lord's goodness in their lives has implications beyond local church services on Sunday nights. Interreligious dialogue is one such possibility.

As Ghanaian Pentecostal theologians Opoku Onyinah and Samuel Gakpetor astutely observe, the Apostle Paul's use of testimony in Acts 22-26 may have implications for communicating the gospel or provide lessons for interreligious dialogue.[75] Arrington notes that whenever Paul is pressed to offer a defense for himself and his ministry he repeatedly adopts a biographical (testimonial) approach.[76] Further, each of these four addresses was given to quite different audiences: a Jewish mob, the Sanhedrin, a Roman governor, and King Agrippa.[77] The centrality and versatility of testimony is hereby underscored. Adaptations of the practice of testimony for interreligious environments seem a biblically responsible and logical possibility for Pentecostals.

Utilizing Testimony as Dialogue

The Pentecostal practice of testimony can serve as an effective model for contemporary interreligious dialogue. May Ling Tan-Chow's work connected dialogue and testimony in an Asian plural-

---

[74] E.g. Rev. 12.11 clearly addresses martyrdom for the cause of Christ, John Christopher Thomas, *The Apocalypse: A Literary and Theological Commentary* (Cleveland, TN: CPT Press, 2012), pp. 371-73.

[75] Opoku Onyinah and Samuel Gakpetor, Review of Tony Richie, *Speaking by the Spirit: A Pentecostal Model for Interreligious Dialogue*, pp. 461-62, *Pneuma* 34.3 (2012), p. 462.

[76] Arrington, *The Spirit-Anointed Church*, p. 339.

[77] Arrington, *The Spirit-Anointed Church*, p. 339.

ist societal context.[78] For her, dialogue reflects the missional nature of the Triune God as revealed in the incarnation of Christ and the movement of the Spirit.[79] Interfaith dialogue counters communicational distortions threatening separations that militate against peace.[80] Dialogue is not only conversation but also 'a living encounter' in thought and life of 'listening, generosity of heart and mind, and mutuality and friendship'.[81] My own theology of religions utilizes testimony in dialogue.[82] The functional-practical element of Pentecostal testimony as a means of receiving and retaining divine blessings suggests interreligious dialogue may be a benefit to Pentecostals themselves as much as to others.[83] The energy and vitality of the movement may be enhanced and increased thereby. Isolationism often leads to diminishing relevance. Arguably, the movement of Pentecostals out into the world, including into the world of religions, through a vibrant testimony of God's graciousness, could be critical to their survival.

Testimony is helpful to Pentecostal engagement with religious others because, first, Pentecostal spirituality and theology are such that they can hardly be experienced or expressed purely conceptually, and second, interreligious dialogue often calls for participants to overcome rigid categories of Enlightenment/Western rationalism to arrive together at deeper understanding and appreciation.[84] Otherwise dialoguers take turns talking past each other in sequential monologue. Testimony provides a means to connect at a more universally human level.

---

[78] Tan-Chow, *Pentecostal Theology*, pp. 162-64.

[79] Tan-Chow, *Pentecostal Theology*, p. 162.

[80] Tan-Chow, *Pentecostal Theology*, pp. 162-63.

[81] Tan-Chow, *Pentecostal Theology*, p. 163.

[82] E.g. *Speaking by the Spirit* and 'Translating Pentecostal Testimony into Interreligious Dialogue'.

[83] See Duffield and Van Cleave, *Foundations*, p. 402, and Arrington, *Encountering the Holy Spirit*, pp. 20-21 and 421-66. Cf. Martin, *Tongues of Fire*, p. 167.

[84] Pentecostal publications often intertwine doctrinal discussions and personal testimonies. See David D. Bundy, 'United Methodist Charismatics', in *NIDPCM*, p. 1160. Frank D. Macchia, 'Theology, Pentecostal', in *NIDPCM*, argues that testimony uniquely contributes to and helps shape Pentecostal theology (pp. 1120, 1122, 1131) through an often missed/misunderstood dialectic (pp. 1123-24).

The transformational and participatory nature of Pentecostal testimony fits well with interfaith conversation.[85] A cerebral, document-centered approach to dialogue can all-too-easily degenerate into dry exchanges of information or combative encounters. Through testimony dialogue can become a genuinely life-changing personal encounter informed by a variety of participants rather than only academic experts or special interest groups.[86] Both Pentecostals and their partners can experience mutual growth in a context of people's real, that is, lived lives through dialogue shaped by testimony tuned to the reality of divine-human encounter. Further, as an act of worship, testimony as dialogue is offered for the glory of God.[87] Winning arguments, converting others, and political or social agendas are subsumed under the overarching objective of glorifying God. Testifying in interreligious contexts is worshipfully declaring God's wonderful works before the world, including before the world's religions.

Prayer is an essential component of Pentecostal testimony.[88] Prayer is absolutely essential for testimony as dialogue. Prayer prepares the hearts of participants. It reminds that dialogue is a spiritual enterprise. Prayer brings energy and vitality to dialogue that cannot be incorporated by any other means or method.[89] Furthermore, as Spirit-inspired and Spirit-enlivened speech, testimony, like speaking in tongues and other oracular gifts, transcends class, gender, and race as well as economics, education, power or social status.[90] As

---

[85] Bridges Johns, *Pentecostal Formation*, pp. 126-27, and Martin, *Tongues of Fire*, p. 163.

[86] Cheryl Sanders, *Saints in Exile: The Holiness-Pentecostal Experience in African American Religion and Culture* (Religion in America; New York: Oxford University Press, 1999), p. 84.

[87] Boone, 'Community and Worship', pp. 138-40. Cf. Macchia, 'Theology', p. 1122, and Sanders, *Saints in Exile,* pp. 51, 53.

[88] Walter J. Hollenweger, 'After Twenty Years of Research on Pentecostalism', *IRM* (January 1986), p. 6, relates Pentecostal orality and prayer.

[89] Early Pentecostal chronicler Frank Bartleman, *Azusa Street* (originally *Another Wave Rolls In)* (New Kensington, PA: Whitaker, 1982), recounts Spirited intermingling of prayer, testimony, and praise (p. 21).

[90] For Spirit-empowered egalitarianism in ministry practice, see Estrelda Alexander, 'Introduction', in Estrelda Alexander and Amos Yong (eds.), *Philip's Daughters: Women in Pentecostal-Charismatic Leadership* (Princeton Monograph Series; Eugene, OR: Pickwick, 2008), pp. 3-4. Cf. same volume, Frederick L. Ware, 'Spiritual Egalitarianism, Ecclesial Egalitarianism, and the Status of Women in Ordain Ministry', pp. 214-34 (esp. p. 230). For Bartleman, *Azusa Street*, the prominence

the Spirit moves, all may speak and listen in turn. This brings depth of diversity to interreligious dialogue, enriching and extending it immeasurably.

Telling the right testimony is integral to the shape of substantive dialogue. True interreligious testimony is not anecdotal autobiographical experiences with a generalized moral or spiritual message. It points others to the story of Christ in which one's own story is deeply embedded. It displays intersections of autobiographical and Christological realities through the power of the Holy Spirit.[91] This is done tactfully but should not be left undone. Pentecostal testimonies convey the message that what Christ has done in the past for others Christ still does for those who trust him. Pentecostal testimony demonstrates the ongoing consistency of Heb. 13.8, 'Jesus Christ is the same yesterday and today and forever' and Mal. 3.6, 'For I, the Lord, do not change' (NASB).[92] Thus the autobiographical and Christological narrative is grounded in Scripture through an ongoing dynamic between human experience, the biblical story, and God.[93]

In the congregational context of typically marginalized people groups, Pentecostal testimonies characteristically include dual emphases on pastoral and prophetic concerns.[94] Pentecostal testimony

---

of songs, prayers, and testimonies, along with some diminishment of sermonizing, indicated clerical, ecclesiastical, and hierarchical monopolizing had been overturned (pp. 57, 94-95).

[91] See Plüss, 'Testimony', p. 877. Culpepper, *The Great Commission: The Solution*, firmly fixes personal testimony among Pentecostals in the overarching story of Jesus (pp. 86-88). Cf. Arrington, *Encountering the Holy Spirit*, pp. 20-21.

[92] These texts clearly affirm divine constancy and permanency faithfully expressed in life's vicissitudes and rooted in the unchangeableness of God's character and nature. See Donald A. Hagner, *Hebrews* (NIBC; Peabody: Hendrickson, 1983, 1990), pp. 239-41, and Adam Clarke, *Clarke's Commentary: Malachi* (Wesleyan Heritage Collection; Rio, WI: Ages Software, 2002), p. 12.

[93] Ellington, 'Reciprocal Reshaping', pp. 30-31. Cf. Plüss, 'Testimony', pp. 877-78.

[94] See Russell P. Spittler, 'The Pentecostal View', in Donald L. Alexander (ed.), *Christian Spirituality: Five Views of Sanctification* (Downers Grove, IL: InterVarsity Press, 1988), pp. 145, 147. Cf. Vinson Synan, *Voices of Pentecost: Testimonies of Lives Touched by the Holy Spirit* (Ann Arbor, MI: Servant Books, 2003), esp. pp. 12-13. Kenneth J. Archer, *Pentecostal Hermeneutics: Spirit, Scripture, and Community* (Cleveland, TN: CPT Press, 2009), suggests testimonies represent in part openness to others involving the 'humanization' of those often overlooked or undervalued (p. 28).

addresses the care of souls, family life, and practical day-to-day survival, even physical and emotional healing and battles with temptation. It also addresses critical concerns of the uneducated, of the poor, of women, and of the otherwise needy or disenfranchised and powerless.[95] Accordingly, the use of testimony in interfaith dialogue must not miss the concerns of the life of faith in the contemporary world. Pentecostal testimonies in interfaith settings should candidly address at times difficult or unpleasant realities of daily existence.[96] Adherents of other religions will get to know Pentecostals better by this means than by dogmatic formulations.

The statement regarding Vinson Synan's Pentecostal history, *The Century of the Holy Spirit*, 'This is a powerful testimony of the hand of God', well sums up the general thrust of Pentecostal testimony as it aims to uplift God's activity in praise.[97] Although there are many important concerns involved in doing dialogue, prime is giving glorious praise to God in the tenor of Ps. 96.3: 'Declare his glory among the nations, his marvelous deeds among all peoples' (NASB). The doxological dynamic of testimony as dialogue probably underscores the importance of this model as much or more than any other aspect. Synan says of early Pentecostal worship gatherings that 'the burning, convicting power of Pentecostal testimony filled the room' so that through 'the Pentecostal fire' burning in the heart of a testifier conviction gripped 'spiritually cold' hearts.[98] Frequently accompanying prayer and testimony services are 'manifestations of ecstatic energy'.[99] Testimony transcends common communication. A vital spiritual energy is evident because they testify under inspiration of the Spirit. Pentecostal testimony accesses spiritual experience as much as it expresses it. Although deliveries vary according to environments (e.g. interreligious con-

---

[95] As in Bridges Johns, *Pentecostal Formation*.
[96] Allan Anderson, 'Global Pentecostalism in the New Millennium', in A. Anderson and Walter J. Hollenweger (eds.), *Pentecostals after a Century: Global Perspectives on a Movement in Transition* (JPTSup 15; Sheffield: Sheffield Academic Press, 1999), pp. 210, 214-18.
[97] From a blurb on the back cover of Vinson Synan, *The Century of the Holy Spirit: 100 Years of Pentecostal and Charismatic Renewal* (Nashville, TN: Nelson, 2001).
[98] Synan, *Voices of Pentecost*, p. 78.
[99] Robert Owens, 'The Azusa Street Revival: The Pentecostal Movement Begins in America', pp. 39-68, Synan, *Century of the Holy Spirit*, p. 41.

texts), such testimonies help others outside the Pentecostal tradition experience something of its heart and soul.

Pentecostals bring to the interreligious world their conviction that at its deepest level real religion is about a personal encounter with the presence of God.[100] For Pentecostals engaging in interreligious dialogue perhaps the chief challenge will be to seek humbly thus to be anointed by the Spirit of God and of Christ as instruments or vessels of the Spirit's presence and power. Testifying before religious others ought to be executed in the agency of the Holy Spirit. Natural technique alone is inadequate. A sense of supernatural, spiritual presence is alone sufficient.[101] Listeners may personally experience an encounter with the Holy Spirit through one's testimony.[102] To that end, the testifier draws directly and deeply out of his/her own experience of the Holy Spirit. This is Incarnational ministry in motion. Pentecostal dialogue participants thus make the presence of God real around the dialogue table.

Pentecostals, without behaving brashly, thus can nevertheless boldly tell their spiritual biographies.[103] Pentecostal testifiers should therefore be completely committed to the historical factuality and faith-truth of their testimonies and to the community of faith out of which they arise. Pentecostals should never be anything less than Pentecostal in their relations with religious others. Succumbing to the temptation to tone down their convictions is untrue to their own identity and unfair to the integrity of their dialogue partners. Public testimonies exhibit willingness to stand unapologetically,

---

[100] Thus Harvey Cox, *Fire from Heaven: The Rise of Pentecostal Spirituality and the Reshaping of Religion in the Twenty-First Century* (New York: Addison-Wesley, 1995) speaks of 'primal spirituality' (pp. 81-82, 132). Cf. Sanders, *Saints in Exile,* on Black Pentecostals testifying to the primary reality of the Holy Spirit in their lives (p. 136).

[101] As Russell Spittler, 'Spirituality, Pentecostal' in *NIDPCM,* explains, this is typical of Pentecostals' own testimonials of encounters of 'deepened personal experience with the Lord' (p. 1100).

[102] E.g. R. Marie Griffith, 'A Network of Praying Women: Women's Aglow Fellowship and Mainline American Protestantism', Edith L. Blumhoffer, Russell P. Spittler, Grant A. Wacker (eds.), *Pentecostal Currents in American Protestantism* (Champaign, IL: University of Illinois Press, 1999), pp. 131-51, prayer and testimony in Aglow meetings 'are meant to have a transformative effect on both the storyteller and her listeners' (p. 140).

[103] Pentecostals humbly believe one's 'personal faith stories' bear 'normative implications for others' (Wacker, *Heaven Below,* p. 58).

though hopefully inoffensively, in explicit identification with the Pentecostal worldview.[104] At the dialogue table there is often un-spoken pressure to affirm common ground. While identifying and appreciating commonalities is laudable, it is in 'un-commonalities' where dialoguers may make the greatest progress. Accordingly, Pentecostals should willingly talk about what is most different about their own faith.[105]

Openly expressing one's faith through testifying is for Pentecostals an act of self-consecration to a commitment.[106] The content of interfaith dialogue employing testimony therefore should reasonably express strongly held and dearly loved commitments. Pentecostals who hold stoutly to the distinctive commitments of their movement are actually most effective in interfaith dialogue testimony. However, a dialogue is not a debate. Its objective is not to win an argument with an opponent but to reach out to another pilgrim (broadly speaking). One ought to expect strong commitment in those of other faiths to their understanding of religious reality, and be willing to respect it, even when, as will undoubtedly often be the case, disagreeing – just as one rightly expects respect for their own faith views, especially when they are presented sensitively. Furthermore, it is helpful to avoid confusing possibly esoteric personal convictions with broad commitments held by most members of the Pentecostal movement everywhere. Through the power of the Holy

---

[104] Susie C. Stanley, 'Wesleyan/Holiness and Pentecostal Women Preachers: Pentecost as the Pattern for Primitivism', in Alexander and Yong (eds.), *Philip's Daughters,* p. 23.

[105] Antonios Kireopoulos, 'Reflection on Pope Benedict XVI's Encyclical Letter, *Spe Salvi*' (November 30, 2007), observes,

Oftentimes, Christians are the first in interfaith dialogue to be reticent in affirming their respective truth claims. Ultimately, this is not helpful, because it prevents an honest dialogue on theological differences. More to the point, however, is how such truth claims are expressed in dialogue with others. One of the greatest challenges today for Christians engaged in interfaith dialogue is discussing their own theological beliefs, or to give 'an accounting for the hope that is in [them]' (1 Peter 3:15, NRSV), in a way that is neither triumphalistic nor dismissive of others' beliefs.

See http://www.ncccusa.org/news/071217spesalvi.html.

[106] Spittler, 'Spirituality', explains that Pentecostals 'take their commitment with the utmost seriousness' and convey it through oral testimony and 'sharing' (p. 1102).

Spirit, interfaith testimony points others to the story of Jesus Christ with which one's own story is inseparably intertwined.[107]

Conclusion

Suggesting a procedure for the process of interreligious dialogue has been the chief concern of Chapter 4. Specifically, this chapter has sought to outline for Pentecostals an explicit procedure guiding theology of religions and interreligious encounter and dialogue. The theology and practice of Pentecostal testimony has been plumbed as a paradigmatic resource for engaging religious others in a manner that is consonant with the faith and values of devotees in the Classical Pentecostal movement and effective for encounter with religious others consistent with their faith and values as well. In a sense, this chapter represents a turning point in the book's development. Emphasis has heretofore been on providing a theological rationale for Pentecostal theology of religions and for intentional and informed engagement by Pentecostals with religious others through the practice of dialogue. The next chapter will continue this conversation in partnership with several representative theologians, some who are Pentecostal and some who are not, who have in one way or another interconnected with themes that directly impact Pentecostal theology of religions.

---

[107] See Plüss, 'Testimony', p. 877; Culpepper, *The Great Commission: The Solution*, pp. 86-88; and Arrington, *Encountering the Holy Spirit*, pp. 20-21.

5

CONTINUING CONVERSATIONS ON PENTECOSTAL THEOLOGY OF RELIGIONS (PENTECOSTAL PARTNERS)

Introduction

From Paul's writings to the Galatians (1.18-19) we learn that Peter and he, as well perhaps as James, engaged in conversation – and at times quite strong debate – regarding the place of Gentiles in the New Testament church in other contexts over time. In a sense, this ongoing conversation and its attendant conundrums were initiated by Peter's encounter with Cornelius (Acts 10) and had pivotal significance at the Jerusalem Council (Acts 15.6-11). However, it apparently continued, even later, on a more personal and direct basis and resulted in a kind of apostolic agreement (Gal. 2.7-10). Although sometimes strained, this ongoing conversation about the Gentiles reveals the struggle of the New Testament church to come to grips with the scope of the gospel of Jesus Christ (Gal. 2.11-21; cf. 2 Pet. 3.15-16). This chapter endeavors to continue that tradition of conversation in the context of Pentecostal theology of religions. Veli-Matti Kärkkäinen and Amos Yong are selected as Pentecostal conversation partners on the basis of their widely recognized contributions to Christian theology of religions in conjunction with some point of interaction with my own work in the discipline.

On Veli-Matti Kärkkäinen's Suggestion

In the Assemblies of God theological journal, *Encounter,* Veli-Matti Kärkkäinen did an affirmative review of my *Speaking by the Spirit.*[1] He also offered a suggestion for the next move forward:

> ... the proposal remains at a quite abstract and general level. What I mean is this: theology of religions can only get us so far. In order to make the discussion more 'practical' – and certainly more complicated – one should move to the comparative theology discourse. That conversation does not treat religions as one big 'thing', but rather looks at some definite Christian themes in relation to some specific teachings of another particular religious tradition. Hence, a further task for Richie's continuing scholarship would be to take the Pentecostal resource of testimony and relate it to some specific Buddhist, Muslim, or Hindu traditions.[2]

Considering Kärkkäinen's extensive expertise in the discipline of Christian theology of religions (see Chapter 3), his suggestion is to be taken all the more seriously.[3] Accordingly, this section will give due attention to his remarks. Its goal is to move the conversation on Pentecostal theology of religions forward a bit.

I wish to make three responses to Kärkkäinen's insightful suggestion. First, it is agreed that the next move going forward in Pentecostal theology of religions beyond laying out a general theological framework for its justification and for participation in various forms of encounter and cooperation, especially dialogue through testimony, is a move from the general and abstract to the specific and concrete. Second, it is also agreed that at some point at least this move may involve comparative theology discourse or relating Pentecostal theology of religions, in this case particularly regarding the utilization of testimony, to concepts and practices in other reli-

---

[1] Veli-Matti Kärkkäinen, Review of Tony Richie, *Speaking by the Spirit: A Pentecostal Model for Interreligious Dialogue* (Lexington, KY: Emeth Press, 2011), *Encounter,* (Summer 2012) http://www.agts.edu/encounter/book_reviews/2012summer/review_karkkainen.html.

[2] Kärkkäinen, Review, *Speaking by the Spirit.*

[3] Noteworthy is that Kärkkäinen views other theologies of religions, for example, that of Amos Yong, as verging on the overly abstract as well (*An Introduction to the Theology of Religions,* p. 281). Perhaps in part, such statements by Kärkkäinen are indicative of his commitment to concreteness in the discipline.

gious traditions. Kärkkäinen's own able work in comparative theology is instructive in this regard. It certainly demonstrates its potential productivity.[4]

However, it is not agreed that a move to comparative theology discourse in general or the application of testimony is *necessarily* the *next* move. From the perspective of demonstrating the desirability and effectiveness of Pentecostal engagement in theology of religions and interreligious dialogue quite another move should perhaps occur previously. I suggest that before Pentecostal theology of religions dives headlong into comparative theology discourse, which is, as Kärkkäinen readily, and rightly, admits, 'certainly more complicated', it should address already existing interreligious concerns by contemporary Pentecostals. Over the next several paragraphs I will unpack what I mean by that assertion.

Before tackling the topic of why Pentecostal theology of religions could and should address contemporary interreligious concerns prior to doing comparative theology proper, it should be readily acknowledged that the (at least, for some, eventual) movement of Pentecostal theologians of religions into the comparative theological discourse is legitimate and laudable. For example, Kärkkäinen himself demonstrates the practical missiological benefits of exploring the meaning of suffering and the release from its power in the Christian and Buddhist traditions for doing Pentecostal mission in a Buddhist environment.[5] Since both Christianity and Buddhism have prominent concerns over liberation or salvation from suffering, doing Pentecostal mission in a Buddhist environment can become more effective through the mutual understanding gained by comparing and contrasting their respective concepts of suffering.[6] In particular, a Pentecostal theology informed by an acceptance of miraculous divine interventions and of divine healing tempered by the reality of human suffering that can skillfully negotiate this dynamic in frequently animist Buddhist environments promises to be

---

[4] E.g. see Veli-Matti Kärkkäinen, '*Dukkha* and *Passio*: A Christian Theology of Suffering in the (*Theravāda*) Buddhist Context', in Yong and Clarke (eds.) *Global Renewal*, pp. 97-116.

[5] Kärkkäinen, '*Dukkha* and *Passio*', p. 97.

[6] Kärkkäinen, '*Dukkha* and *Passio*', pp. 97-98.

more sensitive to human needs and more effective in Christian mission.[7] That is a very helpful observation.

It is also the case that Yong, as with Kärkkäinen in conversation with Buddhism, has demonstrated that, among other dynamics, phenomenological and theological concerns of interreligious dialogue may often overlap.[8] Admittedly, a too sharp cut-off between diverse approaches to dialogue bordering on exclusivity is neither desirable nor possible. Thus what follows is not a denial or negation of the potential of Pentecostal involvement in comparative theology discourse at some point and at some level. Yet it does seem a bit incongruous when calls for avoiding the overly abstract and moving into the realm of the more concrete nevertheless focus on abstract discussions of esoteric comparisons between religions without addressing existing concrete conditions between the religions in the public arena.

Rather, my suggestion is that after establishing the integrity and validity of Pentecostal theology of religions and thereby Pentecostal involvement in interreligious dialogue through testimony, the next best move is not to introduce highly theoretical discussions of comparative theology but rather to address already existing concerns many Pentecostals have with important topics of an interreligious nature. My reasoning is threefold. First, it is reassuring. Second, it is simpler. Third, it is necessary. It is reassuring in that it can help allay any remaining suspicions, which are still strong at least at the popular level, that theology of religions inevitably leads to a pluralistic compromising amalgamation of world religions in which Christian distinctiveness is diminished if not destroyed.[9] An incautious move to comparative theology may actually fuel those fears, although clearly ungrounded, among those who conceive of

---

[7] Kärkkäinen, 'Dukkha and Passio', p. 108. Cf. Amos Yong's extensive treatment of pneumatology in conversation with Buddhism in *The Cosmic Breath: Spirit and Nature in the Christian-Buddhism-Science Trialogue* (Leiden and Boston: Brill, 2012) and *Pneumatology and the Christian-Buddhist Dialogue: Does the Spirit Blow through the Middle Way?* (Leiden and Boston: Brill, 2012).

[8] Amos Yong, 'From Azusa Street to the Bo Tree and Back: Strange Babblings and Interreligious Interpretations in the Pentecostal Encounter with Buddhism', in Kärkkäinen (ed.), *Spirit in the World,* pp. 203-26.

[9] Cf. popular Pentecostal evangelist and author Perry Stone, *Unleashing the Beast: The Coming Fanatical Dictator and His Ten-Nation Coalition* (Lake Mary, FL: Frontline, 2009, 2011).

global history primarily in terms of religious competition and conquest. Contrariwise, observing the effectiveness of Christian theology of religions in other capacities, as, for example, that which is discussed below, may encourage other endeavors as well; or, at least it may allow sufficient space for valuable contributions.

It is simpler because it does not require immediate immersion in the complex tenets of other religious traditions before applying preliminary benefits of the unique contributions of Pentecostal theology of religions to the broader discipline within Christian parameters. Obviously, there is a vast difference between developing a Christian understanding of and approach to the reality of other religions and in developing sufficient expertise in the beliefs and practices of other religions to be able to compare and contrast these with those of Christian theology at the profound level required for comparative theological discourse.[10] Conceivably, a too soon or inevitable move in that direction could discourage Pentecostal participation in theology of religions. This possibility does not limit those so disposed from following the course of comparative theology; however, it does invite those not so inclined to participate in Pentecostal theology of religions without necessarily following the same strategy.

Finally, it is necessary because of the practical reality that today's world brims with difficult and potentially dangerous encounters between individuals, groups, and nations that have interreligious components demanding intelligent and immediate attention.[11] Addressing these topics from a perspective informed by Pentecostal theology of religions demonstrates the value of such theological contributions in practical and political contexts. By offering a constructive paradigm by which contemporary Pentecostals concerned about global and local crises that are fueled on multiple levels by interfaith components can respond intelligently and ethically, theology of religions provides a real service to Spirit-filled believers and others everywhere. In any case, Pentecostal contributions toward alleviating the potentially, and at times, really, dangerous tensions

---

[10] As even an introductory text like Francis X. Clooney, *Comparative Theology: Deep Learning across Religious Borders* (Oxford: Blackwell, 2010) suggests.
[11] Former Secretary of State Madeleine Albright offers provocative discussion of this controversial religious reality in *The Mighty & the Almighty: Reflections on America, God, and World Affairs* (New York: Harper, 2006).

inherent in critical encounters of the religions is urgently incumbent.

To employ just a couple of examples, most Pentecostals, with many others of course, are concerned about issues such as the instability of the Middle East and the volatility of Christian–Muslim relations throughout the world.[12] Obviously, both are rife with Jewish–Christian–Muslim (and secularist) relational dynamics. Can Pentecostal theology of religions offer any assistance on these perennially thorny problems? If so how? Can the tool of testimony offer anything distinctive? And if so how? I answer in the affirmative and propose a possible path toward these objectives.

A number of factors come into play, including theologies of Israel and of Judaism and interpretations of eschatology as well as political theology. For instance, Peter Ochs, Judaic philosopher and theologian, suggests that Christian theologies of Judaism take into account attitudes toward Shoah (the Holocaust), shared scriptures, overlapping histories, and the history of supercessionism (doctrine that the Church has replaced Israel as God's covenant people).[13] Among other things, the correlation of Yahweh, God of Israel, and the Christian Trinity is critical. Ochs points out that some Christian theologians are wrestling with ways to relate Judaism's worship of the God of Israel with Christianity's worship of the Triune God.[14] Judaism and Christianity obviously have very different understandings of the nature of God; but, it is nonetheless argued that Yahweh is the Triune God.

The Reformed theologian from Germany, Jürgen Moltmann, argues persuasively for Christianity's enduring indebtedness to Israel.[15] He suggests the history and destiny – the redemption – of Israel, of the Church, and of the world, that is, of creation, is insepara-

[12] See Eric Newberg, *Pentecostal Mission in Palestine: The Legacy of Pentecostal Zionism* (Eugene, OR: Pickwick, 2012).
[13] Peter Ochs, 'Judaism and Christian Theology', pp. 645-62, in Ford (ed.), *The Modern Theologians*.
[14] Ochs, 'Judaism and Christian Theology', pp. 650-51. Cf. Kendall R. Soulen, *The God of Israel and Christian Theology* (Minneapolis, MN: Augsburg Fortress, 1996); and Bruce Marshall, 'Israel', in James J. Buckley and David S. Yeago (eds.), *Knowing the Triune God: The Work of the Spirit in the Practices of the Church* (Grand Rapids: Eerdmans, 2001), pp. 231-64.
[15] Jürgen Moltmann, *The Church in the Power of the Spirit: A Contribution to Messianic Ecclesiology* (London: SCM, 1977), pp. 136-50.

bly linked permanently.[16] Furthermore, he affirms the distinctive continuing calling and vocation of Israel, suggesting that Judaism and Christianity (quoting Rom. 11.11, 14) serve to provoke each other in redemptive and eschatological hope.[17] To the extent that the Church distances itself from Israel, especially in its anti-Judaic tendencies, it becomes pagan and corrupt.[18] Yet even Moltmann admits that the restored State of Israel in the ancient homeland presents both Jewish and Christian theologians with difficulties.[19] Is it a sign of the end of the dispersion and Israel's homecoming or the tragedy of Israel becoming like any other nation and a curse to the people of Palestine? Is it the sign of the end of the era of the Gentiles and of the Church's messianic mission? Or can it be that both Israel and the Church will look beyond these events in hope while they 'wait for the coming God and his redeeming kingdom'?[20]

Yet these puzzling theological (and political) conundrums need not be the main focus of Pentecostal theology of religions as it addresses the interreligious dynamics of the Middle East crisis and international Christian–Muslim relations. In fact, one must here settle for an implicit direction rather than an explicit directive. Unfortunately, time and space in this chapter do not allow for a full explication of all of these topics. That would require a rather extensive monograph in itself. However, perhaps enough can be said to indicate how Pentecostal theology of religions may inform and energize concerned Pentecostal Christians relative to interreligious conundrums.

Nevertheless, as an important qualifier it is incumbent to remember an observation by twentieth-century American ethical and political theologian Reinhold Niebuhr. Niebuhr's theology is particularly helpful in dealing with religious pluralism in civic contexts.[21] He observed that the Jewish people present a special case before

---

[16] Moltmann, *The Church in the Power of the Spirit*, p. 144.
[17] Moltmann, *The Church in the Power of the Spirit*, pp. 148-49.
[18] Moltmann, *The Church in the Power of the Spirit*, pp. 135-36.
[19] Moltmann, *The Church in the Power of the Spirit*, p. 149.
[20] Moltmann, *The Church in the Power of the Spirit*, pp. 149-50 (p. 150).
[21] See Tony L. Richie, 'A Politics of Pluralism in American Democracy: Reinhold Niebuhr's Christian Realism as a National Resource in a Post-9/11 World', *JES* 45.3 (Summer 2010), pp. 471-92.

the world partly because of rampant Anti-Semitism.[22] Niebuhr suggests that the Jewish minority is the victim of a 'profounder prejudice' derivative of 'a double divergence' from majorities on both racial and religious grounds.[23] This presents a complex scenario beyond simplistic resolutions. However, to begin with a democratic society must, on the one hand, affirm the virtues of minorities, including Jews, and on the other hand, confess the sinful reality of the universality of racial pride and prejudice.[24] The ancient and continuing background of racial and religious prejudice against the Jewish people throughout the world must be borne in mind when searching for solutions regarding the State of Israel, with which they are intimately associated (although not absolutely defined by or absolutely identified with). Christians should remember Jesus' teaching in Jn 4.22 that 'salvation is from the Jews' and Paul's reminder that Christ came, so far as his human ancestry is concerned, from the Jews (Rom. 9.5).[25] Accordingly, in terms of Western civilization, Niebuhr referenced 'the historical dynamism of the Judeo-Christian religious tradition'.[26]

Niebuhr also argues that finally differences between Judaism and Christianity should be assessed on fundamentally theological grounds.[27] He outlines these differences under three headings of problems: first, Messianism, second, grace and law, and third particularity and universality.[28] Messianism centers on the person and place of Jesus Christ, grace and law on the nature of redemption and its moral demands, and particularity and universality on the Jewish people as an ethnic and religious group and on the State of

---

[22] Niebuhr, *Children of Light and Children of Darkness*, pp. 141-45. Richard Crouter, *Reinhold Niebuhr on Politics, Religion, and Christian Faith* (Oxford: Oxford University Press, 2010), p. 137, suggests that Niebuhr's thought was significantly shaped not only by Christian theology but also by Judaism.

[23] Niebuhr, *Children of Light and Children of Darkness*, p. 142.

[24] Niebuhr, *Children of Light and Children of Darkness*, pp. 143-44.

[25] Crouter, *Reinhold Niebuhr on Politics, Religion, and Christian Faith*, p. 139, observes that Niebuhr broke with traditional supercessionism (the view that Christianity totally supplants Judaism).

[26] Niebuhr, *Children of Light and Children of Darkness*, p. 51.

[27] Reinhold Niebuhr, *Pious and Secular America* (New York: Charles Scribner's Sons, 1958), p. 98.

[28] Niebuhr, *Pious and Secular America*, pp. 98-112.

Israel – which he does not see as a religious state.[29] Niebuhr suggests that

> Many Christians are pro-Zionist in the sense that they believe that a homeless people require a homeland; but we feel as embarrassed as anti-Zionist religious Jews when Messianic claims are used to substantiate the right of the Jews to the particular homeland in Palestine; or when it is assumed that this can be done without injury to the Arabs.[30]

For Niebuhr, 'the thrilling emergence of the State of Israel' functions as 'a kind of penance of the world for the awful atrocities committed against the Jews' for a strange configuration of secular and religious forces.[31] Yet the Jewish ethic and faith impressively demonstrated in the universality of the Diaspora becomes problematic when in embodied in a particular state engaged in a battle for survival with Arab forces.[32] For this reason, Niebuhr argues that as a bi-national state Israel will fail.[33] Presumably, he thus expresses support for a two state solution, consisting of Israel and Palestine respectively. Nevertheless, he considers the history of the Jewish people to be nothing short of miraculous.

> We ought to recognize that among the many illogical emergences of history (that is, configurations that do not fit into our logic) there is the strange miracle of the Jewish people, outliving the hazards of the diaspora for two millennia and finally offering their unique and valuable contributions to the common Western civilization, particularly in the final stage of its liberal society. We should not ask that this particular historical miracle fit into any kind of logic or conform to some historical analogy. It has no analogy. It must be appreciated for what it is.[34]

Now to return to an earlier thread: Pentecostal theology of religions (especially as outlined herein) can assume that a variety of positions are held on Israel and eschatology while addressing the in-

[29] Niebuhr, *Pious and Secular America*, p. 110.
[30] Niebuhr, *Pious and Secular America*, p. 109.
[31] Niebuhr, *Pious and Secular America*, p. 109.
[32] Niebuhr, *Pious and Secular America*, p. 110.
[33] Niebuhr, *Pious and Secular America*, p. 110.
[34] Niebuhr, *Pious and Secular America*, pp. 111-12.

stability of the Middle East and the volatility of Christian–Muslim relations throughout the world only from the insights of its own discipline. However, it is significant that the discussion above from Niebuhr ignores the obvious fact that many Evangelicals and Pentecostals prevalently view the post-World War II (re)establishment of the State of Israel in terms of prophetic fulfillment with profound eschatological implications.[35] Yet if the theological work of Althouse and the sociological study of Miller and Yamamori are accurate indicators, contemporary Pentecostal eschatology is fast transforming itself from a dispensationalist system with an individualistic fetish and fatalistic proclivities to a more historic form of premillennialism that is able to address and then embrace concerns about broader social needs and demands with a certain hopeful optimism.[36] These Pentecostals tend to support the continuing existence of the State of Israel with a different set of foci. Since Pentecostals arguably range across a broad spectrum of views on eschatology, Pentecostal theology of religions can, while noting this fact, nevertheless address the Middle East from the possibility of a variety of perspectives. That is, Pentecostal theology of religions is not tied to or bound by a particular eschatological framework for its explication of the situation in the Middle East. Thus it can make valuable contributions for a variety of observers.

First a qualifier is needed. The following focuses on theological insights into interreligious aspects of the situation in the Middle East and of Christian–Muslim relations throughout the world predominately as an example of doing Pentecostal theology of religions in a concrete and specific mode. There are myriad geo-political, economic, historical, and other areas of legitimate emphasis that will nevertheless not be addressed because of our necessarily more narrow interests.[37] Yet they must be part of a satisfactory solution. At the least, here I note that efforts should be made by Christians

---

[35] D.J. Wilson, 'Eschatology, Pentecostal Perspectives On', in *NIDPCM*, pp. 601-605.

[36] See Althouse, *Spirit of the Last Days*, and Miller and Yamamori, *Global Pentecostalism*.

[37] See Robert O. Smith, 'Toward a Lutheran Response to Christian Zionism', *Dialog* 48.3 (Fall 2009), pp. 279-91; and Tony Richie, 'Can Any Good Thing Come Out of Premillennialism: A Response to Robert O. Smith', *Dialog* 48.3 (Fall 2009), pp. 292-300.

in the West to understand better the causes and their sources of Muslim differences on these vital issues and to give due consideration accordingly.[38] That being said, the discussion now proceeds to tease out a few brief applications of Pentecostal theology of religions (as herein envisioned) for the Middle East and Christian–Muslim relations.

Of course, Pentecostals are called to involvement in resolving the conundrums of the Middle East and international relations between Christians and Muslims as a result of their theological commitments. These situations are not simply worldly political and economical concerns that harbor little or no interest for spiritually minded people; they are fraught with theological faith and values. Additionally, Pentecostals can and should approach the process of working out a way of contributing to the resolution of problems in the Middle East and the improvement of global relations between Christians and Muslims *as* Christians. Nothing can be gained by downplaying commitment to Christ or the efficacy of his redemptive work. Yet making Christ central does not require relegating other religious founders or leaders to pejorative stature. Expressing respect for Moses and the rabbinical tradition of Judaism as well as for Mohammed and the importance of the imam in Islam does not take away anything from the uniqueness of Jesus Christ as Savior and Lord. Petty rivalry over religious founders is disgracefully immature. No one is comparable to Christ, but it is essential to understand that Moses and Mohammed hold an important place in the lives of Jews and Muslims, respectively. An attitude of mutual appreciation and respect is essential for progress. Pentecostal Christians should take the initiative in helping make that happen. Here is one place that testimony can be a helpful tool. Testifying to God's glory about life in Christ repudiates anyone's supposed desire or need to denigrate others. Testimony is by nature, although perhaps at times honest and transparent to an almost embarrassing degree, positive and uplifting. It does not attack others. It exalts Christ.

If, as herein asserted, God's Spirit is graciously present and active to some extent among all peoples, then that includes both Israelis and Palestinians, both Jews and Muslims. Therefore, neither

---

[38] Carl Medearis, *Muslims, Christians, and Jesus: Gaining Understanding and Building Relationships* (Grand Rapids: Bethany House, 2008), p. 126.

group should be demonized but should be treated as human beings who are loved by God and for whom Christ died. Of course, the reality of original sin means that neither should be divinized either. Members of both groups have virtues and vices which can and do show up in their policies and practices. Realistic help recognizes this fact and endeavors to find ways of coming together through overcoming challenges on all sides. Pentecostals, because of eschatological interpretations, have sincerely struggled with maintaining this balance.[39] Pentecostals unfortunately allowed themselves to be perceived as 'pro-Israel' and 'anti-Palestinian'. That perception must be replaced with a stance that expresses God's love in Christ toward all. This in no way should be caricatured as abandonment of support for the right of the State of Israel to exist in peace and security. In that sense, Pentecostals are indeed decidedly 'pro-Israel'.[40] They deplore terrorism and condemn terrorists without reserve. Yet this does not justify uncritical support of the secular State of Israel either. Pentecostals ought not to dismiss out of hand the need for the Palestinian people to live in peace and security or ignore human rights violations against them. Pentecostals must insist that both Israelis and Palestinians prosper together. As long as aggressive factions in either group can pit the rest of the world against each other, whether fundamentalist Muslims or fundamentalist Christians, progress toward lasting peace can never take place. And eventually the rest of the world will be (even more than ever) infected (and afflicted) with the violent results.

Furthermore, Pentecostal churches, denominations, and mission organizations should see offering assistance and support to the peace process in the Middle East, and to improving Christian–Muslim relations worldwide, as an important part of their mission in the world for Christ today. As already stated, the Middle East crisis and Christian–Muslim relations throughout the world are intertwined. What is perceived by Arab/Palestinian Muslims and Christians as an unbalanced stance on the Middle East by Western Christians has been a major blockade regarding Christian–Muslim

[39] Wilson, 'Eschatology', in *NIDPCM,* pp. 601-605.
[40] John Hagee, *In Defense of Israel* (Lake Mary, FL: Frontline, 2007), is an admittedly extreme example, but he is able to maintain popularity with his Evangelical and Pentecostal base due to shared presuppositions.

relations in America and throughout the world.[41] Arguably, participating directly in the peace process through gaining mutual understanding and building relationships among these groups, specifically
utilizing dialogical testimony as laid out in the present volume,
could potentially help advance the task immeasurably. Of course, it
does not displace the mandate for evangelism and 'soul winning' by
any means. Yet that the Spirit-filled believer can turn a blind eye or
a deaf ear to the sights and sounds of human suffering without attempting to help is appalling – and ultimately un-Christian. If Pentecostal churches, of all Christian groups probably the most energetic in doing mission, were to begin focusing on peace in the Middle East, rather than rampant eschatological speculations with aggressive cosmic scenarios, conceivably an amazing turnaround
could occur. Pentecostals may thus look for the Lord's return not
only as the time of blessing for a few Christian individuals but also
as the prelude to the establishment God's kingdom among all peoples.

Pre-exilic Israelites charged the prophet Jeremiah with betrayal
because he advised cooperating with Babylonian 'heathens' (Jer.
37.11-16). First-century Jews charged the apostle Paul with blas-
phemy for associating with Gentile 'pagans' (Acts 21.27-32). Yet
Jeremiah and Paul were courageously following God's will – as sacred history has abundantly proved. Might not history, and more
importantly, eternity, likewise prove that it is God's will for coura-
geous men and women of Pentecostal Christian faith to work for
peace in the Middle East and for the improvement of relations between the disciples of Jesus Christ and the rest of the world, including the interreligious world, including Jews and Muslims? Meanwhile, Christian–Muslim relations worldwide likely would be dramatically impacted in positive directions by such demonstrations of
Pentecostal theology of religions in action for the benefit of all. It
may be helpful to remember that in response to Abraham's prayer
for Ishmael God promised to bless Ishmael and his descendants
even though his covenant is with Isaac and his descendants (Gen.
17.18-22). For Pentecostal theology of religions, any proposed 'solution' (or authentic step in that direction) to tensions in the Middle

---

[41] Medearis, *Christians, Muslims, and Jesus*, p. 127.

East must recognize the unique covenant status of the Jews while respecting the divine promise to the Arabs or Palestinians. Of course, Pentecostals, who often have been people from the margins, can identify with others in similar situations and testify to God's gracious sustenance during that difficult journey toward liberation.[42] Testimony can help Pentecostals establish and express solidarity with those of other religions in their at times comparable *Sitz im Leben* (situation in life).

In sum, a Pentecostal theology of religions consistent with a pneumatological approach to prevenient grace based on Christ's atonement with its implications for Christian identity and ecclesial mission and for the providential care and concern of God for all people directs toward a proactive approach to peace in the Middle East. This includes dialogue, especially through testimony. Such may improve relations between Christians and Muslims beyond the Middle East into the rest of the world. Hopefully, in the process of this theological reflection Kärkkäinen's insightful suggestion receives something of a preliminary response. More importantly, it perhaps discovers the humble beginnings of a way forward not only for Pentecostal theology of religions in its next move but for a Pentecostal contribution toward resolving a major crisis of our time that has been stubbornly resistant to all overtures.

It would of course be a gross exaggeration and arrogant over-simplification to assume that Pentecostal theology of religions and interreligious dialogue offer a simple panacea or easy solution to inherent complexities in the Middle East or historically resilient tensions between Christians and Muslims on an international scale. However, it does not seem like too much to suggest that thereby Pentecostals can and should be major contributors to a constructive and positive process toward peaceful co-existence and cooperative concerns. What if Pentecostals could help tip the scales in the perennially irresolvable Middle East context toward authentically hopeful change? What if Pentecostals could help tip the scales in favor of amicable co-existence between Jews, Christians, and Muslims on a global scale? At the least, Pentecostal theology of religions, includ-

[42] Estrelda Alexander, 'When Liberation Becomes Survival', *Pneuma* 32.3 (2010), pp. 337-53.

ing the use of testimony in dialogue, provides a powerful starting point for the attempt. What a difference might Pentecostals make?

On Amos Yong's Observation

In Amos Yong's gracious Foreword to my *Speaking by the Spirit*, he described its contents as 'a powerful theology of witness in a pluralistic world'.[43] As with Kärkkäinen (above), Yong's preeminent place in the discipline of Christian theology of religions, especially in Pentecostal theology of religions (see Chapter 3), inclines one to take such remarks seriously. In this case, I am stimulated by Yong's observation to reflect theologically on the juxtaposition of two concepts that superficially at least may seem to be placed so near each other only with great awkwardness or discomfort: Christian witness and religious pluralism. However, the following paragraphs suggest that Christian witness in a pluralistic world, as I understand Yong to use these terms in his observation, when probed more deeply, is not discordant. More specifically, it will propose that robust and responsible Pentecostal witness is particularly well-suited to the demands and needs of an authentic life of faith amidst the resultant vicissitudes of today's religiously plural world. After all, the word 'witness' and what it signifies should not be taboo in today's world anymore than it was in the pluralistic world of the first century (Acts 14.17).

As explained in the Introduction, *Toward a Pentecostal Theology of Religions* (as does *Speaking by the Spirit*) differentiates between various forms of religious pluralism. Refuting pluralism in its sense of an ideology affirming the more or less equal validity and verity of all religions – through offering a positive alternative for Pentecostals – has been a major objective of this study. Yong's observation challenges it to give some possibly overdue attention to pluralism in the other senses. Multiple religions do exist in the world today, often in close proximity, and many contemporary political systems (e.g. the United States) not only acknowledge and allow but often promote, in the guise of a common civil religion, diverse religious beliefs and

---

[43] Amos Yong, 'Foreword', pp. xi-xii; Richie, *Speaking by the Spirit*, p. xi.

124   *A Pentecostal Theology of Religions*

practices within their purview.[44] Per Yong's comment, I suggest that reflection on Christian witness in a pluralistic world in terms of pluralism in these latter senses may yield fruit for Pentecostal theology and mission. The following approaches this task in three steps. First, it outlines a brief theology of Christian witness as a basis for conversation. Second, it explores implications of the fact of religious pluralism (rather than as a philosophy) for contemporary theology of Christian witness, with special attention to Pentecostals. Third, it offers a few suggestions for further reflection on Christian theology of witness in a pluralistic world. Throughout this section it is assumed that a robust theology of Christian witness will fully affirm the continuing essentiality of evangelistic witness and that a responsible theology of Christian witness will firmly endorse other vital aspects of witness, including the need to serve well in a world of multiple religious persuasions. It also suggests the practice of personal testimony is particularly well suited as Christian witness in pluralistic settings.

Chapter 1 of this work briefly surveyed the distinctive importance of mission for Pentecostals. Certainly evangelistic witness is of central significance. For Steve Land, within a trinitarian framework soteriology, ecclesiology, missiology, and pneumatology all interconnect with Christian witness.[45] So, what is Christian witness? Before describing Christian witness itself, it may be helpful, especially in light of the discussion above from Niebuhr on Israel and the Jews, to note that Niebuhr sees the Christian witnessing tradition both in terms of continuity and discontinuity with its Judaic parentage. He describes Judaism and Christianity as 'two covenant faiths, in which a community of believers propagates the shared faith and seeks to bear witness to its validity even to those who do not share it'.[46] Contrariwise he later argues that 'Obviously the Jewish faith is not universal in the sense of being missionary and offering its way of life to all people'.[47] Niebuhr may simply be somewhat self-contradictory on this point. Likely he intends that

---

[44] Moltmann, *A Broad Place,* identifies messianic and millennarian elements in American civil religion (p. 144). That assessment implies that civil religion in the United States is primarily indebted to Christian categories.
    [45] Land, 'Pentecostal Spirituality', *JPT,* p. 37.
    [46] Niebuhr, *Pious and Secular America,* p. 98.
    [47] Niebuhr, *Pious and Secular America,* p. 107.

the witness of transnational and cross-cultural Christianity is universal in a way that the more ethnically oriented particularity of Judaism does not claim. Notably, Newbigin argues that a significant difference of Judaism and Christianity with Islam is that the former are not universal extensions of Hebrew culture while the last insists on a non-translatable faith inextricable from a universalized Arabic culture.[48] However, one reminds that resolving this struggle is exactly what was underway in early Jewish Christian interaction with Gentile Christians in Acts 10, 11, 15 and Galatians 2! For present purposes, it is enough to note that in a derivative sense Christian witness has something of a 'pluralistic' pedigree. Further, it is important to note that some other religions, including Buddhism and Islam, are in their own ways just as 'missionary minded' as Pentecostal Christianity.[49]

Along this line, according to Jesus, Jews from among the Pharisees already were well known for making many converts (Mt. 23.15). However, clearly Jesus does not commend but rather condemns their inconsistencies. Chrysostom charges that they were careless and traitorous regarding the real intent of winning religious converts.[50] Jerome questions their motives as avaricious.[51] Shelton rightly notes that Jesus does not condemn their making converts (or proselytes) because Israel was expected to be a light to win converts (e.g. Isa. 42.6; 49.6); rather, the negative effect of their proselytizing was found harmful.[52] Doubtless Christians have sometimes fallen into a similar mode in their unbridled zeal. The lessons for Christians include that it is not enough to witness unless witnessing is done wisely and well. Consequently, a sound Christian theology of witness is of paramount importance today (as always).

Now on to Christian witness more directly. For Christians, witnessing is no peripheral endeavor; it is inextricably bound up with the inner core of Christian identity. As neo-orthodox theologian

[48] Newbigin, *Gospel in a Pluralist Society*, p. 145.
[49] Frank Whaling, 'A Comparative Religious Study of Missionary Transplantation in Buddhism, Christianity, and Islam', *IRM* 70 (1981), pp. 314-33, esp. pp. 319-24.
[50] Manlio Simonetti (ed.), *Matthew 14-28* (ACCS; Downers Grove, IL: Inter-Varsity Press, 2002), p. 172.
[51] Simonetti, *Matthew 14-28,* p. 172.
[52] Shelton, 'Matthew', *FLBCNT,* p. 228.

Emil Brunner, arguably one of the greatest Christian thinkers of the early twentieth century, says, 'the matter of greatest significance for the Church is the proclamation of the Gospel'.[53] Further, the Church is under a divine charge to bear witness to the love of God bestowed in Christ on humanity.[54] This witness forms the basis of the Church's existence, and includes not only its testimony to the word of truth but also its demonstration of the life of Christ in the fellowship of the Spirit as the 'Ekklesia' or Church in a 'double witness'.[55] Brunner's description implies that just as the announcement of God's love in Christ toward humanity and the manifestation of Christ's life by the Spirit through the Church is its *raison d'être*, it would be unthinkable to suggest to the Church that it in any way minimize or mute its witness. To do so would be to undermine its own being. The Church does not *do* witness so much as it *is* witness. The Church cannot exist as the Church without bearing witness to Christ. Put another way, in its message and in its existence the Church bears witness to Jesus Christ.

If Brunner is correct, then since Christian witness and Christian existence are so inextricably connected, it is all the more important for the Church to engage constantly in self-examination and honest evaluation to assure that its witness is authentic and legitimate. Otherwise, its own existence runs the risk of distortion or possible denial. To the extent that the Church's witness is distorted or denied then it ceases to be the Church. So then, on the one hand, the Church cannot cease to bear witness in faith, but, on the other hand, it must always take pains to assure the authenticity and validity of its witness. The Church's self examination of its own witness must always first include its message but also extend to its methodology. It is a constant matter of concern whether the pure message of God's love and the Spirit's life in Christ are in any way marred by the method of its presentation before the world through its primary mode of transmission, the Church. However, a critical theology of Christian witness must never become merely a discussion of evan-

---

53 Emil Brunner, *Our Faith* (trans. John W. Rilling; New York: Charles Scribner's Sons, 1936, 1962), p. 123.

54 Emil Brunner, *The Christian Doctrine of the Church, Faith, and the Consummation: Dogmatics III* (trans. David Cairns in collaboration with T.H.L. Parker; Philadelphia: Westminster Press, 1962), p. 135.

55 Brunner, *Dogmatics III,* p. 135.

gelistic techniques; it is above all a call to self-testing for affirmation by the approving presence of Jesus Christ (2 Cor. 13.5).

According to Wilbert Shenk, Mennonite missiologist from Fuller Theological Seminary, the gospel is what Christianity is all about, and the gospel involves announcing the good news and its content, that is, 'God's redemptive action in Jesus Christ for the salvation of humankind'.[56] There is a telling, a testifying, or a witnessing that is inherent in and un-removable from authentic Christianity. Exercising Christian witness may range from spontaneous sharing by individuals out of the overflow of their own joyous experience of Christ to international missionary programs by institutions or organizations existing for the explicit purpose of 'world evangelism'. However, a responsible theology of Christian witness does not reduce witness to personal salvation and preparation for Heaven or an evangelistic formula. Rather, commitment to 'the *whole* gospel' includes 'the larger movement of the kingdom of God' as disciples dedicated to the ethical and social implications of obedience to Christ as well.[57] (Perhaps startling to Pentecostals, who ardently emphasize the full gospel, is that other traditions [e.g. Mennonites] may perceive their full gospel, or at least its customary application, as partial or incomplete!)

Kimberly Thacker notes that closely related New Testament terms for evangelizing (εὐαγγελίζω) and gospel (εὐαγγέλιον), signifying announcing important good news, point to proclamation and witness as 'sharing the good news of Christ with others'.[58] Examples of evangelism by Jesus and his early followers include verbal proclamation, miracles and healing, and personal witness and testimony.[59] The purpose and breadth of evangelism, which requires the participation of the Holy Spirit and cultural understanding and sensitivity, includes several components, and involves different strategies, is to 'enable and encourage people to enter into a relationship with God through Jesus Christ'.[60] Timoteo Gener emphasizes holis-

---

[56] Wilbert R. Shenk, 'Gospel', in Dyrness and Kärkkäinen (eds.), *GDT*, p. 356.
[57] Shenk, 'Gospel', p. 358 (emphasis original).
[58] Kimberly Thacker and Timoteo D. Gener, 'Evangelism', in Dyrness and Kärkkäinen (eds.), *GDT*, p. 297.
[59] Thacker and Gener, 'Evangelism', p. 297.
[60] Thacker and Gener, 'Evangelism', pp. 297-98 (esp. p. 297).

tic evangelism (personal salvation and social action), or words and deeds, functioning in a conjunctive rather than a disjunctive mode.[61] However, he acknowledges that Pentecostal and Charismatic movements' proclamation of Christ as 'Lord of the spirits' (through deliverance type ministries) is impacting global evangelism and contributing to their rapid spread.[62] Gener suggests institutional Christianity per se must be replaced by a more missional approach 'emphasizing both the local and collective (universal) dimensions of witnessing to Christ'.[63]

As already stated above, Pentecostals see witnessing as particularly important to their identity as a movement. Arrington considers an intended result and a main purpose of Spirit baptism, the central distinctive of Pentecostalism, to be endowment of power for bold witnessing (cf. Acts 1.8).[64] Further, Land associates speaking in tongues with prayer and service in witness of redemptive reality.[65] Pentecostal ecclesiology stresses the role of the Church as a community sending forth evangelists and bearing witness to Jesus Christ.[66] The Church's mission, along with worship to God, edification of believers, and social concern for the world, is evangelization of the lost or unconverted.[67] Indeed, Pentecostals are noted for their book of Acts approach to the Christian life, and witness has been presented as a primary theological integrating theme for Acts.[68] Undoubtedly, Pentecostals would likely agree with Roman Catholic Robert Faricy that Christian witness is carried out as the witness of the Holy Spirit, both externally through those who proclaim or testify and internally in the hearts of hearers.[69] Pentecostals also would likely agree with Richard Armstrong in his uncompro-

---

[61] Thacker and Gener, 'Evangelism', p. 299.
[62] Thacker and Gener, 'Evangelism', p. 299.
[63] Thacker and Gener, 'Evangelism', p. 299.
[64] Arrington, *Christian Doctrine*, III, pp. 71-72 and 82-84.
[65] Steven J. Land, 'The Nature and Evidence of Spiritual Fullness', in Robert White (ed.), *Endued with Power: The Holy Spirit in the Church* (Cleveland, TN: Pathway Press, 1995), pp. 69-78.
[66] Arrington, *Christian Doctrine*, III, pp. 182-83.
[67] Higgins, Dunsing, and Tallman, *An Introduction to Theology*, pp. 175-77.
[68] I. Howard Marshal and David Peterson (eds.), *Witness to the Gospel: The Theology of Acts* (Grand Rapids: Eerdmans, 1998). See esp. Chapter 1.
[69] Robert Faricy, 'Witness of the Spirit', in Alan Richardson and John Bowden (eds.), *The Westminster Dictionary of Christian Theology* (Philadelphia: Westminster Press, 1983), p. 603.

mising assertion that the Church's evangelistic task is not optional
and that all Christians (not just clergy or missionaries) are expected
to respond in obedience to the call of witnessing to the world of
Jesus Christ.[70]

And yet Armstrong asserts that a chief challenge to the contemporary Church is 'how to do evangelism in a pluralistic world' while
'affirming the truth of other faiths without compromising the
uniqueness of Christ'.[71] Similarly, Scott Jones argues that Christian
theology of witness flows out of the universal love of God for the
entire world, including persons of other religions, thus enabling
evangelism and dialogue.[72] At its core Christian witness is inseparable from the love of God for everyone, including Jews, Muslims,
Hindus, Buddhists, Sikhs, Bahá'í, and others. Obviously, Christian
witness can take diverse forms. For example, John Howard Yoder
argues convincingly that Christian witness must address the State
and its social order.[73] And Charles Kraft proposes that those engaged in the ministry of Christian witness, at least in a cross-cultural
context, which anymore to some extent means just about everyone,
need a crash course (or more) in anthropology in order to understand the complex identities of their audience![74] Frances Adeney is
surely right both that evangelistic witness is complex and controversial and that what is needed is a more graceful approach.[75] Some
Christians see witnessing as an act of love and obedience while
some non-Christians see it as an arrogant attempt to impose one's
views on others. Surely, not only the content but also the tone of
witnessing should be graceful.

In this text, of course, the concern is with a theology of Christian witness as it relates to living in a pluralistic world (in the sense
that many religions co-inhabit the planet and contemporary society

---

[70] Richard Stoll Armstrong, 'Evangelism', in Richardson and Bowden (eds.),
Westminster Dictionary of Christian Theology, p. 192.

[71] Armstrong, 'Evangelism', p. 193.

[72] Scott J. Jones, *The Evangelistic Love of God and Neighbor: A Theology of Witness
and Discipleship* (Nashville: Abingdon Press, 2003). See esp. Chapter 7.

[73] John Howard Yoder, *The Christian Witness to the State* (Newton, KS: Herald
Press, 2002).

[74] Charles H. Kraft, *Anthropology for Christian Witness* (Maryknoll, NY: Orbis,
1996, 2001).

[75] Frances S. Adeney, *Graceful Evangelism: Christian Witness in a Complex World*
(Grand Rapids: Baker Academic, 2010), pp. xi-xii.

is structured accordingly). Newbigin puts it into perspective when he asks, 'What, then, does it mean to do evangelism in this kind of society?'[76] Evidence indicates that Pentecostal missiologists, such as for example Gary Tyra, are becoming increasingly aware of the need for Spirit empowered witness that is adaptable in and applicable to pluralistic contexts.[77] Therefore, an adequate Pentecostal theology of witness ought to take into account the realities of pluralistic cultures.

In this context, Adeney sees the churches at an impasse and in a battle over the meaning and methods of evangelism.[78] Again, Adeney's assessment is on target.

> In the wider society, the battle takes the form of arguing over religion in the public sphere, including debate about prayer in schools, posting the Ten Commandments in high school hallways, and announcing Christian holidays in schools, shopping malls, or town squares. To protect freedom of religion, our society is moving away from specific Christian references about Christmas, for example, to more general ideas that don't push 'the reason for the season'. Coke ads replace Christian symbols with snowflakes, 'Merry Christmas' becomes 'Happy Holidays', and Tiny Tim's famous line from Charles Dickens' *Christmas Carol* morphs from 'God bless us everyone' to 'Bless us everyone' on street banners in San Francisco.[79]

Adeney goes on to admit that 'There are good reasons to protect people from having religious views foisted upon them and to be careful not to offend the religious sensibilities of others' before adding, somewhat ominously, 'But Christian evangelism no longer has the cultural support of general consensus and struggles to find a fit in our pluralistic society'.[80] This is a startling and disturbing evaluation that is difficult to discount. After a study of the history and theory of evangelism, Part Four of her book suggests reformulation in order to craft a more graceful approach to evangelism. Chapter

---

[76] Newbigin, *Gospel in a Pluralist Society,* p. 4.

[77] Gary Tyra, *The Holy Spirit in Mission: Prophetic Speech and Action in Christian Witness* (Downers Grove, IL: InterVarsity Press, 2011).

[78] Adeney, *Graceful Evangelism,* pp. xi-xii.

[79] Adeney, *Graceful Evangelism,* p. xii.

[80] Adeney, *Graceful Evangelism,* p. xii.

12 in particular probes Christian witness in a world where interfaith marriage is more common, some young people are converting to another religion, there are political questions in the public realm about other faiths, and local pastors must navigate relationships with religious leaders in the community.

Adeney's telling description of 'our pluralistic society' jells well with Newbigin's belief that 'a Christian must welcome some measure of plurality but reject pluralism'.[81] There is a sense in which Pentecostals, with other Christians and with non-Christians, must *own* pluralism. For better or for worse, this is *our* pluralistic society, at least for the present. And it may not be entirely negative. As Newbigin observes, a plurality or diversity of human experiences potentially enriches Christians and provides opportunities to test and demonstrate the sufficiency of Jesus Christ.[82] However, the ideology of pluralism reduces truth to the subjective and relative realm, and is therefore not acceptable to those committed to integrity of the truth of the gospel.[83] Accordingly, one might suggest that a robust and responsible theology of Christian witness must steer a safe course between the Scylla of refusing to acknowledge the reality, and perhaps even beneficial nature, of plurality in the sense of diversity, and the Charybdis of choosing to embrace the destructive, and perhaps even damnable, ideology of religious pluralism.

The insights of Adeney and Newbigin correspond with my explanation above regarding Yong's observation: even though Pentecostals reject the ideology of pluralism they still live with the reality of its presence. This reality affects evangelistic witness. For many Christians there is no question as to whether we do evangelism – we do; but, some are grasping for a way to do evangelism most effectively in today's widely varied settings.[84] The latter trend corresponds to some of my own research and reflections, especially applicable in pluralist settings. For example, several years ago I interacted with Walter Hollenweger's work on Pentecostal evangelism (see the Introduction above) through an article in the *International*

---

[81] Newbigin, *Gospel in a Pluralist Society*, p. 243.
[82] Newbigin, *Gospel in a Pluralist Society*, pp. 243-44.
[83] Newbigin, *Gospel in a Pluralist Society*, p. 244.
[84] A popular level example is John Kramp, *Out of Their Faces and into Their Shoes: How to Understand Spiritually Lost People and Give Them Directions to God* (Nashville: B & H Books, 1997).

Review of Mission titled 'Revamping Pentecostal Evangelism: Appropriating Walter J. Hollenweger's Radical Proposal'.[85] In short, Hollenweger exploits the encounter of Peter and Cornelius in Acts 10 to propose Pentecostals adopt a form of evangelism that is 'dialogical' and 'situational' based upon an inclusive and pneumatological theology of religions.[86] However, as Pentecostal (Church of God) missiologist Grant McClung notes, Pentecostals not only see evangelistic witness as a high priority empowered by the Holy Spirit, they also are often 'aggressive' in their approach to evangelism.[87] As Kärkkäinen has pointed out, this fact has generated problems with evangelism and proselytism, common witness and Christian unity, and relations with other religions.[88] Accordingly, I therefore argue, in a qualified agreement with Hollenweger, that Pentecostals need to review and revise – that is, revamp – their approach to evangelism.[89]

A number of ideas deserve noting. First, revamping must not be understood as repudiating the strong evangelistic and witnessing heritage of Pentecostals. More will be said on this momentarily. Suffice it to say for now that my long term involvement in the formulation of the unprecedented ecumenical statement, involving Catholics and Protestants, and including Evangelicals and Pentecostals, 'Christian Witness in a Multi-Religious World: Recommendations for Conduct', taught me that other Christian communions struggle with maintaining commitment to announcing the gospel in tandem with concerns about contexts of religious pluralism – but that a way forward is possible.[90] Second, ministry is situation specific. There are some situations where proclamation is more appropriate. There are others where dialogue is more so. Words that are altogether appropriate in the local Pentecostal church in the United States might be outright rude when going into someone else's coun-

---

85 Richie, 'Revamping Pentecostal Evangelism', pp. 343-54.
86 Richie, 'Revamping Pentecostal Evangelism', pp. 343-46.
87 Richie, 'Revamping Pentecostal Evangelism', pp. 347-49. See McClung, 'Evangelism', in *NIDPCM*, p. 617.
88 Veli-Matti Kärkkäinen, 'Missiology: Pentecostal and Charismatic', in *NIDPCM*, pp. 882-83.
89 Richie, 'Revamping Pentecostal Evangelism', pp. 349-52.
90 See http://www.oikoumene.org/en/resources/documents/wcc-programmes/interreligious-dialogue-and-cooperation/Christian-identity-in-pluralistic-societies/Christian-witness-in-a-multi-religious-world.html.

try and culture, into their home, so to speak, as cross-cultural guests. Additionally, in some cases a form of cooperation on shared social concerns might be most appropriate at the time.

In any case, revamping Pentecostal evangelism, the way we do witness, is not a matter of losing spiritual ardor. Pentecostals can be fervent without being unfriendly. Perhaps part of the problem is the unfortunate word 'aggressive' when it is attached to evangelism or witness and what it can imply – and therefore the kind of conduct it can, perhaps inadvertently, but almost inevitably, encourage. I have before questioned the appropriateness of this concept in relation to the theology and practice of Christian witness.[91] While for some 'aggressive' may only signify an attitude of overcoming obstacles to get the job done, more often than not it carries connotations of co-ercion. After all, as any dictionary can confirm, the word means 'ready or likely to attack or confront'. Is that really the image that we, speaking as a Pentecostal, wish to project to others when witnessing to the world about God's love in Christ? At its best, aggressive means 'pursuing one's aims and interests forcefully, sometimes unduly so'.[92] Words like 'energetic' or 'enthusiastic' may more adequately describe how Pentecostals could better conceptualize and practice evangelism and witness.[93] Energy speaks of power and enthusiasm speaks of fullness. Power and fullness are certainly more consistent with primary Pentecostal values (Lk. 24.49, Acts 1.8, and 2.4). Furthermore, the Bible advocates responsible, responsive Christian evangelism (e.g. 1 Pet. 3.15). Pentecostal evangelism should rid itself of any impressions, real or imagined, of aggression in the sense of coercion or manipulation. However, Pentecostals should not be asked or expected to mute their energy and enthusiasm for evangelism.

---

[91] See Tony Richie, 'A Pentecostal in Sheep's Clothing: An Unlikely Participant but Hopeful Partner in Interreligious Dialogue', *Current Dialogue* 48 (December 2006), available at http://wcc-coe.org/wcc/what/interreligious/cd48-03.html.

[92] Of course Newbigin is right in arguing that positions of power can add to this impression (*Gospel in a Pluralist Society*, pp. 158 and 226).

[93] Hence Newbigin advocates for energetic efforts in evangelism and social action within a framework of confidence in the gospel but without Pelagian-like dependence on human initiative (*Gospel in a Pluralist Society*, p. 243).

So then, how might a Christian theology of witness work in pluralistic settings? Princeton's Daniel Migliore briefly but straightforwardly tackles the topic of witness to Jesus Christ in a religiously plural world.[94] He offers three theses. First, '*Christians are called to relate to non-Christians in the confidence that the grace of God made known in Jesus Christ is at work by the power of God's Spirit even where it is not recognized as present*'.[95] Accordingly, going forth to proclaim the gospel to the world may in large part involve looking for signs of what the Holy Spirit has been doing in preparation long in advance of the missionary's arrival. Second, '*The encounter of Christians and non-Christians requires genuine dialogue; yet without relinquishing the responsibility to communicate the gospel as faithfully and as compellingly as possible*'.[96] Accordingly, a responsible theology of witness does not present an either/or choice between proclamation and dialogue. Rather, the proper dynamic is both/and. Third, '*The interaction of Christians and non-Christians should be encouraged at the grassroots level and fostered in cooperative efforts on matters of common concern and commitment*'.[97] Evangelism, witness, and dialogue go far beyond words. At their best they are accompanied by and validated through actions manifesting the God's love in concrete forms.

In surveying the preceding, it is evident that certain themes stand out. Christian theology and praxis of witness is rooted in the nature of the gospel itself as good news, involves sharing that good news of God's redemptive love in Christ for all by the power of the Holy Spirit, is central to Pentecostal identity and ecclesial mission, flows out of and reflects the nature of God's love toward the world, and should be holistic in nature, encompassing individual salvation and its implications for humanity and the created order as a whole. It also must be able to adapt to the realities of cultural diversity, including the demands and needs of pluralistic society if it is to communicate the gospel of Jesus Christ effectively in today's world without compromising its own innermost ethos.

One further thought has to do with the nature of the ones who witness. The previous information deals mostly with what witness-

94 Migliore, *Faith Seeking Understanding*, pp. 326-29.
95 Migliore, *Faith Seeking Understanding*, p. 327 (emphasis original).
96 Migliore, *Faith Seeking Understanding*, p. 328 (emphasis original).
97 Migliore, *Faith Seeking Understanding*, p. 328 (emphasis original).

ing is and how it is done. The focus has been on 'knowing' and 'doing'. Now attention to 'being' is appropriate. As Land says, 'The church is being transformed by and for God and thus bears witness in what it is and what it does in the kingdom'.[98] Authenticity in Pentecostal identity is inherently connected to witnessing.[99] However, Christian witness is much more than verbal proclamation or social activism; it is ontological and transformational. In other words, Christian witness is a matter of manifesting holy character before a watching world (see on Mt. 23.15 above). Land expands on this astounding dynamic.

> This development is a progression from *belonging* to a community to *being identified* with Christ wholeheartedly in order to fulfill all righteousness, to *being empowered* to actualize the missionary purpose of God in the world as led and filled by the Holy Spirit who gives his fruit (character of the witness) and gifts (special equipment for the witness).[100]

Pentecostal witness ought to be thought of as much more than communicating propositional truth to the heretofore epistemologically uninformed. While certainly affirming the reality of absolute truth over against relativism, Pentecostals, along with 3 Jn 3-4, tend to understand truth in more subtle and relational terms, including the practice of truth through a holy walk.[101] This perspective is in keeping with the Wesleyan roots of Pentecostalism. Wesley thought the chief hindrance to evangelism among those of other religions was their encounters with so-called Christians failing to live up to the standard of holiness.[102] For Wesley and for Pentecostals, 'the greatest witness to the world of the truth in Christ is a life transformed by the power of the Holy Spirit from the guilt and bondage of sin to a life of holiness and freedom'.[103] As Newbigin phrases it, Christian mission and witness require 'a community which lives

---

[98] Land, 'Pentecostal Spirituality', *JPT*, p. 39.

[99] Land, 'Pentecostal Spirituality', *JPT*, p. 43.

[100] Land, 'Pentecostal Spirituality', *JPT*, p. 37 (emphasis original).

[101] See Tony Richie, 'Approaching Religious Truth in a Pluralistic World: A Pentecostal-Charismatic Contribution', *JES* 43.3 (Summer 2008), pp. 351-69.

[102] Richie, 'Mr. Wesley and Mohammed', p. 91.

[103] Richie, 'Mr. Wesley and Mohammed', p. 91. Cf. *CWJW* (Rio, WI: Wesleyan Heritage Collection; Ages Software, 2002), 6.305; 8.521; 9.34, 180; and 10.190.

faithfully by the gospel'.[104] Even more pointedly, he asserts that 'the only hermeneutic of the gospel, is a congregation of men and women who believe it and live by it'.[105]

Consequently, a key question for Pentecostals in Christian witness has to do with the character of the witness as much or more than the nature of their witness. No one should feel disqualified or be discouraged if they have not yet attained unto 'Christian perfection', to utilize Wesley's way of putting it; but, everyone should display the reality of God's grace in Christ through a life transformed by the Holy Spirit as the ultimate demonstration of the gospel. In 'our pluralistic society', as Adeney put it, this may be even more relevant than ever – if that is possible.[106] As noted, it is becoming increasingly difficult to express Christian faith openly or publically because of radically pluralist (or secularist) assumptions that it will be offensive to others (usually, at least when done reasonably, it is not). Disagree or decry that fact as one may, it is nonetheless the reality of contemporary society. Perhaps that will change; perhaps not. In any case, a well-lived life speaks volumes about one's faith to one and all. As in the first Christian century, the powerful truth of 1 Pet. 3.15-16 will be evident:

> but sanctify Christ as Lord in your hearts, always being ready to make a defense to everyone who asks you to give an account for the hope that is in you, yet with gentleness and reverence; and keep a good conscience so that in the thing in which you are slandered, those who revile your good behavior in Christ will be put to shame. (NASB)

The old adage that believers must 'practice what they preach' is applicable here. Only in this case it might be better said that in interreligious dialogue one's verbal and moral testimonies must match if they are to project an authentic (and attractive) Christian witness in and to a pluralistic society. Perhaps it is not too fantastic to suggest that to an extent willingness to engage in interreligious dialogue testifies to the world of one's moral compass as well. In any case, I propose that a robust and responsible theology of religions is also

---

104 Newbigin, *Gospel in a Pluralist Society*, p. 154.
105 Newbigin, *Gospel in a Pluralist Society*, p. 227.
106 Adeney, *Graceful Evangelism*, p. xii.

responsive (á la 1 Pet. 3.15). That is, our Christian theology of witness should be responsive to our pluralistic society. For Pentecostals, that requires developing a dynamic theology of religions and implementing it through their own distinctive testimony via interreligious dialogue.

Conclusion

This chapter has endeavored to engage in conversation on Pentecostal theology of religions with Veli-Matti Kärkkäinen and Amos Yong. They are Pentecostals widely recognized for their contribution to the field. In particular it has suggested that the next best move for Pentecostal theology of religions, in advancing from the general and abstract to the concrete and specific, may be addressing current shared concerns involving interreligious components, such as the crisis in the Middle East and Christian–Muslim relations worldwide. It has also suggested that a robust and responsible theology of Christian witness in a pluralistic society and Pentecostal theology of religions can be mutually enabling and empowering. The next chapter takes the conversation to a non-Pentecostal partner of note.

6

CONTINUING CONVERSATION ON PENTECOSTAL THEOLOGY OF RELIGIONS (NON-PENTECOSTAL PARTNER)

Introduction

The previous chapter unfolded against a backdrop of continuing conversations in the New Testament (Gal. 1.18-19; 2.7-10) regarding the place of Gentiles in the young church as initiated by Peter's encounter with Cornelius (Acts 10) with its pivotal significance at the Jerusalem Council (Acts 15.6-11). This ongoing conversation revealed the struggle of the New Testament church to come to grips with the scope of the gospel of Jesus Christ (Gal. 2.11-21; cf. 2 Pet. 3.15-16). The present chapter endeavors to continue the conversation of the previous chapter but extends it beyond Pentecostal partners such as Kärkkäinen and Yong. Jürgen Moltmann is selected as a non-Pentecostal conversation partner on the basis of his widely recognized contributions to Christian theology of religions in conjunction with some point of interaction in my own work in the discipline. Moltmann has often been an important partner for Pentecostal theologians.[1] This chapter will provide the necessary background for discussion through an overview and assessment of Moltmann's theology of religions and interreligious dialogue with observations from the perspective of Pentecostal theology. The

---

[1] See Christopher A. Stephenson, *Types of Pentecostal Theology: Method, System, Spirit* (Oxford, UK: Oxford University Press, 2013), pp. 39-40 and 149; Land, *Pentecostal Spirituality*; and Althouse, *Spirit of the Last Days*. See also the dialog between Moltmann and six Pentecostal scholars from five continents in *JPT* 4 (April 1994), pp. 5-70.

next, and final, chapter will engage further with Moltmann through his direct comments about some of my own work in Pentecostal theology of religions. Neither of these chapters is offered as critical analysis of Moltmann's theology in general or his theology of religions particularly. Rather, they are better received as interactive theological reflections focused on Pentecostal priorities.

Overview & Assessments of Jürgen Moltmann's Theology of Religions & Interreligious Dialogue

Although complex and continually evolving, in brief Jürgen Moltmann's theology is organized around the theme of divine promise in terms of future eschatological fulfillment; simply put, it is a theology of hope.[2] Moltmann has been described as the world's 'leading living constructive theologian'.[3] Notably, he has engaged in significant interaction with Pentecostal theologians at several levels.[4] Readers should not be surprised to discover much in Moltmann that is affirmed as fruitful while also frequently calling for discerning qualifications. In particular, universalistic tendencies in Moltmann are problematic, to put it mildly, for Pentecostals. In spite of this obvious divergence, Pentecostals can yet draw with benefit from Moltmann's theology, specifically, in the case of theology of religions, on his Christological and charismatic and pneumatological ecclesiology with its energetic and innovative missiology enabling partnerships of integrity with religious others through dialogue. To put it somewhat colloquially, Pentecostals may well wish to be fellow travelers with Moltmann on his journey in theology of religions but most likely will want to get off the bus a bit before he does.

---

[2] E.g. Jürgen Moltmann, *Theology of Hope: On the Ground and the Implications of a Christian Eschatology* (London: SCM Press, 1967), and *Ethics of Hope* (Minneapolis: Fortress Press, 2012). Cf. Ryan A. Neal, *Theology as Hope: On the Grounds and Implications of Jürgen Moltmann's Doctrine of Hope* (Princeton Theological Monograph Series, 99; Eugene, OR: Pickwick, 2009).

[3] Veli-Matti Kärkkäinen, 'Introduction: Pentecostalism and Pentecostal Theology in the Third Millennium: Taking Stock of the Contemporary Global Situation', in Kärkkäinen (ed.), *The Spirit in the World*, p. xxiv.

[4] Kärkkäinen, 'Taking Stock', p. xxiv.

Jürgen Moltmann offers an intriguing summary of his theology of religions in *The Church in the Power of the Spirit*.[5] This foundational and paradigmatic book is a sustained study of ecclesiology in light of pneumatology. However, as the subtitle, *A Contribution to Messianic Ecclesiology*, clearly indicates, the text is Christologically centered. Further, in keeping with the general tenor of Moltmann's theology, it has a strong eschatological emphasis. As an ecclesiological study, its content is heavily concerned with Christian mission as well. Notably, Moltmann sets his theology of religions discussion in a chapter on extra-ecclesial relationships, titled 'The Church of the Kingdom of God', which is an expansive treatment of the 'the breadth of the horizon of hope' offered in Christ.[6] The Church of Jesus Christ exists and acts in terms of the grand purposes of God's coming kingdom. In other words, the Church is beckoned by realities beyond itself. In everything it must be related, on the one hand, to the Triune God, and on the other hand, to all creation. As Moltmann puts it early in this text, thereby defining much of what is to follow, 'the church stands for God to the world, and it stands for the world before God'.[7] Yet Christians can never lose sight of Christ; for, 'ecclesiology can only be developed from christology, as its consequence and in correspondence with it'.[8] Nonetheless, hope in Christ is more than the hope of Christianity. The Christian conversation on hope includes Israel's hope, the hope of the world religions, of human society, and of nature because 'Christian eschatology is not merely eschatology for Christians' but also the eschatology of 'the all-embracing kingdom'.[9] Therefore, Moltmann begins his theology of religions from an expansive position. Since by very definition Christian hope is in a sense all-encompassing, Christian theology of religions cannot be rigidly exclusive without surrendering essential elements of its own hopeful identity.

For Moltmann, Christianity's relationship with the world religions is indelibly stamped by its origin in Israel and its orientation toward the future of all humanity.[10] He proposes that a new world

[5] Moltmann, *The Church in the Power of the Spirit*.
[6] Moltmann, *The Church in the Power of the Spirit*, pp. 133-96 (p. 133).
[7] Moltmann, *The Church in the Power of the Spirit*, p. 1.
[8] Moltmann, *The Church in the Power of the Spirit*, p. 66.
[9] Moltmann, *The Church in the Power of the Spirit*, p. 135.
[10] Moltmann, *The Church in the Power of the Spirit*, p. 150.

situation is emerging in which a new community of singularity for nations and cultures requires world religions, including Christianity, to adopt commitment to a common humanity.[11] Decentralization and de-Westernization of Christianity is leading to development of more indigenous forms of the faith in which Christianity enters into living relationships with other religious faiths, uniquely shaping both Christianity and others in dialogues not driven by previous power dynamics.[12] Mission emphasis shifts from its traditional quantitative thrust on making converts to one that qualitatively influences the atmosphere of life in various religious cultures via Christian faith and values.[13] Qualitative mission requires mutually transformative dialogue through vulnerable and open relationships allowing the distinctive identity of each to continue untarnished and yet inviting it to emerge with a new profile.[14]

If what Moltmann deems as the necessary progress toward a single community or common world is to occur, he suggests that several prejudices of Christianity toward other religions must be abolished. First is the exclusive absolutism of the Church, the view that the Church is the sole arbiter of salvation, in favor of a more relational view founded on the universality of Christ himself.[15] Second is the absolute equation of faith with religion which fails to escape an absolutist misunderstanding of the Christian faith in efforts to avoid the compulsion to level all religions down to the same general concept.[16] Third is the Enlightenment relativism which is at times little other than disguised skepticism; but, it is not so much a productive type of tolerance as more of a cloak for absolutizing relativism that actually hinders Christianity from entering authentically into living relationships with world religions.[17]

However, it would perhaps be a mistake to assume from the preceding that Moltmann rejects out of hand all absolutes. He does, in a carefully qualified sense, affirm the absolute nature of Christianity. Moltmann presents a theological model for the relationship

---

[11] Moltmann, *The Church in the Power of the Spirit*, pp. 150-51.

[12] Moltmann, *The Church in the Power of the Spirit*, pp. 151-52.

[13] Moltmann, *The Church in the Power of the Spirit*, p. 152.

[14] Moltmann, *The Church in the Power of the Spirit*, pp. 152-53.

[15] Moltmann, *The Church in the Power of the Spirit*, pp. 153-54.

[16] Moltmann, *The Church in the Power of the Spirit*, pp. 154-55.

[17] Moltmann, *The Church in the Power of the Spirit*, pp. 155-57.

of Christianity to other religions that juxtaposes the natural world religions, obviously containing some elements of truth, with the supernatural religion of Christianity that has come into being as divine mystery.[18] According to this model, Christianity incorporates and completes elements of truth found in other religions but Christianity alone is the absolute religion 'because it lives from the absolute self-manifestation of God and the eschatological presence of the Spirit'.[19] Other religions may be thought of as historically interim processes with Christianity the goal of divine religious history.[20] Moltmann refrains from explicitly endorsing this theological model for the relationship of Christianity to other religions; however, his treatment of it seems quite sympathetic. In any case, he approvingly notes that this model allows for that which is beneficial and positive in 'the provisional religions' to be measured against the standard of the absolute self-manifestation of God.[21] Somewhat dialectally or paradoxically, Moltmann argues that it is actually in its syncretistic openness to other religions that Christianity excels other religions and thereby proves itself to be the absolute religion.[22]

Nevertheless, clearly Moltmann does visualize Christianity's immediate future in terms of a theological model in which it serves as a catalyst for a post-absolutist era. The 'simple presence' of Christians in multi-faith environments, 'provided that Christians live, think, and act differently', will infect other religions and their adherents with Christian ideas, values, and principles.[23] Already this 'indirect infection' is happening with Christianity in relation to Hinduism and Buddhism, as well as Islam and others.[24] However, Christian influence in religiously plural contexts, admittedly containing equivocal or ambiguous elements, should never be confused with Westernization of non-Western cultures or defined as indirect Christianization of other religions.[25] In any case, the models discussed have the drawback of beginning from an intra-Christian

---

[18] Moltmann, *The Church in the Power of the Spirit*, p. 157.
[19] Moltmann, *The Church in the Power of the Spirit*, p. 157.
[20] Moltmann, *The Church in the Power of the Spirit*, p. 157.
[21] Moltmann, *The Church in the Power of the Spirit*, p. 158.
[22] Moltmann, *The Church in the Power of the Spirit*, p. 158.
[23] Moltmann, *The Church in the Power of the Spirit*, p. 158.
[24] Moltmann, *The Church in the Power of the Spirit*, p. 158.
[25] Moltmann, *The Church in the Power of the Spirit*, p. 158.

conversation, and Moltmann insists that Christian participation in interreligious dialogue is critical for Christian relationships with the world religions.[26] Accordingly, Moltmann's next step, and apparently an essential and inevitable step, is to set forth his theological rationale of dialogue and for relationships in dialogue.

One of the most important aspects of Moltmann's Christian theology of religions, and certainly containing some of its more profound implications, is his theology of dialogue. Jürgen Moltmann suggests that while dialogue is still in its modest beginnings (still true more than 30 years after the initial publication of *The Church in the Power of the Spirit*) setting forth its first steps is important, envisioning not only bi-lateral dialogues but eventually multi-lateral dialogues which 'can be the genesis of the tension-fraught universal community of religions for a universal society', although 'no one yet knows what it will look like'.[27] He admits that Christian 'mission' has become a threatening term (and practice) for many non-Christians, and suggests that Christians need to exercise more respect for the sense of mission in other religions as well as their own in a genuinely reciprocating relationship.[28] This approach to dialogue requires not only admitting but embracing that Christians can receive something from others – for example, from Islam's total submission to the divine lordship and their rejection of idolatry, from the liberating power of Buddhism's practice of meditation, and even from animists' preservation of ecological and genetic knowledge.[29] In each of these relational partnerships, Christian participants both contribute their own gifts and accept the gifts of others.

Moltmann suggests dialogue among the Abrahamic faiths can address common history and existing parallels while Christian-Buddhist dialogue can concentrate on the problem of human suffering and the analogy of the feast can guide dialogue among the popular religions.[30] Finding the many starting points require dialogue, but Christians alone cannot determine the nature of the dia-

---

[26] Moltmann, *The Church in the Power of the Spirit*, p. 159.
[27] Moltmann, *The Church in the Power of the Spirit*, p. 159.
[28] Moltmann, *The Church in the Power of the Spirit*, p. 159.
[29] Moltmann, *The Church in the Power of the Spirit*, pp. 159-60.
[30] Moltmann, *The Church in the Power of the Spirit*, p. 160.

logue process without the participation of religious others even though they (both Christians and others) must be clear in advance about their own goals and priorities.[31] For Christians, dialogue is not merely a means to an end but an expression of love meaningful for the present as it arises out of their understanding of God as love.[32] Interestingly (see Chapter 5 of the present volume), Moltmann depicts Christian participation in dialogue with religious others as testifying to who God is and to one's own openness to God's presence and action in others; furthermore, the healing and transformation that can occur in dialogue testifies before all and to all of the healing and transforming power of God in the suffering of God's Son Jesus Christ.[33]

Human suffering is a universal problem and one with which dialogue can offer help. Moltmann is emphatic that dialogue, vulnerability, and suffering lead interreligious dialogue onward into the social situations of humans in the world thereby taking it beyond the theoretical and academic to the realm of the practical.[34] He insists that indigenized Christianity must address and alleviate human suffering wherever it is encountered and in whatever form.[35] This indigenized Christianity should transcend culture and geography. Moltmann says, 'a truly Indian, Chinese, Japanese, Indonesian, Arabic and African Christianity must come into being' – adding that, 'Moreover, in the dialogue with world religions a Buddhist, Hindu, Moslem, animist, Confucian, Shintoist Christianity will come into being'.[36]

In light of the preceding, syncretism naturally becomes a pressing concern. Therefore, Moltmann explains that he is not advocating syncretism but that just as Christianity can be colored by different civilizations without becoming 'a cultural mixture', so it can be tinged with different religions without producing 'a religious mixture'.[37] He disavows a syncretism that dissolves Christian distinctiveness, describing instead a 'charismatic quickening' or 'charis-

---

[31] Moltmann, *The Church in the Power of the Spirit*, p. 160.
[32] Moltmann, *The Church in the Power of the Spirit*, p. 160.
[33] Moltmann, *The Church in the Power of the Spirit*, p. 161.
[34] Moltmann, *The Church in the Power of the Spirit*, pp. 161-62.
[35] Moltmann, *The Church in the Power of the Spirit*, p. 162.
[36] Moltmann, *The Church in the Power of the Spirit*, p. 162.
[37] Moltmann, *The Church in the Power of the Spirit*, p. 162.

matic activation' of the gifts, powers, and potentialities of other religious forces in which, most significantly, Christian involvement is guided forward and guarded from error during the advance journey by its calling and vocation toward the kingdom of God and its messianic future.[38] In other words, so long as the eschatological destiny of Christianity in Christ is kept firmly in mind Christians will be faithful to their authentic identity. Here messianic ecclesiology and messianic eschatology meet and merge to form a point on the compass of human history in God's future that offers Christians a reliable directive for all interreligious dialogue and relationships.

Moltmann is not using the charismatic terminology and the categories it suggests loosely. He relates it directly to pneumatology as well. Moltmann argues that the religious cultures 'can be charismatically absorbed and changed in the power of the Spirit'.[39] Whatever this may mean, it does not mean they will become the Church or become Christians; but, they will be directed toward the messianic kingdom, bringing along their own contributions as Christianity shares its hope with them.[40] This breadth of hope may even include those of no religion since the Christian dialogue with world religions is part of its concern for all creation in terms of the coming kingdom with its liberating and redeeming power.[41] Finally, Moltmann concludes that the profile of Christianity open to the breadth of hope guiding Israel, the world religions, and all of creation can be acquired only in dialogue with others.[42]

In general it may be said that Jürgen Moltmann's theology of religions is overdue some sustained attention by Pentecostals. Probably because Christian theology of religions is not really the primary focal point of Moltmann's theology, neither Veli-Matti Kärkkäinen nor Amos Yong treat Moltmann's theology of religions in their major texts on the topic. Kärkkäinen's *The Trinity and Religious Pluralism* does reference Moltmann's theology on several points other than theology of religions as they come up somewhat tangentially in discussion. More importantly, Kärkkäinen credits Moltmann, along

---

[38] Moltmann, *The Church in the Power of the Spirit*, p. 163.
[39] Moltmann, *The Church in the Power of the Spirit*, p. 163.
[40] Moltmann, *The Church in the Power of the Spirit*, p. 163.
[41] Moltmann, *The Church in the Power of the Spirit*, p. 163.
[42] Moltmann, *The Church in the Power of the Spirit*, p. 163.

with Wolfhart Pannenberg, with taking the theological renewal of the doctrine of the Trinity led by Karl Barth and Karl Rahner to another level.[43] Since that development helps form the basis for Kärkkäinen's own trinitarian approach to Christian theology of religions, this is no small comment. He also finds support in Moltmann for refuting the relativism of pluralist John Hick.[44] Kärkkäinen, however, expresses reservations about Moltmann's extremism on the theology of the Incarnation, especially in dealing with radical religious pluralism.[45] Yet aside from such incidental references there is no sustained discussion of Jürgen Moltmann's theology of religions as such.

Yong, in his *Discerning the Spirit(s)*, does admit that following Moltmann's approach to the *filioque* question on the Trinity (the double procession of the Holy Spirit; that is, from the Father and the Son) leads him to a position that is supportive of a pneumatological theology of religions.[46] Yong also lists Moltmann as among those who have presented parallels to his own doctrine of pneumatological imagination which undergirds his pneumatological theology of religions.[47] Finally, Yong suggests Moltmann's theology exemplifies serious attention to a theology of ancestors such as is necessary in comparative theology discourse for cultures where the status of ancestors is an issue for converts to Christianity.[48] Other brief references in *Discerning* apply to passing issues as they arise in other discussions. In *Beyond the Impasse*, Yong has more of these kinds of references but he also finds support in Moltmann for his own assertion that Christian proclamation and interreligious dialogue are not mutually exclusive in the mission of the Church.[49]

The Anglican biblical scholar and theologian Richard Bauckham, in *The Theology of Jürgen Moltmann*, offers an excellent overview and introduction of Moltmann's theology that does not refrain from

---

[43] Kärkkäinen, *Trinity and Religious Pluralism*, p. 5.
[44] Kärkkäinen, *Trinity and Religious Pluralism*, p. 167.
[45] Kärkkäinen, *Trinity and Religious Pluralism*, p. 173.
[46] Yong, *Discerning the Spirit(s)*, pp. 69-70.
[47] Yong, *Discerning the Spirit(s)*, p. 148.
[48] Yong, *Discerning the Spirit(s)*, p. 293 n. 49.
[49] Yong, *Beyond the Impasse*, p. 52 n. 17. This text also has references or footnotes regarding *filioque* and pneumatological imagination in Moltmann (p. 79 n. 33 and p. 87 n. 9) similar to those mentioned above in *Discerning*.

assessing and engaging his thought critically when the occasion calls for it.[50] In terms of our discussion a number of Bauckham's observations are most notable. According to Bauckham, Moltmann's dialectic of the Christological center through the cross and resurrection suggest to Moltmann the particular history of Jesus of Nazareth in tension with the universal direction of the eschatological promise of hope for the whole world.[51] This tension between the particular and the universal in the cross and resurrection leads Moltmann to an ecclesiology in which the Church is a particular relating to other particulars (including world religions) on the way to the universal (Kingdom of God).[52] Thus Moltmann sets up the principle of relationality or the concept of the Church's openness to others that is essential to his theology of religions.[53] Christian eschatology in this paradigm is not simply the desire for believers to be taken out of the world but rather the hope that the whole world will be different or better through the fulfillment of the divine promise by God's own transforming action.[54] In the meanwhile, or on the way, the Church is in relationship, a kind of 'open friendship', with others in the world, partners as it were, including world religions.[55]

Of interest to Pentecostals is Bauckham's observation that Moltmann's ecclesiology, although Christologically centered, has a strong pneumatological perspective, and can even be called 'a charismatic ecclesiology'.[56] For Moltmann, Christology, pneumatology, eschatology, and ecclesiology come together in complementary ways: it is the Holy Spirit who ultimately fulfills the promise of God in Christ.[57] The emphasis on pneumatology sustains openness to other religions because there is no need for suspicion or jealousy from within the Church regarding the Spirit's working outside the Church because it is still always the same Spirit working both within

---

50 Richard Bauckham, *The Theology of Jürgen Moltmann* (Edinburgh: T & T Clark, 1995, 1996).
51 Bauckham, *The Theology of Jürgen Moltmann*, p. 5.
52 Bauckham, *The Theology of Jürgen Moltmann*, p. 126.
53 Bauckham, *The Theology of Jürgen Moltmann*, p. 126.
54 Bauckham, *The Theology of Jürgen Moltmann*, p. 10.
55 Bauckham, *The Theology of Jürgen Moltmann*, p. 14.
56 Bauckham, *The Theology of Jürgen Moltmann*, p. 123.
57 Bauckham, *The Theology of Jürgen Moltmann*, p. 124.

and without the Church.[58] Therefore, obviously the Church should work in open partnership with others.

However, Bauckham does not agree with the limits that Moltmann applies to the Church in its relations with the world religions (or other partners).[59] Moltmann assumes that neither Israel nor the religions nor human society will ever become the Church. That is, they will not convert. For him, the nature of the partnership requires that they maintain their distinctiveness or their own identities. Else instead of existing as complements to each other one (i.e. Christianity) would supplant the others (i.e. Israel, the religions, the world). But they exist in order to provoke and perfect each other; as particular entities none could absorb the others, but should all move together toward the universal reality of the messianic kingdom.[60] Accordingly, there is mutual transformation but not actual conversion.

Yet Bauckham points out that by giving to its partners the messianic direction of the kingdom which has been described as the Church's own distinctive or uniquely special calling and vocation, they could in fact effectively become the Church.[61] Why could not they believe on Jesus as the Messiah? If they did do so, then, as Bauckham says, 'as liberating movements of the Spirit, oriented to the kingdom and confessing Jesus Christ as Lord, they will, by definition, be his church'.[62] Bauckham finally suggests 'that Moltmann's ecclesiological concerns can be maintained without setting any limits on the church's mission to call people to faith in Jesus Christ'.[63] As a contemporary ecclesiological or missiological strategy of working with non-Christian partners the need to maintain the distinctive identity of each partner may be respected without insisting that none can change or convert if they so choose or that the Church must mute its evangelistic witness.

---

[58] Bauckham, *The Theology of Jürgen Moltmann*, p. 125.
[59] Bauckham, *The Theology of Jürgen Moltmann*, pp. 149-50.
[60] Bauckham, *The Theology of Jürgen Moltmann*, pp. 149-50.
[61] Bauckham, *The Theology of Jürgen Moltmann*, p. 150.
[62] Bauckham, *The Theology of Jürgen Moltmann*, p. 150.
[63] Bauckham, *The Theology of Jürgen Moltmann*, p. 150.

Observations on Moltmann's Theology of Religions & Interreligious Dialogue

There are several observations that may be made from a Pentecostal perspective through my general reading of Moltmann's theology of religions as here presented. Couching ecclesiology and Christian mission in Christology and pneumatology brings balance and breadth to Christian self-understanding while eschatology supplies necessary direction and motivation. An exposition of eschatology as hope, that is, potentiality for an attractive future, is a helpful corrective which makes last things a beneficial and positive topic rather than one overwhelmed almost entirely with the fear and dread of catastrophic judgment so often prevalent in Pentecostal (and other) forms of apocalyptic scenarios. Setting the relationship of the Church to the world, including world religions, within the larger purposes of the Kingdom of God is helpful for validating extra-ecclesial relationships, including those with world religions. Further, this approach is amicable with the Pentecostal distinction between the Church and the Kingdom (see Chapter 1). Yet there must be important clarifications.

The song of eschatological hope is off key and its music out of tune unless it includes notes on the real possibilities of an undesirable future – that is, of judgment.[64] In spite of excessive intellectual wrangling on it, Brunner is at least right about this: the doctrines of universal salvation and final judgment must always be kept together.[65] Separating them and thereby swallowing one up in the other is perhaps satisfying in its simplistic solution but it is not faithful to the record of revelation. Brunner is also likely right in his opinion that contemporary trends to ignore the judgment side of this tension are probably due to previous tendencies too far in the opposite

---

[64] Moltmann argues in favor of universalism in *The Coming of God: Christian Eschatology* (Minneapolis: Fortress Press, 1996), especially Chapter 2. Important to distinguish in his work is an emphasis on universalism, prominent in his pneumatology, but that is not synonymous with soteriological universalism. See his *The Spirit of Life: A Universal Affirmation* (Minneapolis: Fortress Press, 2001). It is quite possible to agree with Moltmann that the Holy Spirit is universally present and active while disagreeing with him that everyone will eventually be saved and there is in effect no eternal judgment.

[65] Brunner, *Dogmatics III*, pp. 415-24 (pp. 421-24).

direction.[66] In any case, the message of judgment teaches humans to take God seriously, because there are consequences for not doing so, and it teaches the true depth of forgiveness, which can only be appreciated vis-à-vis the real possibility of judgment.[67] Here Moltmann clearly comes up short.[68]

Although the Kingdom is larger than the Church it is not synonymous with the cosmos. There is another kingdom at odds with God's reign, satanic and demonic in its resilient love of evil (Eph. 2.2). It is true that God in Christ graciously grants deliverance from evil and translation into Christ's Kingdom (Col. 1.13-14). It is also true that obstinate loyalty to the opposition results in failure to benefit from the blessings of God's benevolent reign (1 Cor. 6.9-10; Eph. 5.5). Pentecostal theology of religions appropriately reaches out in hope to others but it does not offer a false hope that all is well with everyone anyway (contra universalism). Therefore, worth remembering, and retaining, is Yong's emphasis on discerning the presence and absence of the divine as well as of the demonic.[69] Rather than undermining developing theology of religions this honesty ought to add urgency to it.

Qualitative mission, mission as the gradual influence of Christian faith and life on nearby others in multi-faith settings, concurs with a Christian theology of Christian witness (see Chapter 5) that includes not only words and deeds but also being. It seems conformable to Jesus' parables of the mustard seed and the yeast (Mt. 13.31-33), both of which signify gradual, initially unobservable, growth that eventually becomes dramatic and open. Pentecostals can under-

---

[66] Brunner, *Our Faith*, pp. 147-48.

[67] Brunner, *Our Faith*, pp. 148-50.

[68] Crip Stephenson reminds me that Moltmann's universalism does not necessarily preclude judgment. It does preclude eternal judgment but not divine temporal judgment. At issue is Moltmann's refusal to juxtapose judgment and love. Rather, the opposite of judgment is apathy. Judgment is still an expression of divine love, an indication that God still engages humans. The absence of judgment/love is apathy, and God is not apathetic. See Jürgen Moltmann *et al.*, *Love: The Foundation of Hope: The Theology of Jürgen Moltmann and Elizabeth Moltmann-Wendel* (ed. Frederic B. Burnham, Charles S. McCoy, and M. Douglas Meeks; New York: HarperCollins, 1988). Cf. Stephen N. Williams, 'Moltmann on Jesus Christ', in Sung Wook Chung (ed.), *Jürgen Moltmann and Evangelical Theology: A Critical Engagement* (Eugene, OR: Wipf & Stock, 2012), pp. 122-24.

[69] E.g. see Yong, *Discerning the Spirit(s)*.

stand that in some contexts at some times it may be best to take such a subtle approach to witnessing. And perhaps in our pluralistic society it should often be the preferred method. However, the inherent nature of Christian witness as sharing the gospel of God's love in Christ for the world suggests verbal proclamation cannot be abandoned. If in the past it has been a mistake to neglect the dialogical dimension of doing mission in favor of evangelistic witness through proclamation it would certainly only be an equal and opposite error to now neglect proclamation in favor of dialogue. True enough, responsible evangelistic witness can be accomplished best probably in a responsive mode (1 Pet. 3.15). Yet a holistic theology of Christian witness (suggested in Chapter 5) requires word *and* deed *and* being. Nevertheless, perhaps at times a mistake has been to invert the appropriate order. Should not witnessing more often than not begin with being before proceeding to word and deed? That approach will surely slow down an evangelist's 'head count' but it would also likely close the 'revolving door' through which new converts often too quickly enter and almost as quickly depart many churches. Of course, there are still those times when the Spirit immediately directs witness in marvelous ways with miraculous results (e.g. Acts 8.26-40).

In any case, the primary consideration in adopting a particular evangelistic method for a certain time or place cannot be merely avoidance of conflict – as eminently desirable as is nonconfrontational coexistence. At times, conflict may indicate a kind of power encounter in which the demonic resists the Holy Spirit. These cases require deliverance and healing through the operation of spiritual gifts and often result in immediate church growth.[70] Arguably, according to impressions from the book of Acts, if early Christians had successfully sought to avoid all conflicts with evil forces in their witnessing, there would have been no Christianity as we have come to know it. A dramatic case in point is Acts 16.16-

---

[70] Paul A. Pomerville, 'The Pentecostals and Church Growth', in Grant L. McClung, Jr. (ed.), *Azusa Street and Beyond: Pentecostal Missions and Church Growth* (South Plainfield, NJ: Logos International, 1986), pp. 151-55. Cf. Donald Gee, 'Spiritual Gifts and World Evangelization', in McClung, *Azusa Street and Beyond*, p. 113.

18.[71] Missionary confrontation with demonic powers led to violent persecution by pagan authorities and that in turn led to dramatic conversions and church growth (vv. 25-34). However, although there has long been exegetical ambiguity about Paul's inner motives and intentions,[72] he apparently attempted to avoid outright conflict by delaying any recognition and response to the demonized girl, only reacting directly when it became almost impossible to do otherwise. Paul certainly did not court trouble.

As a general rule, therefore, Christians always ought to attempt to share their witness of Christ in non-combative ways. Put another way, they ought to avoid giving offense as much as humanly possible. When they sense by the Holy Spirit that a demonic presence is resisting the gospel, then they must speak and act to overcome it for the sake of the salvation of human beings. And Christians should never compromise the gospel to please anyone (Gal. 1.10).

Moving toward a single common world community with a universal community of religions promises to be problematic for Pentecostals. Pentecostals have been heirs to the dispensationalist teaching that the end times preceding the Second Advent would be marked by the rise of a one world religion seducing the nations of humanity into blasphemous and damnable apostasies.[73] Pentecostal scholarship has questioned association with 'dispensationalism' and its frequent attendant, nearly unrestrained wild speculation about the specifics of end time events.[74] Nevertheless, warnings of apos-

---

[71] For background on this unusual occurrence, see French L. Arrington, 'Acts', in *FLBCNT*, pp. 619-20.

[72] E.g. Ammonius suggests Paul may have intentionally given the demon time to testify to Christ but Origen insists Paul was grieved at demonic witness to Christ while Chrysostom implies that Paul allowed the demon to establish a witness before credulous pagans before demonstrating Christ's superior power by casting it out (Francis Martin [ed.], *Acts* [ACCS; Downers Grove, IL: InterVarsity Press, 2006], pp. 202-03).

[73] E.g. popular bestsellers such as Hal Lindsey, *The Late Great Planet Earth* (Grand Rapids: Zondervan, 1970), or the *Left Behind* series by Jerry B. Jenkins and Tim LaHaye (Colorado Springs, CO: Tyndale House, 1995-2007).

[74] E.g. R. Hollis Gause, *Revelation: God's Stamp of Sovereignty on History* (Cleveland, TN: Pathway Press, 1983); Faupel, *The Everlasting Gospel*; Althouse, *The Spirit of the Last Days*; and Thomas, *The Apocalypse*. Other important works with strong eschatological emphases, such as Steve Land's *Pentecostal Spirituality*, and Frank Macchia's *Baptized in the Spirit*, have suggested eschatological alternatives to traditional dispensationalism as well.

tate and idolatrous entities survive (to an extent, doubtlessly rightly so).[75] Consequently, it appears clear that Pentecostals will never accept any form of a one world religion – not for religious, political, or economic reasons, and not for all-too-elusive promises of world peace.

Nevertheless, as Moltmann notes, governments and businesses now find vast cooperative networks necessary for their very survival. What about the religions? It is obvious that religions are not exempt from the contemporary global situation. Much of the animosity toward religions today may not only be traceable to the long and bloody history of religious wars but probably also to an ever-increasing frustration with the failure of the major religions to coexist in harmony. A religion that is isolationist is typically thought of as dangerous. Anymore it is not just a half comical, half serious impression that some 'don't play well with others'; rather, we are considered a threat to the safety of our neighbors and to the stability of our planet. From a pragmatic and political perspective, they are most likely right (see the Introduction of this volume), at least regarding religious extremists. That seems a far cry from Christ's calling to be salt and light for this world (Mt. 5.13-16). Yet imperatives to live holy lives (1 Pet. 1.15-16) and to avoid compromise (Rev. 3.15-16) are essential and honorable as well.

But is Moltmann's vision of a single common world community with a universal community of religions the only path to obeying these apparently (at least, superficially) competing callings and commands? More to the point, is one world religion the only way to go? Of course it is not. Perhaps maintaining the distinctions between the religious 'partners' is the key idea. If Christianity does not become Islamic or Buddhist and so on but remains clearly and firmly *Christian* then there is no one world religion after all. That would entail cooperation but not identification. The concept of 'open friendship' is even better; it does not convey the loss of freedom that may come with partnerships. From 1 Cor. 9.19-23 it is clear that Paul was perfectly willing to go quite far in connecting with non-Hebraic or Hellenistic culture for the sake of the gospel. Yet even that telling passage is bracketed with careful qualifiers.

---

[75] Most recently is Thomas, *Apocalypse,* esp. pp. 490-518.

And Paul also warned those same Corinthian Christians in the starkest and sternest of terms against inappropriate liaisons with unbelievers (1 Cor. 6.14-18). Actually, Scripture is replete with complex relationships, and with checks and balances guiding their conduct.[76] For a few examples, Joseph, Daniel, Mordecai, and Esther were high-ranking officials in what can only be called pagan empires. And Paul taught that relationships with those outside the Christian faith should be considered opportunities (Col. 4.5), that Christians should win their respect (1 Thess. 4.12), and establish a good reputation with them (1 Tim. 3.7).

The straightforward insistence that believers not be 'unequally yoked' with unbelievers (2 Cor. 6.14 NKJV) clearly excludes ill-advised alliances or inappropriate partnerships.[77] The main concern seems to be eschewing relationships which inevitably lead to spiritual compromise, particularly idolatry.[78] Worth remembering is that these instructions arose out of the Torah prohibition against yoking an ox and a donkey together when plowing (Deut. 22.10).[79] Implied is that God's people establish and protect a distinct moral and spiritual identity as God's 'special' people (Exod. 19.5; Tit. 2.14; 1 Pet. 2.9 NKJV). To push the symbolism just a bit, the prohibition does not preclude donkeys and oxen from working on the same farm or even in the same field so long as they are not yoked together. They simply do not fit together in the same harness. They never were meant to pull together. In other words, cooperative relationships with those of other religions are possible, and potentially productive, within clear boundaries.

So what are the clear boundaries for Christians in interreligious dialogue and cooperation? How far toward 'a universal community of religions' can, or should, Pentecostals go? As seen above, Moltmann argues that abiding commitment to the messianic calling of the eschatological Kingdom of God, essentially the special purpose of Christianity's vocation in the world, will keep Christians on target in their interreligious relations. I agree – with qualifications. If

---

[76] See Tony Richie, 'Cooperating with Other Religions: How Far Can Christians Go?' *Evangel* 101.10 (October 2011), pp. 22-23.

[77] James Hernando, '2 Corinthians', in *FLBCNT,* p. 944.

[78] Hernando, '2 Corinthians', p. 944.

[79] Christopher Wright, *Deuteronomy* (NIBC; Peabody, MA: Hendrickson, 1996, 2003), p. 242.

they fix their eyes firmly on the ultimate goal in Christ (Phil. 3.14; Heb. 12.2), then they should not get off track. However, it is not simply the end which keeps one running well. Sometimes it seems so distant. The 'great cloud of witnesses' is essential to the endurance necessary for finishing well (Heb. 12.1). This refers to the present and ongoing encouragement and accountability of the community of faith. How does one discover if one is still faithful to the messianic calling of the Kingdom of God? Does one wait until the eschaton hoping everything will turn out well in the end? No! The forward look is all-important but not all-sufficient. Is it not necessary in the present tense to glance around, to look toward the bleachers, to listen for the cheers, to check yourself and your progress against that of others, if one is to continue the race to the finish line and so win the prize?

Therefore, our eschatological vision of the Messianic Kingdom must be tempered by our present accountability to and responsibility for our own community of faith. Perhaps this is why Moltmann insists on the permanent or impermeable distinction between the partners in the single community he envisions. If it is acknowledged that the Church's partners may become the Church, then what is to prevent the Church from becoming the others? If the borders are porous, then identities may morph either way. Yet this legitimate ecclesiological concern can be taken care of through committed and accountable relationships *within* the churches. Rather than the churches being diminished by expanding mission toward dialogue with other religions, their vital role in the lives of the faithful is ever more affirmed. Pentecostals will want to add that the mission of the Spirit of Truth to lead and guide believers (Jn 16.13; Rom. 8.14) will more emphatically assure that they can participate in a process of dialogue and cooperation with religious others without losing sight of their own calling and commitment. However, as more specific attention will be given to pneumatology subsequently, this statement alone will need to suffice without further commentary.

Acceptable, that is, healthy reciprocation in dialogue between religions can begin with exchange of information and knowledge but extend further into the broadening and deepening of character and behavior. Probably best of all it is relational. Through personal interaction and relationship building the way people of different faiths feel about and act toward each other often changes for the better. Surely Abraham and Abimelech learned to look at each other differently (Genesis 20). This is a process of mutual and beneficial transformation. Unless some degree of reciprocating occurs it is difficult to imagine what the purpose of dialogue may be after all. Conceivably, some amount of cooperation on shared concerns may occur. And Moltmann certainly sees cooperative social activism as a major component of or consequence of interreligious dialogue. Jesus certainly stresses the importance of social ministry (Mt. 25.31-46). Why not cooperate with others for a good cause? However, it is perhaps, with Moltmann also, even better to understand interreligious dialogue as an expression of the overflowing love of God in Christ toward the world. The temptation to gauge the success of dialogue by some sort of measurable that is, concrete, results helpful as it is, cannot compete with the simple concept that it is really just another way of faith expressing divine love (Gal. 5.6). In answer to 'Why do dialogue?' one may aptly reply, 'Because God loves "us" and God loves "them" and it pleases God when we love each other too'.

One form that unacceptable or unhealthy reciprocation might take is that of syncretism, or the inappropriate mixing of religions. Among the ancient Israelite kings, the assessment of history that one served the Lord wholeheartedly, or not, indicated whether they had tried to mix Yahweh worship with that of Baal or some other idolatrous rival for the loyalties of the nation (e.g. 2 Kgs 25.2, 14-15; 2 Chron. 31.21-22). Interreligious reciprocation must not be allowed to degenerate into syncretism. On the spiritual level, syncretism is sinful in making divine truth relative rather than absolute, inspiring rather than inspired, and manageable rather than authoritative. On the theological level, syncretism is inconsistent and incoherent in ignoring the distinctive voices and their truth claims for each religious worldview in making a patchwork quilt out of the profundities of faith. On the practical level, it is self-defeating and self-destructive in robbing each religious faith of its unique ability to offer guidance and sustenance to its adherents.

Moltmann struggles with syncretism. He defends his desire for a Buddhist, Hindu, Muslim, animist, Confucian, Shintoist Christianity to come into being on the grounds that it is little different than the cultural colorings that come with Christianity that has been indigenized in Asia or Africa or America or any other place. That hardly seems like an accurate assessment. Whether one prefers a particular food or style of dress or speaks a certain language is not the same as whether one believes in one God or many or none. Therefore, I have reservations about Moltmann's indigenization model of interreligious reciprocation. At its best, it may work well enough with those carefully on guard against error. More often than not it will probably degenerate into syncretism.

However, Moltmann is right about reciprocation. Perhaps he goes too far, possibly unwittingly, toward syncretism. Yet that is not to say that Christianity cannot be informed by, say, Confucianism. The family values and respect for relationships that Confucianism promotes is clearly compatible in many respects with Christianity, and not surprisingly can expand and develop common Christian perceptions or alter misconceptions.[80] Yet what results is not so much a hybrid Confucian Christianity as a more holistic Christianity informed by Confucian insights regarding that which may have been more or less dormant within itself but not non-existent. Even in cases where there possibly may be something apparently 'new' discovered in another religion, unless there is a corresponding 'echo' in Christianity with which to resonate how could there be authentic mutual conversation much less transformation? As Pentecostals are fond of quoting in other contexts but perhaps appropriate here also 'Deep calls to deep' (Ps. 42.7).

If Christians who experience reciprocation through engaging in dialogue with religious others (speaking only from the Christian side) were to say that some new kind of Christianity is coming into being thereby, so that now they must prefix the name of the other to their own, then that really would be an actual change of identity. Does not a name change imply a change of identity (Mk 3.16; cf. Rev. 3.4)? That is not possible for those called by the name of Christ (Acts 4.12). Buddha and Jesus Christ are not consorts. But when an echo, however faint, from another devout heart, and however deep within the Christian bosom, occurs, mutual transformation occurs that does not threaten the identity of either. God has set eternity in the human heart (Eccl. 3.11). Accordingly, when de-

---

[80] A trip to China (June 2012) that included fellowship and worship with fully indigenous (non-Western originated or supported) Chinese Christians convinced me of reciprocity regarding Confucianism and Christianity.

vout hearts genuinely talk to each other an echo of divine truth reverberates back and forth from one to the other – and back again. The Christian becomes, not some sort of hydra-headed Buddhist, Hindu, Muslim, animist, Confucian, Shintoist Christian, but a fuller, richer, better Christian through his/her encounter with the religious other. A conscious Christian aim in interreligious dialogue must be to become a better Christian.

In spite of concerns with Moltmann's movement toward, or at least too close to, religious syncretism, and cautions regarding a single community of world religions, there is no need to reject automatically his concept of 'charismatic quickening' or 'charismatic activation' of the gifts, powers, and potentialities of other religious forces. Here is the pneumatological side of his theology of religions and of interreligious dialogue. The term 'charismatic' commonly signifies gifts of divine grace often associated with the working of the Holy Spirit (1 Cor. 12.1-11). The terms 'quickening' and 'activation' suggest a bringing out in life and action that which is already in some sense present but perhaps to an extent dormant or underdeveloped. These gifts, powers, and potentialities in the religions may become points of contact and conversation with Christians and with each other for open friendship and mutual growth toward God's Messianic Kingdom. Although not without need for cautionary clarifications, this can be a good approach for interreligious dialogue.

For Pentecostals, charismatic quickening and charismatic activation sound a lot like prevenient grace, that is, the working of the Holy Spirit in humanity prior to and in anticipation of actual conversion to Jesus Christ (see Chapter 1 of this volume). Yet Moltmann makes a remarkable move that is not necessarily identified with prevenient grace: he applies the Spirit's gracious gifting and working not only to individuals, human beings, but to religions, organized and systematic religious worldviews. This is a bold but complex and potentially problematic notion. We have already seen with Newbigin (Chapter 2) and Pinnock (Chapter 3) that the world's religions are not considered as vehicles of salvation. Neither does Moltmann seem to be saying that they are vehicles of salvation. His suggestion appears more along the line that within the parameters of their own distinctive (i.e. non-Christian) religious identity the Spirit has imparted gracious gifts for further development together with the Church in open relationship. That description is in conformity with his view that the various religions are like 'thorns' in one another's sides that provoke spiritual growth. The Spirit's gifts provide a basis for conversation, provocation, and transformation.

Of course, Moltmann's Reformed heritage may be moving him along more in terms of common grace than prevenient grace. Common grace would simply affirm that God had graciously gifted all but not necessarily in anticipation of Christian salvation, as in prevenient grace. Accordingly, as Moltmann has maintained, the religions would not become the Church, would not convert. Their charismatic gifts and potentialities would benefit them within the context of their own religious identities and in dialogue with others, including Christians. This may be similar, perhaps even an antecedent, in some ways to Mark Heim's argument for affirming multiple or plural religious ends.[81] However, as noted above, Bauckham has challenged Moltmann's consistency on this point, arguing that conversion to Christ is possible (and desirable).[82] A challenge Pentecostals might present to Moltmann could be that in utilizing charismatic terminology not only are Christian pneumatological categories explicit but Christian soteriological categories of grace are also at least implicit. In other words, it is difficult, if not impossible, to speak of 'charismatic quickening' and 'charismatic actualizations' among other religions without thinking of the Holy Spirit's preeminent work in Christian salvation.

Pentecostal theologian Frank Macchia has approvingly referenced Moltmann's idea in *The Spirit of Life* of 'the divine *inhale* that draws people together in communion and praise' and the '*exhale* of the Spirit that drives one vocationally and charismatically into the world'.[83] At first glance this statement appears to be directed entirely toward Christians. Indeed, Macchia goes on to say, 'The accent

---

[81] Mark S. Heim, *Salvations: Truth and Difference in Religions* (Maryknoll, NY: Orbis Books, 1995, 2000). If so, it would be an unknown antecedent. Heim does not build on Moltmann's theology.

[82] Macchia, *Baptized in the Spirit*, p. 95, also presses Moltmann to recognize the category of conversion. As Macchia notes, Moltmann utilizes conversion in other ways (*Baptized in the Spirit*, p. 279); cf. Moltmann, *Coming of God*, pp. 22-23.

[83] Macchia, *Baptized in the Spirit*, pp. 76-77; quoting Moltmann, *Spirit of Life*, p. 45 (emphasis original).

on spiritual gifts highlights the freedom of the Spirit eschatological-
ly in driving God's people toward a more expansive witness'.[84]
However, Macchia immediately adds, 'As Moltmann notes, through
the gifts of the Spirit, the Spirit exercises eschatological freedom to
expand, diversify, and proliferate the many expressions of divine
grace in the world'.[85] Further, for Moltmann, as Macchia approvingly notes, God cannot be God without being God of the other, and
God cannot be God without being Creator and Redeemer.[86] Accordingly, as also shows in Moltmann's treatment (above) of models for relating Christianity with other religions, there is dialectical
continuity and discontinuity that tries to enable thinking of the Spirit as working graciously in gifting other religions without either diminishing the Spirit's distinctive working in the Church or making
other religions some kind of closet Christianity. (Moltmann is un-
derstandably ambiguous about Karl Rahner's 'anonymous Christianity'.[87] Although sympathetic to Rahner's effort to recognize the
presence of God's grace outside the Judeo-Christian tradition, and
agreeable to his attempt to relate non-Christians to Christ,[88] I fear
his denominational commitment to rigid ecclesiology forced him
into an untenable position undermining distinctions between Chris-
tianity/the Church and other religions and insulting the identities of
other religions.)[89]

There is a sense in which Christians experience in Christ the Holy Spirit that the world, including world religions, simply does not
participate in (Jn 14.16-17; Rom. 8.9). Pentecostal theology of religions must maintain that distinction. The Spirit's life manifested in
the risen Son of God also shines in those who belong to Jesus
Christ (Rom. 1.4-6). Yet the 'God of the spirits of all flesh' (Num.

---

[84] Macchia, *Baptized in the Spirit,* p. 77. Cf. pp. 100-101.

[85] Macchia, *Baptized in the Spirit,* p. 77.

[86] Macchia, *Baptized in the Spirit,* p. 263. Macchia is referencing Moltmann's
The Trinity and the Kingdom: The Doctrine of God (San Francisco: Harper & Row,
1981), pp. 52-56.

[87] As Bauckham, *Theology of Moltmann,* p. 153, notes. See Karl Rahner, *Foundations of Christian Faith* (New York: Crossroad, 1978, 2002), pp. 311-21.

[88] See William V. Dych, SJ, *Karl Rahner* (Collegeville, MN: Liturgical Press,
1992), pp. 34, 86, 98.

[89] For further discussion of Rahner's theology of religions, including objections and responses, see D'Costa, 'Theology of Religions', pp. 632-33 and pp.
635-36.

16.22; 27.16), 'the Lord God of the spirits of the prophets', (Rev. 22.6), who creates and renews all (Ps. 104.30), is present and active everywhere (139.7). Like the wind, the Spirit is mysterious but not absent and certainly not passive (Jn 3.8). With Moltmann and Hollenweger (see the Introduction), Yong (Chapter 5), and others, therefore, Pentecostals can readily recognize and respect the Spirit's gifts in religious others but only in light of the incomparable and unparalleled gifting of the Spirit in those who through faith in Christ with obedient hearts are indwelled and filled with the Holy Spirit. And yet even this enables and invites Pentecostals Christians to meet religious others in open friendship, dialogue, a degree of partnership, social cooperation, mutual or reciprocal transformation – and more – in expressing and testifying to God's love in Christ for all.

Conclusion

The present chapter extended the conversation on theology of religions in the previous chapter with Pentecostal partners Veli-Matti Kärkkäinen and Amos Yong to a non-Pentecostal partner, Jürgen Moltmann. It provides the necessary background for discussions in the next chapter. Partly because of the complexity and subtly of Moltmann's theology of religions and interreligious dialogue, and partly because of its special import for Pentecostal theology, it has been the longest and in some ways most advanced discussions of this volume. The next, and final, chapter will engage further with Moltmann through his direct comments about some of my own work in Pentecostal theology of religions.

7

CONSIDERING RAMIFICATIONS FOR PENTECOSTAL THEOLOGY OF RELIGIONS

Introduction

The ongoing nature of the conversation in the New Testament church in coming to grips with the scope of the gospel of Jesus Christ (Gal. 2.11-21; cf. 2 Pet 3.15-16), pivoting on the Peter–Cornelius encounter (Acts 10, 11, 15), continues to provide inspiration for the present conversation regarding Christian relations with other religions. The immediate past chapter engaged Jürgen Moltmann as a non-Pentecostal conversation partner on the basis of his widely recognized contributions to Christian theology of religions and interactions with Pentecostal theology. This chapter builds on its overview and assessment of Moltmann's theology of religions and interreligious dialogue with relevant observations from the perspective of Pentecostal theology. It engages further with Moltmann through his direct comments about some of my own work in Pentecostal theology of religions. Perhaps worth repeating is that neither the last chapter nor this one is offered as critical or in depth analysis of Moltmann's general theology or theology of religions, but as interactive theological reflections focused on a few of the more obvious Pentecostal priorities.

Issues Raised by Jürgen Moltmann for Pentecostal Theology of Religions & Dialogue

In their critical evaluation of Jürgen Moltmann's theology, Stanley Grenz and Roger Olson offer a somewhat mixed preliminary judgment about his admittedly pioneering thought. They describe his overall theological work as constructive and innovative but 'riddled with tensions'.[1] As can be noted from the previous chapter that tendency toward tension shows in his theology of religions as well. Yet tension is not necessarily contradiction. Moltmann wrote the Preface to a volume edited by Veli-Matti Kärkkäinen, *The Spirit in the World: Emerging Pentecostal Theologies in Global Contexts,* which included a chapter of mine.[2] As part of his comments for that Preface, Moltmann addressed my chapter on 'Azusa-era Optimism: Bishop J.H. King's Optimistic Theology of Religions as a Possible Paradigm for Today'.[3] (Cf. study of King in Chapter 2 of the present volume.) As it provides the basis for the discussion in this chapter, the following relates his paragraph from that work in full.

Finally, the problem of particular faith and universal grace awaits a theological solution. Bishop King (chapter 12) has offered a solution: The 'religion of Christ' is universal and was there from the beginning; it appears, restricted in time and space, in the 'Christian religion'. So the Christian religion must always be related to the religion of Christ. It does not bring Christ to the peoples of the world, but discovers him among them, for he is already there. That is a good approach for interfaith dialogue. God's relationship to human beings is universal. In his love they are his children on earth, in the self-giving of Christ they are already reconciled; the seed of the Spirit who redeems is in them all. But the relation of human beings to God is particular. When God's Spirit is experienced and faith is awakened, then they respond to God's relationship to them. Trusting in God's relationship to all human beings, believers understand their experience of the Spirit as the beginning and pledge of its outpouring 'on all flesh'. The experience is particular; the expectation is universal.[4]

Moltmann's statement raises a number of theological issues. Uppermost is the perennially troublesome relationship between the

---

[1] Stanley J. Grenz and Roger E. Olson, *20th Century Theology: God & the World in a Transitional Age* (Downers Grove, IL: InterVarsity Press, 1992), p. 185.

[2] Moltmann, 'Preface', in Kärkkäinen (ed.), *The Spirit in the World*, pp. viii-xii.

[3] Tony Richie, 'Azusa-era Optimism: Bishop J.H. King's Optimistic Theology of Religions as a Possible Paradigm for Today', in Kärkkäinen (ed.), *The Spirit in the World*, pp. 227-44.

[4] Moltmann, 'Preface', p. xi.

particular and the universal, especially here in terms of faith and grace. Also raised are implications for theology of religions for Christian mission and for interfaith dialogue, the prominent role of pneumatology therein, the scope of the redemption and reconciliation in Christ, the nature of coming to faith, and, of course, overall eschatological orientations. A hint of universalism may be hidden in Moltmann's comments (see Chapter 6 of this volume). Except for the last, which would (con)fuse universality and universalism (see the Introduction) in a way that surely he would reject, all of these points are more or less implicitly drawn from King's theology of religions. Nevertheless, as a reading of Moltmann's own theology of religions in the preceding chapter (6) suggests, he appears to have read into King recurring themes from his own theological perspective too. If so, a legitimate question would be whether that is a valid reading. I argue that indeed there are valid connections between Bishop J.H. King and Jürgen Moltmann, perhaps implicit and undeveloped, but that they are far from identical.

The following analyzes these themes arising out of Moltmann's impressions of my treatment of Bishop King's theology of religions more specifically from the perspective of Pentecostal theology of religions with some attention to their broader applications. Before tackling that endeavor, it was necessary to survey briefly (in the previous chapter) Moltmann's own theology of religions. In this chapter it will be necessary as well to summarize the background and development of key categories inherently involved in his affirmative and far-reaching evaluation of King. Then perhaps we will be better prepared to benefit from the evaluation itself by this important theologian with its value for contemporary Pentecostal theology of religions.

Clearly, Moltmann frames his comments primarily around the problem of relating the particular and the universal. Particularities refer to specific and historical realities, in all their distinctiveness, over against that which is generalized and abstract. Universals describe that which is common to all (i.e. its 'essence'). The tension between the universal and the particular, or the One and the Many, is a special concern of the branch of philosophy known as metaphysics.[5] Metaphysics is concerned with explaining the fundamental nature of being and the world. Since the time of Plato (5th century BCE) philosophers have struggled to relate the particular and the universal. Partly at issue is that the particular is evident but the universal is assumed; yet it is difficult, if not impossible, to think or talk about the reality of the obvious particular without some concept of the not-so-obvious universal with which to relate it. Sometimes this problem is expressed by saying things are particulars but their qualities are universals, but do universals exist apart from the particular things? A favorite example is how to think or speak of a particular chair without some universal idea of what kind of reality constitutes 'chairness'. Metaphysical concerns became most prominent for Christian theology during the medieval age through the rise of scholasticism, a movement that reached its zenith with the great Catholic theologian, Thomas Aquinas. Concern with the fundamental nature of reality is of continuing interest for Christian theology today.[6]

As Moltmann rightly notes, discussing Bishop King's theology of 'the religion of Christ' (a universal) in relation to Christianity (a particular) took me into the problem of the particular and the universal. More importantly, Moltmann affirms that it offers one approach to a theological solution. Below I will address this topic further. Here I wish to list further other issues for discussion raised by Moltmann's comments. The main two are how the paradigm affects ecclesial identity (ecclesiology) and the performance of mission and how it informs the divine-human relationship. Along the way, insights into Christology and pneumatology as well as the eschatological nature of religious experience also surface. I discuss these topics more or less in order below but not in a designedly systematic template.

A few words of clarification may be helpful. First, this discussion centers on Moltmann's reading of my reading of Bishop King. Readers of this volume are advised to read King for themselves.

[5] Hugo A. Meynell, 'Universals', in Richardson and Bowden (eds.), *Westminster Dictionary of Christian Theology*, p. 592.
[6] A helpful book on this problem from a perspective sympathetic with Pentecostal and Charismatic Christians is J.P. Moreland, *Universals* (Central Problems of Philosophy; Kingston, Ontario: McGill-Queen's University Press, 2005).

Similarly, they would be well-served to read Moltmann directly. I have no idea if Moltmann has ever read King directly, but I would rather doubt it. In any case, the present exchange arises out of a particular (!) reading of a prominent Pentecostal thinker in the movement's early years in conversation with a leading Christian theologian of today as an exploration of its implications for contemporary Pentecostal theology of religions.

Second, this exercise does not aim to be anything like an exhaustive treatment of the issues raised. It certainly does not offer any kind of final word on anything. As the chapter title indicates, it is part of a conversation with a highly respected partner who was kind enough to offer a few words on his thoughts regarding my take on Bishop King's theology of religions and its possibilities for Pentecostals today. Hopefully, this conversation will at least provide stimuli for development and productivity in the fertile field of Christian theology of religions.

Interacting with Jürgen Moltmann on Issues in Pentecostal Theology of Religions & Dialogue

In the previous chapter (6) it was noted that Moltmann's own theology is constructed in terms of the central importance of the particular and the universal. Moltmann's dialectic of the Christological center through the cross and resurrection suggests the particular history of Jesus of Nazareth in tension with the universal direction of the eschatological promise of hope for the whole world. This tension between the particular and the universal in the cross and resurrection in Moltmann impacts his theology of religions. It is important to an ecclesiology in which the Church is conceived of as a particular relating to the world religions as other particulars on the way to the universal reality of the Kingdom of God. The principle of relationality or the concept of the Church's openness to others is essential to his theology of religions. The Church therefore exists in relationship, in open friendship, with others in the world, partners as it were, including world religions.

When Moltmann described Bishop King's theology of the 'religion of Christ' as offering a solution to the problem of the particular and the universal quite possibly a great deal of the preceding was in mind. Here one can argue that Bishop King's much earlier and mostly embryonic theology of religions has visible similarities to a more developed form of theology of religions in Moltmann. (Interestingly, Dietrich Bonhoeffer, frequently referenced in many of Moltmann's works on a variety of topics, also spoke of 'the religion of Christ' in a context of distinguishing the particular religion of Christianity from its universal essence in the person of Jesus Christ.[7] Bonhoeffer argued that Christianity as a religion is in its humanity in many ways comparable to the world religions; not Christianity itself but Christ and his cross bring God to us and bring the gift of God's grace and love.)[8] For a Pentecostal theologian, this alone is encouraging and a bit exhilarating. Pentecostals, have not generally been noted for sophisticated theology. Yet here Moltmann, by any judgment one of the greatest theologians of the last century, is apparently glad to identify with King's theology, or with a certain aspect of it anyway. Perhaps closer attention to King (and other early Pentecostals) will discover further cause for celebration and, more importantly, for maturation of Pentecostal theology through ongoing interaction with the broader church. In any case, in what follows I suggest both a comparison and a contrast and urge in favor of King's helpful contribution. However, first it is helpful to work through Moltmann's comments on King's theology of religions thematically for in-depth comprehension prior to exploring it categorically.

To begin, one of the issues faced in considering the reality of other religions is the relative youth of Christianity. Christianity is a comparative latecomer on the world religions scene. Along with Judaism, Canaanite fertility religions, Babylonian astrology, and Greco-Roman paganism, Hinduism, Buddhism, Taoism, Confucianism, and of course many indigenous religious expressions, all predate the rise of Christianity. As early as the New Testament, Paul was obliged to explain that the Jewish religion functioned as a 'tutor' leading to the faith in Christ subsequently taught by Christianity (Gal. 3.24-25). Even farther back, the gospel was announced in advance to the patriarch Abraham (3.8) as a sort of preparatory precedent. For Paul, the mystery of God's eternal purpose planned

---

[7] E.g. Bonhoeffer, 'Jesus Christ and the Essence of Christianity', p. 51. I am not suggesting any kind of interdependence but only complementariness.

[8] Bonhoeffer, 'Jesus Christ and the Essence of Christianity', p. 53.

that all things would eventually culminate in Christ (Eph. 1.10). Early Church apologists such as Justin Martyr and others argued that the 'seeds of the Logos/Word' had always been present and that in all of the previous religions, anything that was good and true was actually 'Christian' even before Christianity came along.[9] Arguably, for Paul and Justin authentic religious reality preceded but came to permanent fruition in Christianity. This reality that comes together in Jesus Christ can well be called the religion of Christ.

The doctrine of the religion of Christ as the universal religious reality that is reflected to a greater or lesser degree in particular religious expressions, most copiously in the ancient Hebrew monotheistic faith and in Christianity but also hinted at in others, addresses the pre-existence of 'Christian' faith and values theologically.[10] It sets Christianity and other religions in the context of God's eternal and abiding providential care and purposes and provides a basis for relationship between world religions before Christ as well. On one hand, as the religion which was specifically anticipated Christianity is then genuinely unique and necessary. On the other hand, to the extent that they participate in the seeds of Christ other religions are partially validated in their historical development. Yet both Christianity and the world religions are challenged to self-critical examination in the light of that which they discover within themselves that is transcendent and universal, and also to dialogue with each other in the mutual task of identifying the universal and developing it in their particular religious expressions.

The religion of Christ, however, is always Christological. It is always the religion *of Christ.* It is formed and guided by Jesus Christ, both in his eternal deity and his historical Incarnation and his eschatological reign. The historical revelation of God's saving love in Christ was the eschatological objective of the pre-Incarnation witness of the religion of Christ. The eschatological consummation of the historical revelation in the Incarnation of God in Jesus of Nazareth is the ongoing objective of the religion of Christ. Accordingly, Christianity is always related to Jesus Christ. Further, other religions

---

[9] *The First Apology of Justin Martyr. Ante-Nicene Fathers* I (Peabody, MA: Hendrickson, 1999), 1.46, 2.10.

[10] See Tony Richie, 'Hints from Heaven: Can C.S. Lewis Help Evangelicals Hear God in Other Religions?' *ERT* 32.1 (January 2008), pp. 38-55.

always relate to Christianity as it relates to Jesus Christ. Even further, Christians must relate to other religions as they also relate to the religion of Christ which is for Christians the sign of Jesus Christ. However, Christians recognize and respect that for other religions in all their particularities to relate to the universal religion of Christ is not synonymous with Christianity per se. Christianity recognizes that it is not yet in the full and final form of the religion of Christ; it is still on a journey toward an eschatological or future fulfillment of its own being and destiny. Christianity can therefore travel with other religions into the future to the extent that they both potentially share in the religion of Christ although they may critically assess each other as being at different points in their journey. Naturally, that entails interreligious encounter and dialogue. Nonetheless, each religion, especially Christianity, will want to bear witness to its own (particular) experience of universal religious reality (the religion of Christ). For Christians that can only be expressed in terms of God's saving love in Jesus of Nazareth, in his cross and resurrection, and in the life-giving power of the Holy Spirit. Yet even this very particular and specific message can be presented against the backdrop of the eternal and universal religion of Christ.

Two problems pertaining to theology of religions arise in light of the preceding paragraph. The first is in the Christian assumption that other religions are required to relate to the religion of *Christ.* This appears to be thinly disguised Christian imperialism. The second is in the Christian concern not to mute or tone down their distinctive testimony. This implies a compromise of Christian identity and mission. However, much of the force of these problems dissipates with understanding that the religion of Christ and *Christianity* are not synonyms. Since the religion of Christ and Christianity are not synonymous then neither is it arrogantly implied that the most devout of other religions are somehow anonymous Christians or anonymous members of the Church.[11] As Christians, we are totally convinced in faith that when the present age of partial understandings of provisional truth passes into the eschaton of universal perfect love (1 Cor. 13.8-12)[12] then God will be all in all through the

---

[11] Contra Rahner, *Foundations of Christian Faith*, pp. 311-21.
[12] Wolfhart Pannenberg is helpful here (*An Introduction to Systematic Theology* [Grand Rapids: Eerdmans, 1991, 1992], pp. 4-8).

submissive self-presentation of the resurrected and exalted Son
(15.20-28). And everyone everywhere will know and acknowledge
the place of Jesus Christ in the purposes of God (Isa. 45.23; Rom.
14.11; Phil. 2.10). Yet until the eschaton Christians must exercise
their unique gifts in love while being drawn forward into God's future for us, as Moltmann might put it, and so act and speak toward
other religions in faith, hope, and love (1 Corinthians 13).

   Christian mission and witness (see Chapter 5 of this volume)
therefore at times may be a matter of discovering together where
Christ is already present throughout the world in its various faith
cultures. There may indeed be occasions where cultural conditions
indicate that love of darkness has become so strong and love of
light so weak (Jn 3.19-21) that one cannot discern Christ in the
midst. There was good reason for Paul to be cut sharply within his
spirit – aroused, distressed, or exasperated (παρωξύνετο) – when
he observed the pervasiveness of Athenian idolatry (Acts 17.16). In
such cases, Christian witness must be given accordingly. Amazingly
enough, Paul's Athens encounter with idolatry eventually led to a
paradigmatic interreligious encounter characterized by intelligent,
articulate, sensitive, and unadulterated sharing of the gospel with
those of a very different faith tradition (17.22-34). There may also
be many occasions where the Christian missionary finds that Christ,
who has been there ahead of him or her, and in spite of perhaps
encountering stiff opposition, already has 'many people' in that
place (Acts 18.10 NASB). Discovering Christ in a non-Christian
culture will undoubtedly require spiritual discernment (1 Cor.
12.10). Yet when successful it could dramatically change the tone of
evangelistic ministry and stimulate growth (conversionary and otherwise) in response.

   If, as Pentecostal missiologist Corky Alexander says, at times
Christian evangelistic mission is more of 'a treasure hunt than a de-
livery system',[13] then the tone and strategy of witness is transformed. As much has been said on this topic in this volume already
(see Chapter 5, etc.), it will not be belabored here. Suffice it to say
that while at times it is necessary to confront evil, both in individu-

---

[13] I am indebted to a conversation with Pentecostal missiologist Corky Alexander, author of *Native American Pentecost: Praxis, Contextualization, Transformation*
(Cleveland, TN: CPT Press, 2012), for this poignant phrase.

als and in societal structures, usually a gracious and non-pejorative approach may be more effective. Per human nature, most people are probably more likely to be receptive when they are approached with kindness and sensitivity. Further, it will be encouraging for many if they can see points of contact between their traditional faith and the gospel.

However, it will still be necessary at some point and in some way to lead them to see the contrasts and contradictions. Else, why change (or convert) at all? If all is well then why take the trouble and risk of presenting the gospel in potentially hostile faith environments? Brunner is surely correct that the whole of Scripture teaches the necessity of conversion as a turning away from the previous way and life of one's own choosing and turning to God's way and will.[14] Yet it must be borne in mind that religion and culture are often so intertwined throughout the world that it is almost impossible to extricate religious influences on hosts of issues ranging from family relationships to rules of etiquette to attitudes toward government. Unless European and North American Christians want unwittingly to westernize the world, it is essential to distinguish between the gospel and their own cultural assumptions as well.[15] The gospel has within it inherent power to critique prophetically any culture or moral and spiritual climate. The responsibility of the Church to challenge the world to turn from the emptiness of idolatry to serve the living God and creator of all is therefore always universally relevant (Acts 14.15).

A theology of the religion of Christ and attendant commitment to interreligious dialogue do not diminish the importance or dilute the responsibility for Christians to share the good news of Jesus Christ in multi-faith environments (Acts 17.23). One may expect that results will often be mixed, but the successes will have lasting value nonetheless (vv. 32-34). Human response to God's Word is shaped by the inward condition of the heart (Mk 4.1-20). That finally decisive factor cannot be avoided. As Brunner has summarily suggested, Christian conversion involves God's eternal election of

---

[14] Brunner, *Dogmatics III*, p. 277.
[15] William Placher, *A History of Christian Theology: An Introduction* (Philadelphia: Westminster Press, 1983), pp. 307-08.

those who freely choose to believe on Jesus Christ.[16] (Readers will recall Moltmann's reference above to 'particular faith' and 'universal grace'.)

Here it is helpful to remember with Brunner that the Christian understanding of faith as the basis of existence and as a total way of life is unique among the religions and directly derivative from the Bible alone.[17] Faith in this special sense of 'dependence on God and trust in Him alone occurs only and solely in Jesus Christ'.[18] In typical fashion, Brunner does not deny that people of other religions experience some kind of faith and through it some real relation with God. However, he argues that only the Christian faith relationship with God as 'absolute surrender to God' and 'unconditional trust in God' is faith's true form.[19] One might, with some justification, argue that Brunner defines faith in Christian terms and then excludes other forms of faith by his a priori definition. But that is not my point. Christians' volitional act of placing faith as trust in Jesus Christ is such a unique and nontransferable, or perhaps better, nontranslatable, event that those of other religions are probably hard pressed to process it. When Christians ask someone from another religious faith background to 'put your faith in Jesus' they more than likely do not have any idea what is meant. Worse still, they may have an outright wrong idea that is not meant. Again, here is an example of an area in which interreligious dialogue can help build better understanding for more effective communication.

Moltmann's interpretative application of Bishop King's theology of the religion of Christ to the divine-human relationship naturally enough assumes Christian anthropology. The beginning and grounding of Christian anthropology is that human beings are created by God in God's image.[20] Therefore, in spite of fallenness and sinfulness human beings are enabled by God's graciousness to en-

---

16 Brunner, *Our Faith,* pp. 29-33.
17 Brunner, *Dogmatics III,* pp. 140-41.
18 Brunner, *Dogmatics III,* p. 147.
19 Brunner, *Dogmatics III,* pp. 147-48.
20 Arrington, *Christian Doctrine,* I, pp. 197-99. Emil Brunner, *Christian Doctrine of Creation and Redemption: Dogmatics II* (trans. Olive Wyon; Philadelphia: Westminster Press, 1952), notes that the significance of anthropology is highlighted by its unique status as a common concern of Christians with the unbelieving world and also as the basis for all social ethics (p. 46).

joy genuine relationship with God. A theological anthropology suggests that living in relationship with God and with others is at the heart of what it means to be human. Furthermore, Jesus Christ is the decisive and definitive representation of what that means.[21] Moltmann is directly concerned with the divine-human relationship, or more specifically, with how God and humans relate to each other. More specifically still, he discusses how God and humans relate to each other in terms of the philosophical categories of the universal and the particular.

Addressing Moltmann on the Particular–Universal Problem in Pentecostal Theology of Religions

Notably, Moltmann appears to be applying possible insights from King's theology of religion of Christ and not articulating his own theological position. In other words, if one accepts King's theology on this point, here is one direction it might lead. Yet as has been seen, Moltmann, perhaps inevitably, views King through the lens of his own theology, particularly regarding, first, his understanding of the categories of universals and particulars, and second, although less so, through his tendency toward universalism.[22] I suggest the latter is not a necessary implication of King's theology but that the categories of universal and particular, widely used throughout Christian theology, are pertinent and helpful. Primarily for that reason I will not discuss universalism further in any depth and also because it has already received sufficient treatment herein for the purposes of this volume. The particular and universal will require more attention, however.

First, on the divine side the relationship is universal in its scope and trinitarian in its shape.[23] It is initiated by God's all-encompassing love, accomplished by Christ's reconciliatory cross,

---

[21] Migliore, *Faith Seeking Understanding,* pp. 139, 141-42.

[22] Cf. Brunner, *Dogmatics III,* who insists that the doctrines of universal salvation and final judgment be kept in tension, with neither eclipsing the other (pp. 421-24).

[23] One of the challenges of Trinitarian Pentecostal theologies of religions is Pentecostalism's own internal debate with Oneness Pentecostals. E.g. see David K. Bernard, *The Oneness of God* (Series in Pentecostal Theology, Volume One) (Hazelwood, MO: Pentecostal Publishing House, 1986).

and actualized by the Spirit's gestational presence. Pentecostal theology might sum up the preceding as God loves everyone, Christ died for everyone, and the Holy Spirit is drawing everyone. The point is that on the God side everything that is required for divine-human relationship is already in effect toward all and for all on the basis of God's saving love in Christ by the Holy Spirit. God's side of the relationship is universal.

Second, the human side of the divine–human relationship is particular. The relationship of God and human beings is not a generic or generalized encounter between the category 'Divine' and the category 'Human', but of free subjects or persons acting with liberty in relationship. Accordingly, it is particular in the sense of individual specificity. It requires human responsiveness to the divine initiative (i.e. faith). God's Spirit therefore graciously works in every human being to generate and cultivate spiritual life. That which is dormant rouses in willing response to the Spirit's nudging and prompting. Bare belief becomes confidence and reliance in God's care and kindness. One's initial pneumatological experiences are recognized as anticipatory of further and, finally, full experiences of the eschatological Spirit available for all. The human side of the relationship is particular.

The role of religious or spiritual experience is prominent in the preceding schema. In his presidential address to the Society for Pentecostal Studies, Terry Cross persuasively argued that in the divine–human encounter the role of experience is a valid and fruitful theological topic when examined in light of traditional theological categories.[24] The question, 'What happens when the Holy Spirit meets the human spirit, when the infinite touches the finite?' cries out for a considered response.[25] Significantly, Pentecostal theology needs to address that question not only in light of charismata in their understanding of spiritual experience in the Spirit-filled life but also in pre-conversion work of the Spirit in every human being. Here it is proposed that the Spirit graciously works in an anticipatory fashion (prevenient or preceding grace) in all people and by

---

[24] Terry L. Cross, 'The Divine-Human Encounter: Towards a Pentecostal Theology of Experience', *Pneuma* 31 (2009), pp. 3-34.

[25] Cross, 'The Divine-Human Encounter', p. 9.

definition that anticipatory work includes those who presently adhere to other religions.

Moltmann is very helpful in his rendering of King's theology of the religion of Christ in terms of the particular and the universal and in reminding that there is ample space in Christian pneumatology, specifically Pentecostal pneumatology, for an understanding of the work of the Spirit beyond the Church in the hearts of those living in a multi-religious culture. However, it is worth noting that one of the challenges of Christian theology is that its categories are not always airtight. In the Incarnation the universal entered the particular as true God became true human without ceasing to be true God. In Pentecost the universal enters the particular as God the Holy Spirit indwells and fills human hearts and lives. Again, Cross' question, 'What happens when the Holy Spirit meets the human spirit, when the infinite touches the finite?' is crucially important but must always leave room for the answer such as that of Jesus to Nicodemus in Jn 3.8: 'The wind blows where it wishes and you hear the sound of it, but do not know where it comes from and where it is going; so is everyone who is born of the Spirit' (NASB). It is perhaps precisely at that point in which the universal touches the particular that the mystery of the Spirit appears the most profound and impenetrable. As Paul Tyson rightly suggests, ecclesial and institutional Christianity must always beware of succumbing to the temptation of 'taming the Spirit'.[26] One might aver that since the Spirit of Almighty God is in fact untamable, those who attempt the taming inevitably will suffer defeat and loss.

By way of comparison, both King and Moltmann assume that Christianity and other religions are in some sense particular expressions of a more universal reality. There are several implications that may be inferred from this assumption alone. For one thing, it offers a basis for critiquing one's own Christian religion. For another, it offers a basis for dialogue with non-Christian religions. And finally, it offers a basis for affirming the uniqueness of Christianity. Since Christianity is not its own highest ideal and destiny, it can critique itself in the light of that which is higher than itself. With Barth it is here agreed that Christian theology must always *'feel itself responsible'*

---

[26] Paul G. Tyson, 'Taming the Spirit', *Pneuma* 34.2 (2012), pp. 229-44.

to the 'living command' of the Word of God.[27] Again with Barth, we acknowledge easily enough that, due to human fallibility and frailty, in the work of theology 'critical testing is constantly demanded'.[28] Accordingly, Christianity in all its ecclesiastical and institutional forms, as well as every individual Christian disciple, should constantly gauge themselves by their consistency with God's Word (Ps. 119.105; Jn 1.1).

Both the previous chapter and this one as well have already amply averred that the religion of Christ provides a substantive basis for interreligious dialogue. Although already intimated as well, perhaps here is a place to affirm and reaffirm the uniqueness of Christianity in light of the religion of Christ. If *Christianity* is true to its own innermost identity and ethos it will endeavor to, and in fact accomplish, even if imperfectly, reveal Christ to itself and to the world. To the extent that Christianity is true to that high and holy calling, it and only it can be the true religion. Without any intended insult to other religions Christianity cannot but affirm its own distinctive and unparalleled standing in relation to Jesus Christ. Christianity is the only religion that has Jesus Christ as its 'foundation' (1 Cor. 3.11; Eph. 2.20) and therefore itself is supportive of and foundational to the service of the truth (1 Tim. 3.15). To the extent that it disdains or ignores that holy calling it becomes more false than any other religion could ever be. As Barth puts it, the Church is authentic '*in that it submits to sole rule by Jesus Christ, in whom it is founded*', adding, '*that it also aims to live solely in the fulfillment of its service as ambassador, that it recognizes its goal in its hope, which is its limit*'.[29]

By way of contrast, King's 'religion of Christ' suggests a more direct or energetic focus on the person of Jesus Christ than Moltmann's more general 'messianic kingdom' does. Of course, technically Christ (Χριστός) and Messiah (Μεσσίας) are interchangeable. However, it is well known that Judaism and Islam, especially, as well as other religions have messianic themes.[30] Yet 'Christ' has be-

---

[27] Karl Barth, *Dogmatics in Outline* (New York: Harper Torchbook, 1959), p. 5 (emphasis original).
[28] Karl Barth, *Church Dogmatics: A Selection with an Introduction* (ed. Helmut Gollwitzer; Louisville, KY: Westminster/John Knox Press, 1961, 1994), p. 82.
[29] Barth, *Dogmatics in Outline*, p. 141 (emphasis original).
[30] Gershom Scholem, *The Messianic in Judaism: And Other Essays on Jewish Spirituality* (New York: Random House, 1971, 1995). See Yehoiakin Ben Ya'ocov, *Con-*

come the universal designation for Jesus of Nazareth. The religion of *Christ* immediately brings to mind Jesus Christ; the messianic kingdom not so much so. Also, messianic kingdom, true to Moltmann's overall theological emphasis, places the heaviest accent on the eschatological character of identity while the religion of Christ is more open to the historical movement toward eschatological consummation. Doubtless both terms are correct enough. The messianic kingdom is certainly a strong biblical and theological theme.[31]

The point is to keep the focus on Jesus Christ. Chapter 5 of this volume related Kärkkäinen's focus on the Trinity for doing theology of religions and Yong's suggestion that Christology presents an impasse for interreligious dialogue that perhaps can best be avoided by belaying the topic. Kärkkäinen is correct that the distinctive Christian doctrine of the Trinity is its surest and longest standing theological principle and therefore provides immense instruction for Christian theology of religions. Yong is pragmatically correct that the best starting point of dialogue between very different partners is usually some point of commonality; then, when relationships are established and a level of trust has been earned, the move is made toward difficult and controversial areas. And Moltmann is surely correct that Christianity is called to witness to the world and it's religions of the coming Kingdom of God inaugurated in and to be consummated by the Messiah and therefore not inaccurately described as 'messianic' in nature.

None of the above approaches present Pentecostals with insurmountable theological hurdles. And yet the early Pentecostal theology of the religion of Christ appears to be stronger, more robust in its focus on the face of Jesus Christ, so to speak (1 Cor. 4.6). The religion of Christ does not suggest that Christians should be abrasive and offensive in their interaction with non-Christian religions. It does not suggest that trinitarian insights will not inform Christian theology of religions. It does not suggest that Christianity or the Church constitute the entire reality of God's Kingdom. It certainly does not suggest any diminishment of eschatological movement

---

cepts of Messiah: A Study of the Messianic Concepts of Islam, Judaism, Messianic Judaism, Christianity (Bloomington, IN: WestBow, 2012).

[31] E.g. George Eldon Ladd, *The Gospel of the Kingdom: Scriptural Studies in the Kingdom of God* (Grand Rapids: Eerdmans, reprint 2000).

toward God's hopeful future for all humanity. What it does do is to keep the focus on Christ. In Pentecostal theology of religions, the Christ of interreligious dialogue and cooperation is not a diminished lord but one who transcends history and culture to be Lord of all!

Conclusion

The present chapter of this book has engaged Jürgen Moltmann rather directly on his comments about my reading of Bishop J.H. King's theology of religions. Special focus has been on his use of the religion of Christ and its contribution to the philosophical–theological problem of the particular and the universal. In connection with the previous chapter, on Moltmann's own theology of religions and dialogue, it appears that Moltmann has much to offer for Pentecostal reflection in the discipline of theology of religions. The upcoming Conclusion looks at some issues possibly lying ahead for Pentecostal theology of religions.

CONCLUSION

Throughout the course of this book it has been argued that there is urgent and legitimate need for Pentecostal theology of religions in forms familiar to classical Pentecostal categories of belief and practice. A guiding thesis has been that Pentecostal theology can make significant contributions to Christian theology of religions in a manner clearly congruent with distinctive Pentecostal faith and values. Interreligious dialogue as an extension of the practice of Pentecostal testimony has been described as an effective and viable option. This work has also offered some conversation on the discipline of Christian theology of religions with leading Pentecostal and non-Pentecostal partners. These conversations not only recount something about the current status of the discipline but also raise possibilities about future directions. However, this concluding section offers some specific discussion about issues lying ahead for Pentecostal theology of religions and for Pentecostal participation in interreligious dialogue. Sometimes earlier themes are interwoven and applied with this objective in mind. It does not claim to be a complete sampling but only representative possibilities. Yet it proposes some possibilities on the shape of dialogue with religious others from the perspective of Pentecostal theology.

Exploring Theology Together with Religious Others

Of course, the comparability of various sacred texts is a critical issue among the world's religions. David Ford goes so far as to assert that 'Conversation about scriptures is at the heart of interfaith relations'.[1] Emil Brunner, an early twentieth-century theologian, was ahead of his day in taking the time to relate the Bible to the status

---

[1] Ford, *The Modern Theologians,* p. 761.

of sacred texts in other world religions. Brunner argued that the Bible is distinctively and uniquely the Word of God because it speaks of Jesus Christ who himself '*is* the Word of God' (cf. Jn 1.1).[2] In terms of the technology of his day, Brunner compares this process to that of a phonograph. The Master's voice is heard on the record but one knows it is not to be mistaken for the Master Himself. One also knows not to be distracted by the scratching of the needle or other secondary sounds not made by the Master's voice. Yet one listens attentively to the Master's voice.[3]

But Brunner did not deny that Muslims consider the Quran to be the Word of God and Hindus consider the Bhagavad-Gita the Word of God.[4] How are Christians to consider those other books which claim to be God's word also? Brunner offers a twofold reply. First, for Christians these texts are simply not applicable because Christians are not Muslims or Hindus. Here he is obviously talking about the Christian's own faith life rather than his/her relationships with religious others. Second, if one is still curious, Brunner explains that a different voice is heard on the phonograph of the Quran or the Bhagavad-Gita. It is not the voice of the Good Shepherd (John 10). It is not the same God but a stranger.[5] Yet it may nevertheless somehow be God's voice in a scarcely recognizable form, just as a poor photograph can resemble someone but not show their real appearance.[6]

Quite a dialogue could be carried on about the resemblances and differences in the Bible, the Quran, and the Bhagavad-Gita. How do we explain the resemblances? Do they represent the religion of Christ showing through? Are they due to mere human religiosity? What about the differences? Are they human distortions? Or, are they demonic inventions? How should Christians go about arguing the superlative clarity and authority of the Bible? How would Mus-

---

[2] Brunner, *Our Faith,* p. 9 (emphasis original).

[3] Brunner, *Our Faith,* pp. 10-11.

[4] Brunner, *Our Faith,* p. 7.

[5] Brunner, *Our Faith,* p. 11.

[6] Brunner, *Our Faith,* p. 11. J. Edward Humphrey points out that Brunner believed that behind every religion 'there is at least a rudimentary idea of an all-encompassing law behind which stands an inexorable divine will' (*Makers of the Modern Theological Mind: Emil Brunner* [ed. Bob E. Patterson; Waco, TX: Word Books, 1976], p. 74).

lims or Hindus respond? Perhaps possessing even more potential than these general preliminary questions would be considerations of specific points of contact between the Bible and sacred texts of the world religions. Almost irrespective of the conclusions drawn, the discussion itself could hardly help but prove productive if carried out authentically.

For another instance, recall that in Chapter 6 it was pointed out that the correlation of Yahweh, God of Israel, and the Christian Trinity can be a critical discussion between Jews and Christians.[7] Judaism and Christianity have very different understandings of God's name and nature. Yet Christians believe that Yahweh is the Triune God. In other words, the God of the Jews and the God of the Christians is one and the same God. To suppose otherwise suc- cumbs to an ancient heresy known as Marcionism (rejecting the world's creator and Israel's lawgiver as the God revealed in Jesus through the Spirit). Therefore, two different religions with quite varied understandings of God nevertheless worship the same God albeit not in the same manner. Of course, this is a unique case be- cause of Christianity's parental Jewish heritage (see Chapter 5 of this volume). Still, it calls for collaborative deliberation about how differing perceptions of God do not preclude an amount of authen- ticity in other religions.

Identifying or distinguishing a common deity is also important for the future of Christian theologies of the other Abrahamic reli- gion: Islam.[8] Islamist scholar Ataullah Siddiqui explains that 'The divide between Islam and Christianity that most needs bridging de- rives from their different understandings of God and relationship with him'.[9] Could it be the case that just as Christians admit to shar- ing with Judaism the worship of the same God, although through vastly differing faiths with different names for God and differing views of God's nature, that they also ought to extend to Islam this same possibility? This is a good question for dialogue.

---

[7] Peter Ochs, 'Judaism and Christian Theology', pp. 650-51. Cf. Soulen, *The God of Israel and Christian Theology*; and Marshall, 'Israel', pp. 231-64.

[8] E.g. Miroslav Volf, *Allah: A Christian Response* (New York: HarperOne, 2011).

[9] Ataullah Siddiqui, 'Islam and Christian Theology', pp. 663-81, Ford, *The Modern Theologians,* pp. 663-64.

More to the point, interreligious dialogue might lead to a suggestion that neither Jews nor Muslims be considered inevitable idola-
ters by Christians (or vice versa). Arguably, only Christians, with
their understanding of God as Father, Son, and Holy Spirit would
be expected to develop an in depth theology of a communal or relational God or of the life of faith as primarily loving relationship
with God and with one's neighbor. Accordingly, Siddiqui explains
that relating to God in terms of intimacy or interpersonal fellowship is foreign to 'mainstream Islam' and suspected as bordering on
tawhid (compromising God's transcendence and otherness; i.e. idolatry).[10] Yet exploring Muslim devotion to God through total submission to the divine will, or radical monotheism of Jewish devotion to God through righteous observance to Torah, could certainly
have the potential to provide much material for mutually beneficial
conversations. In so doing, interreligious dialogue could serve to
call attention to the presence of the religion of Christ in all of the
Abrahamic religions.

Throughout the present work there has been a recurring affirmation of the definitive uniqueness of Jesus Christ. As Chapter 1 explains, Pentecostal Christians are completely and uncompromisingly
committed to the absolute and utter uniqueness of Jesus Christ. Jesus is at the center of what Pentecostals are, of what they believe,
and what they do. Pentecostals believe Jesus preexisted from all
eternity, that he is God incarnate, fully divine and fully human, that
his sacrificial death provides atonement for sins, and that he rose
bodily from the dead and is coming again. In short, Jesus alone is
Lord and Savior. Christianity is fundamentally about how one answers the pair of questions posed by Jesus, 'Who do people say the
Son of Man is?' and 'Who do you say that I am?' (Mt. 16.13, 15)
Pentecostal theology of religions retains and reinforces the centrality of Jesus Christ. It cannot compromise the basic confession that
'Jesus is Lord' (Rom. 10.9; 1 Cor. 12.3).

How then do Pentecostals perceive other religions' founders?
The quite obvious answer is that they are not on a par with Jesus.
They are not God. They are not the Savior. Only Jesus is rightly
described in such terms. For purposes of dialogue one might well

---

[10] Siddiqui, 'Islam and Christian Theology', p. 664.

ask, 'Does the non-divine status of other religions' founders necessarily entail that they could have had no divine encounters?' Or, 'Does the non-salvific nature of other religions' founders necessarily entail that they could not have been deliverers that may have been in some sense sent by God?' (cf. Neh. 9.27; Obad. 21)

Pentecostal Old Testament scholar Wilf Hildebrandt observes that in ancient Israel God often raised up charismatic deliverers and leaders through whom the Lord could help and guide the people.[11] Sometimes, as in the book of Judges for example, these leaders were both highly gifted and deeply flawed individuals.[12]Pentecostal Old Testament scholar Lee Roy Martin candidly admits that this apparently incongruent combination of divine power and human weakness has long troubled Pentecostals; indeed it has become a source of both affirmation and embarrassment.[13] Is not this kind of bifurcation similar to what is experienced with other religions' founders? Their mighty achievements must be acknowledged although human frailty is often all too evident. Might this biblical precedent provide a possible paradigm for viewing other religions' figures as well?

At times, God's Spirit inexplicably anointed foreign rulers, who attained an almost messianic aura, to deliver and lead Israel, as in the cases of Cyrus and Artaxerxes I.[14] These amazing figures were not Christians. Some of them were not Jews either. While neither Hildebrandt nor Martin make an explicit connection, for the purposes of dialogue might other religions' founders be compared and contrasted with such historic charismatic leaders? Is it conceivable for Pentecostals that God may have anointed, in some limited sense, religious figures in other religious cultures for the purpose of fulfilling God's own providential objectives? If so, what might be learned in this way? How would religious others respond?

Perhaps one of the most germane discussions for interreligious dialogue is on the respective views of Christians and Muslims re-

---

[11] Wilf Hildebrandt, *An Old Testament Theology of the Spirit of God* (Peabody, MA: Hendrickson, 1995, 1999), pp. 149-50.

[12] Hildebrandt, *An Old Testament Theology of the Spirit of God,* pp. 112-14, 117-18, and 201-204.

[13] Lee Roy Martin, *The Unheard Voice of God: A Pentecostal Hearing of the Book of Judges* (JPTSup 32; Dorset, UK: Deo, 2008), pp. 3-8.

[14] Hildebrandt, *An Old Testament Theology of the Spirit of God,* pp. 135-37.

garding Jesus and Mohammed. After all, some comparison between Jesus and religious founders and figures is undoubtedly inevitable. Earlier in this section it was suggested that exploring various understandings of sacred texts holds potential for interreligious dialogue. From the Muslim point of view, these ideas come together in the doctrine that the Prophet Mohammed, in his personality and character, embodies the teaching of the Quran.[15] Although it must be understood that Muslims do not think of their prophet in divine categories, this teaching nevertheless sounds similar to some Christian claims about Jesus Christ (e.g. Jn 1.1). How are Christian views of Jesus and Muslim views of Mohammed similar? How are they different? To go even further, what do Muslims think of Jesus? What do Christians think of Mohammed? Where are we mistaken about each other? How might we clear up misunderstandings? What radical differences nevertheless remain unresolved? Dialogue on these questions could prove productive.

Timing & Structure of Dialogue & Comparative Theology Discourse

Astute readers will observe that the subject of comparative theology discourse temporarily shelved in Chapter 5 has again been broached in this closing section. However, it is with something of a difference. Three observations are offered. First, Chapter 5 did not disparage the comparative theology discourse. Rather, it only argued that Pentecostals might be better served first to address matters of shared interreligious concerns from the perspective of Christian theology of religions before launching extended abstract discussions with the theologies of other religions. Therefore, it is expected that at some point comparative theology discourse may well occur. It is nonetheless not assumed that it is the primary objective of Christian theology of religions. Second, arguably the common heritage (or parentage?!) of the Abrahamic religions poses a special case. What might with Buddhist or Hindu partners, for examples, be called *comparative* theology discourse for Christians might within the Abrahamic religions be called *common* theology discourse because so

---

[15] Siddiqui, 'Islam and Christian Theology', p. 664.

much of what must be discussed is shared. But of course there are vastly differing conceptions even about the commonalities. The same might apply in Hindu–Buddhist dialogue settings.[16] Third, in searching for occurrences, or perhaps better, appearances, of the religion of Christ among the religions, one is not so much engaging in comparative theology discourse, as valuable as that may admittedly be, at least not directly, as much as one is exploring a commonality together. As Paul Ingram, a participant in the Christian–Buddhist dialogue, argues, specific dialogue must be tailored to the needs of the engaged religions in the contexts in which they are involved.[17] Alertness to appearances of the religion of Christ is appropriate in all interreligious encounter and dialogue.

Yet theology of religions must neither ignore radical differences among the religions nor downplay their significance. These differences are decisive for self-understanding and for mutual dialogue. Even in the common appearances of the religion of Christ one must readily acknowledge different angles that are observed among the respective religions' approaches to each. This argument is not a revised version of the longstanding pluralist philosophical assumption that all religions have a common universal core that merely has to be uncovered in all and embraced by all.[18] As I argued in the Introduction, that leads to religious relativism and ultimately undermines the validity of any religion. Rather, it derives from the biblical teaching that God has not left God's Self without witness in the world, including the world's religions (Acts 14.17), and God is not far from any human being, including human beings in other religions (17.27). Accordingly, a Christian theology of religions must ever emphasize the importance of interreligious dialogue as a means of discovering the religion of Christ wherever it may found.

Islamist scholar Ataullah Siddiqui likewise wrestles with the best approach for the future of interreligious dialogue, including elements of comparative theology discourse. He suggests that understanding of God, the role of the Prophet Mohammed, the relations

---

[16] For an example of some distinctive demands of dialogue beyond the Abrahamic traditions, see Paul O. Ingram, 'Buddhism and Christian Theology', in Ford (ed.), *The Modern Theologians,* pp. 682-702.

[17] Ingram, 'Buddhism and Christian Theology', p. 699.

[18] E.g. William W. Quinn, *The Only Tradition* (Albany, NY: State University of New York Press, 1997).

of sacred scriptures to secular historical scholarship, and the role of dialogue are uppermost among issues of contemporary and pressing importance between Christians and Muslims.[19] For him, dialogue, often focusing more on social, communal, and only general religious issues, has avoided the tough questions and needs finally to establish enough trust and respect to tackle the more difficult topics in a sincere and serious manner.[20] To get past preconceptions about each other will require honest discussion of scripture, the devices and strategies of mission, historical narratives, the role of religion in society, including its relation to the state and with economic structures and systems.[21] Yet he makes the striking suggestion that success in *inter*-faith dialogue requires more energetic *intra*-faith dialogue about religious others.[22]

A number of affirmations appear appropriate. First, it is agreed that interreligious dialogue progresses best when it begins as a conversation among co-religionists and then extends to those of other religions. Second, it is agreed that interreligious dialogue begins with the simple and advances to the more complex in its selection of issues and their implications. Third, it is agreed that to be satisfyingly effective interreligious dialogue must eventually carry on in-depth conversation at the points of greatest divergence with humility and sincerity.

Furthermore, these observations affirm and further clarify previous positions in this text on several key points. First, the movement of Pentecostal theology of religions begins within the Pentecostal family of faith and does so in a manner respectfully employing the grammatical syntax of that tradition. Then it may move to addressing issues of vital public concern that have interreligious components. This step, however, should include some level of familiarization with the positions of the various faith traditions directly involved as well as fresh examination of the basis and character of one's own tradition's interest and involvement. Next Pentecostals may directly engage in conversations with those of other religions. Here it is probably wisest, at least in a pragmatic sense, to

---

[19] Siddiqui, 'Islam and Christian Theology', pp. 676-78.
[20] Siddiqui, 'Islam and Christian Theology', pp. 677-78.
[21] Siddiqui, 'Islam and Christian Theology', p. 679.
[22] Siddiqui, 'Islam and Christian Theology', p. 679.

begin working with those most like ourselves, for example in the Abrahamic faiths, and there probably first with Jews then with Muslims, and move on to include engaging non-Abrahamic traditions, such as Hindus, Buddhists, Taoists, and others. Topics of interest ought to be those which are most germane to building relationships and understanding between the respective faith traditions. Finally, it will eventually be possible and desirable for Pentecostals to join with differing faith traditions in engaging secular culture and even to partner in addressing shared social concerns not only dialogically but also in cooperative efforts. Surely C.S. Lewis is right that Christianity's real battle is against the foes of faith, that is, against aggressive unbelief.[23] Therefore, to an extent Christianity can join with other faiths against the rampant anti-belief inherent in contemporary culture. It is here that justice, tolerance, and peace, that is, righteousness, potentially can be most widely realized on an earthly plane.

A concern of this volume is that Pentecostal theologians of religions not rush through the first step, the intra-Pentecostal conversation, and skip the second, addressing general needs or current events with strong interreligious components, or at best collapse it with the third, comparative theology discourse, and perhaps never even make it to the fourth, cooperative interfaith dialogue with global societies and secular cultures. In a relatively recent update on the status of interfaith dialogue, Moltmann insists that two kinds of dialogue, direct dialogue about different religions' ideas, and indirect dialogue about shared ethical, social, and ecological concerns, are both necessary.[24] He is doubtless correct. However, he is quite concerned that the history of interfaith dialogue suggests it is lacking in self-critical motivation and becoming imbalanced.[25] It is too Western oriented and too Christian dominated. It is too lacking in lasting results. It too often fosters a false dichotomy and contradic-

---

[23] Cf. Michael H. MacDonald and Mark P. Shea, 'Saving Sinners and Reconciling Churches: An Ecumenical Reflection on *Mere Christianity*', in David Mills (ed.), *The Pilgrim's Guide: C.S. Lewis and the Art of Witness* (Grand Rapids: Eerdmans, 1998), pp. 47-48.

[24] Moltmann, 'Dialogue or Mission? Christianity and the Religions in an Endangered World', pp. 172-87, in John Hick and Brian Hebblethwaite (eds.), *Christianity and Other Religions* (Oxford: One World, 2001), pp. 180-82.

[25] Moltmann, 'Dialogue or Mission?', pp. 178-80.

toriness with evangelistic mission.[26] Yet Moltmann is no less convinced that without interreligious dialogue no one will be able to attain any understanding or actualize their own identity either.[27] Isolationism is not an option.

Moltmann therefore argues that interfaith dialogue and Christian mission must be revitalized together as an invitation to life; that is, through the gifting of the Spirit of life, the source of all life, people of faith everywhere should work together for the life of the planet and all its inhabitants.[28] In a world endangered by such things as nuclear war and ecological vulnerability, that is, by the abolition of life, in short, by death, the wisdom and strength of the world's faith traditions can become a common resource for survival, and for more than survival, for the thriving of the Spirit's life in the world. I argue that Moltmann's suggestion is in some ways similar to my proposal that Pentecostal participation in interfaith dialogue include areas of common concern. At the least, rather than an esoteric theological exercise among academicians interreligious dialogue could be an active theological engagement of the pressing issues of the day.

Relating Freedom of Religion & Religious Pluralism

The Introduction of this work affirms the freedom of religion in the sense of a legal and moral right of people to choose and practice their religion, within appropriate ethical boundaries. Freedom of religion means that people may freely and voluntarily convert to another religion. It distinguishes the sort of religious pluralism inherent in the principle of religious freedom from that which views all religions as equally valid. In other words, people should have the right to choose their religion though they may not make the right choices. As always, the ability to make alternate or even wrong choices is the necessary liability of liberty. Issues of religious liberty promise to be increasingly critical in today's pluralist societies. Pentecostal theologies of religions shall have to confront and define the extent and limits of freedom of religion. Important to remember is

---

[26] Moltmann, 'Dialogue or Mission?', pp. 172-73.
[27] Moltmann, 'Dialogue or Mission?', pp. 173-74.
[28] Moltmann, 'Dialogue or Mission?', pp. 186-87.

that international efforts at regulatory management of religion, or forms of so-called religious freedom attempting to privilege one religion, tend to become increasingly complex and problematic for Pentecostals as well as for others.[29] A hearty affirmation of egalitarian religious freedom is the healthiest option for Pentecostal Christians (and others).

As Butler points out, religious freedom in Colonial America was not only the hope of Christians but those of other religions as well.[30] He also informs that religious diversity has been a prominent component of American culture from its early days – although it was at times worn only as an uncomfortable cloak.[31] Nevertheless, the Jeffersonian influence helped make freedom of religion an American right in a way unprecedented and unparalleled in any nation in previous history.[32]

Wacker reminds us that religious freedom and separation of Church and State were new ideas that did not win the day without a fight.[33] Nevertheless, based on reasons of principle, conscience, and practicality, America's Constitution, including Article Six, and its First Amendment made religious freedom the law of the land.[34] Significantly, the historical context of the battle for religious freedom in the United States does not suggest that religion was deemed unimportant but that there was a desire to de-politicize religion; many of the nation's founders continued to express, even in and through public office, strong religious commitments.[35] This proclivity eventually led to the more or less unofficial establishment of American civil religion, a kind of generic appeal to God and affirmation of religion that does not privilege one religion over another, even if arising mostly out of a predominantly Christian cultural heritage.[36] Interestingly, although at times inviting Americans to drift

---

[29] E.g. Christine E. Gudorf, 'Religion, Law, and Pentecostalism in Indonesia,' *Pneuma* 34.1 (2012), pp. 54-74.
[30] Butler, 'Worlds Old and New', p. 13.
[31] Butler, 'The Flowering of Religious Diversity', pp. 73-74 and p. 88.
[32] Butler, 'Religion and the American Revolution', pp. 145-49.
[33] Grant Wacker, 'Prophets for a New Nation', in Butler, Wacker, and Balmer (eds.), *Religion in American Life,* p. 158.
[34] Wacker, 'Prophets for a New Nation', p. 160.
[35] Wacker, 'Prophets for a New Nation', pp. 160-62.
[36] Wacker, 'Prophets for a New Nation', pp. 162-63.

away from traditional Christianity, religious freedom as also enabled Americans to experience ongoing waves of revival.[37]

In the United States, the current societal acceptance and enactment of the reality of religious pluralism and the national tradition of religious freedom are closely linked. Indeed, President Dwight Eisenhower insisted as far back as a public speech on October 12, 1958 that American political freedom and religious freedom and religious pluralism are inseparable.[38] Evangelical scholar John Wilsey argues that there is a progression of religious pluralism inherent within the American Constitution itself.[39] Freedom of conscience in the exercise of religion inevitably affirms religious pluralism.[40] Although it was not until the mid-twentieth century that religious pluralism as it is known today really became prominent, partly through immigration, the American system of government has always accepted religious pluralism in principle in one form or another.[41] Not surprisingly, even a large majority of Evangelical Christians, who tend to be conservative, still affirmed religious pluralism and accepted the need for interreligious dialogue.[42]

By and large religious pluralism seems to have become an acceptable alternative to secularism. Most Americans do not reject religion or religious considerations. There is currently an ongoing struggle to determine the place of religion in civic affairs and public life, but religious skepticism and indifference are not common American characteristics. Quite contrary to predictions by sociologists, 'Americans cling stubbornly to faith at the end of the twentieth century'.[43] And this legacy of tenaciously enduring faith continues strong well into the twenty-first century.[44] 'Despite industrialization, modernization, and even secularization', Balmer notes, 'Americans cling stubbornly to religion and spirituality'.[45] However, reli-

---

[37] Wacker, 'Prophets for a New Nation', pp. 168-69.

[38] Balmer, 'In God We Trust', p. 355.

[39] John D. Wilsey, *One Nation Under God? An Evangelical Critique of Christian America* (Eugene, OR: Pickwick, 2011), pp. xv, 12-14.

[40] Wilsey, *One Nation Under God?*, p. 136.

[41] Wilsey, *One Nation Under God?*, pp. 142-44.

[42] Wilsey, *One Nation Under God?*, p. 146.

[43] Balmer, 'Religion for the New Millennium', p. 410.

[44] Balmer, 'Religion for the New Millennium', p. 426.

[45] Balmer, 'Religion for the New Millennium', p. 426.

gious faith in America is increasingly complex and diverse.[46] In other words, American religious life is culturally pluralistic. True enough, individual Americans may greet these developments with varying attitudes ranging from hostility to indifference to enthusiasm.[47] Yet the American Constitutional and cultural tradition of religious freedom and religious pluralism appears to be amazingly resilient.[48]

Pentecostals tend to affirm freedom of religion rather soundly. Hollis Gause argues that the unprecedented example of the joining of scepter and censer in Melchisedek (see Hebrews 7) as a messianic foreshadowing, coupled with the traditional Israelite separating of the same, dramatically exemplified in Uzziah's disastrous attempt to combine the two (2 Chron. 26.16-21), affirms the political doctrine of the separation of Church and State on biblical and theological grounds.[49] Not until the coming again and millennial reign of Jesus Christ can a theocracy be legitimately expected. In the meanwhile, Pentecostal Christians may conscientiously affirm the essentials of democracy, including separation of Church and State with its emphasis on freedom of religion.

Moltmann, although rightly warning against replacing religious absolutism with secular absolutism, nevertheless argues that freedom of religion and separation of Church and State are necessary presuppositions for interreligious dialogue.[50] One of the ongoing barriers to the progress of interreligious dialogue is the ominous fact that many nations still do not endorse or authentically embrace freedom of religion or separation of Church and State. Religious freedom makes a difference not only with other religions but even within the context of Christianity itself. Thus John Newport notes that when the well-known German theologian Paul Tillich immigrated to the United States after living under socialist and Nazi regimes, the newfound freedom he encountered influenced his writ-

---

[46] Balmer, 'Religion for the New Millennium', p. 410-11.
[47] Balmer, 'Religion for the New Millennium', p. 411.
[48] Balmer, 'Religion for the New Millennium', p. 426.
[49] R. Hollis Gause, lecture on the Book of Hebrews at Pentecostal Theological Seminary, Cleveland, TN (Fall 2012). Gause's *Commentary on Hebrews* is forthcoming.
[50] Moltmann, 'Dialogue or Mission?', pp. 174-78.

ings to take on a more direct and open theological tone.[51] (Tillich himself expressed concerns that Americans might diminish the inherent dynamic of their freedom by radically absolutizing their tradition.)[52]

Religious freedom, then, is part of the warp and woof of the fabric of American political and religious culture and society. Pentecostals, along with other American Christians, affirm freedom of religion and separation of Church and State in principle. With Moltmann above, many are concerned with the encroachment of secularism. Few would likely dispense with the religious liberties provided by the American Constitution even if they were able to do so. However, if freedom of religion and separation of Church and State are to work well for the nation as a whole, then certain principles will need to be employed. First, freedom of religion and separation of Church and State must not be interpreted in an anti-Christian or anti-religious manner. It is not a basis for radical secularist teaching. Second, freedom of religion and separation of Church and State must apply equally to all. It embraces and empowers not only Christians, Catholic and Protestant, but also Jews, Muslims, Hindus, Buddhists, and so on. Third, freedom of religion and separation of Church and State must not be held captive to anyone's political or religious agendas or biases. It does not endorse Christian imperialism any more than it imposes Muslim *sharia* law (Islamic moral code).

How to accomplish this gargantuan task? I suggest Jesus' admonition in Lk. 6.31 to 'Treat others the same way you want them to treat you' (NASB) be used as a simple standard in guiding attitudes and conduct on religious liberty in a pluralistic context. This saying often finds counterparts in other religions as well. In fact, 'In its negative form ("Do not do to others what you do not want them to do to you"), this was a common ethical saying in the ancient world'.[53] Jesus' transformation of this pluralistic principle into positive form is vitally significant. It is not enough to abstain from bad

---

[51] John P. Newport, *Makers of the Modern Theological Mind: Paul Tillich* (ed. Bob E. Patterson; Waco, TX: Word Books, 1984), pp. 59-61.

[52] Paul Tillich, *Systematic Theology: Volume One* (Chicago, IL: University of Chicago Press, 1951), p. 87.

[53] See Lk. 6.31 in Craig S. Keener, *IVP Bible Background Commentary: New Testament* (Downers Grove, IL: InterVarsity Press, 1993).

behavior. One must actively promote and participate in good, that is, godly, behavior and action. For example, any reasonable person would want to be able to practice and promote their religion without interference or prejudice. He or she should willingly extend the same privilege to others. For another example, no reasonable person would want to be coerced or forced against his or her will to participate in religious observances against their beliefs. They should willingly extend the same privilege to others. One final example: any reasonable person who becomes genuinely convinced of the truth and goodness of another religion would want to be able to convert without fear of violent retaliation from co-religionists. The same privilege should be extended to all.

This concluding chapter sought to discuss some specific issues lying ahead for Pentecostal theology of religions and for Pentecostal participation in interreligious dialogue. It proposed some possibilities on the shape of dialogue with religious others from the perspective of Pentecostal theology through a few representative examples. This book has argued that there is urgent and legitimate need for Pentecostal theology of religions in forms familiar to classical Pentecostal categories of belief and practice. It suggests that Pentecostal theology can make significant contributions to Christian theology of religions and do so in a manner congruent with traditional Pentecostal identity. Interreligious dialogue can be approached as an extension of the practice of Pentecostal testimony. Conversations on the discipline of Christian theology of religions with leading Pentecostal and non-Pentecostal partners suggest the growing theological depth and dynamism of the movement. Hopefully, it does not appear arrogant or presumptuous to conclude that Pentecostalism has within itself rich resources for contributing to the developing field of Christian theology of religions.

BIBLIOGRAPHY

Adams, John Wesley, 'Hebrews', in French L. Arrington and Roger Stronstad (eds.), *FLBCNT* (Grand Rapids: Zondervan, 1999), pp. 1295-1399.

Adeney, Frances S., *Graceful Evangelism: Christian Witness in a Complex World* (Grand Rapids: Baker Academic, 2010).

Alexander, Donald L., *Christian Spirituality: Five Views of Sanctification* (Downers Grove, IL: InterVarsity Press, 1988).

Alexander, Estrelda, 'When Liberation Becomes Survival', *Pneuma* 32.3 (2010), pp. 337-53.

Alexander, Estrelda and Amos Yong (eds.), *Philip's Daughters: Women in Pentecostal-Charismatic Leadership* (Princeton Monograph Series; Eugene, OR: Pickwick, 2008).

Althouse, Peter, *The Spirit of the Last Days: Pentecostal Eschatology in Conversation with Jürgen Moltmann* (JPTSup 25; New York: T & T Clark, 2003).

Anderson, Allan, *An Introduction to Global Pentecostalism: Global Charismatic Christianity* (Cambridge: Cambridge University Press, 2004).

Anderson, Allan *et al.* (eds.), *Studying Global Pentecostalism: Theories and Methods* (Berkeley, CA: University of California Press, 2010).

Anderson, Sir Norman, *Christianity and the World Religions: The Challenge of Pluralism* (Downers Grove, IL: InterVarsity Press (1984).

Arrington, French L., *Christian Doctrine: A Pentecostal Perspective* (3 vols.; Cleveland, TN: Pathway Press, 1993).

—'Acts', in French L. Arrington & Roger Stronstad (eds.), *FLBCNT* (Grand Rapids: Zondervan, 1999), pp. 535-692.

—*Encountering the Holy Spirit: Paths of Christian Growth and Service* (Cleveland: Pathway Press, 2003).

—*The Spirit-Anointed Church: A Study of the Acts of the Apostles* (Cleveland, TN: Pathway Press, 2008).

Balmer, Randall, 'In God We Trust', in Jon Butler, Grant Wacker, and Randall Balmer (eds.), *Religion in American Life: A Short History* (New York: Oxford University Press, 2008), pp. 340-59.

—'Religion for the New Millennium', in Jon Butler, Grant Wacker, and Randall Balmer (eds.), *Religion in American Life: A Short History* (New York: Oxford University Press, 2008), pp. 409-29.

Barth, Karl, *Dogmatics in Outline* (New York: Harper Torchbook, 1959).

—*Church Dogmatics: A Selection with an Introduction* (ed. Helmut Gollwitzer; Louisville, KY: Westminster/John Knox Press, 1961, 1994).

Bartleman, Frank, *Azusa Street* (originally *Another Wave Rolls In*) (New Kensington, PA: Whitaker, 1982).

Bauckham, Richard, *The Theology of Jürgen Moltmann* (Edinburgh: T & T Clark, 1995, 1996).

Boddy, A.A., *To Kairwan the Holy: Scenes in Mohammedan Africa* (London: Kegan Paul, Trench & Co., 1885)

Booze, Joyce 'Africa, North, and the Middle East', in Stanley M. Burgess and Eduard M. Van Der Maas (eds.), *NIDPCM* (Grand Rapids: Zondervan, 2002), pp. 6-11.

Bowdle, Donald (ed.), *Ellicott's Bible Commentary in One Volume* (Grand Rapids: Zondervan, 1971, 1980).

Boyd, Gregory A. and Paul R. Eddy, *Across the Spectrum: Understanding Issues in Evangelical Theology* (Grand Rapids: Baker Academic, 2002).

Britt, George L., *When Dust Shall Sing: The World Crisis in the Light of Bible Prophecy* (Cleveland, TN: Pathway Press, 1958).

Brunner, Emil, *Our Faith* (trans. John W. Rilling; New York: Charles Scribner's Sons, 1936, 1962).

—*Christian Doctrine of Creation and Redemption: Dogmatics II* (trans. Olive Wyon; Philadelphia: Westminster Press, 1952).

—*The Christian Doctrine of the Church, faith, and the Consummation: Dogmatics III* (trans. David Cairns with T.H.L. Parker; Philadelphia: Westminster Press, 1962).

Bundy, David D., 'United Methodist Charismatics', in Stanley M. Burgess and Eduard M. Van Der Maas (eds.), *NIDPCM,* pp. 1158-60.

Butler, Jon, 'Worlds Old and New', in Jon Butler, Grant Wacker, and Randall Balmer (eds.), *Religion in American Life: A Short History* (New York: Oxford University Press, 2008), pp. 1-20.

—'Religion and the American Revolution', in Jon Butler, Grant Wacker, and Randall Balmer (eds.), *Religion in American Life: A Short History* (New York: Oxford University Press, 2008), pp. 132-51.

—'The Flowering of Religious Diversity,' in Jon Butler, Grant Wacker, and Randall Balmer (eds.), *Religion in American Life: A Short History* (New York: Oxford University Press, 2008), pp. 71-90.

Cartledge, Mark J., *Testimony: Its Importance, Place, and Potential* (Cambridge: Grove, 2002).

Congar, Yves, *I Believe in the Holy Spirit* (3 vols.; trans. David Smith; New York: Seabury, 1983).

—*The Word and the Spirit* (trans. David Smith; San Francisco: Harper & Row, 1986).

Conn, Charles W., *Like a Mighty Army: A History of the Church of God* (Cleveland, TN: Church of God Publishing House, 1955).

Cook, Robert F., *Half a Century of Divine Leading and 37 Years of Apostolic Achievements in South India* (Cleveland, TN: Church of God Foreign Missions Department, 1955).

Copan, Paul, *True for You, But Not for Me: Overcoming Objections to Christian Faith* (Bloomington, MN: Bethany House, 2009).

Coulter, Dale, 'The Development of Ecclesiology in the Church of God (Cleveland, TN), A Forgotten Contribution?' *Pneuma* 29.1 (2007), pp. 59-85.

Cox, Harvey, *Fire from Heaven: The Rise of Pentecostal Spirituality and the Reshaping of Religion in the Twenty-First Century* (New York: Addison-Wesley, 1995).

Cross, Terry L., 'A Proposal to Break the Ice:' What Can Pentecostal Theology Offer Evangelical Theology?' *JPT* 11.2 (2002), pp. 44-73.

—*Answering the Call in the Spirit: Pentecostal Reflections on a Theology of Vocation, Work and Life* (Cleveland, TN: Lee University Press, 2007).

—'The Divine-Human Encounter: Towards a Pentecostal Theology of Experience', *Pneuma* 31 (2009), pp. 3-34.

Daniels III, David D., '"Gotta Moan Sometime": A Sonic Exploration of Earwitnesses to Early Pentecostal Sound in North America', *Pneuma* 30.1 (2008), pp. 5-32.

Dyrness, William A. and Veli-Matti Kärkkäinen (eds.), *Global Dictionary of Theology* (Downers Grove, IL: InterVarsity Press, 2008).

Duffield, Guy P. and Nathan M. Van Cleave, *Foundations of Pentecostal Theology* (Los Angeles: L.I.F.E. Bible College, 1983, 1987).

Dych, William V. SJ, *Karl Rahner* (Collegeville, MN: Liturgical Press, 1992).

Eck, Diana L., *A New Religious America: How A 'Christian Country' Has Become the World's Most Religiously Diverse Nation* (New York: HarperCollins, 2001).

Faupel, D. William, *The Everlasting Gospel: The Significance of Eschatology in the Development of Pentecostal Thought* (JPTSup 10; Sheffield: Sheffield Academic Press, 1996).

Ford, David F. (ed.), *The Modern Theologians: An Introduction to Christian Theology Since 1918* (Malden, MA: Blackwell Publishing, 2005).

Gaines, Margaret, *Small Enough to Stop the Violence* (Cleveland, TN: Cherohala Press, 2011).

Garrard, David J., 'Guinea, Republic of', in Stanley M. Burgess and Eduard M. Van Der Maas (eds.), *NIDPCM*, pp. 113-15.

—'Uganda', in Stanley M. Burgess and Eduard M. Van Der Maas (eds.), *NIDPCM*, pp. 273-76.

Gause, R. Hollis, *Living in the Spirit: The Way of Salvation* (Cleveland, TN: Pathway Press, 1980).

—*Revelation: God's Stamp of Sovereignty on History* (Cleveland, TN: Pathway Press, 1983).

—*Commentary on the Book of Hebrews* (Cleveland, TN: Deo Publishing, forthcoming).

Gudorf, Christine E., 'Religion, Law, and Pentecostalism in Indonesia,' *Pneuma* 34.1 (2012), pp. 54-74.

Hagner, Donald A., *Hebrews* (NIBC; Peabody: Hendrickson, 1983, 1990).

Heim, Mark S., *Salvations: Truth and Difference in Religion* (Maryknoll, NY: Orbis Books, 1995, 2000).

Hick, John, *The Metaphor of God Incarnate: Christology in a Pluralistic Age* (Louisville, KY: Westminster John Knox, 1993).

Hick, John and Brian Hebblewaite (eds.), *Christianity and Other Religions: Selected Readings* (Oxford: One World, 1981, 2001).

Higgins, John R., Michael L. Dunsing, and Frank D. Tallman, *An Introduction to Theology: A Classical Pentecostal Perspective* (Dubuque, IA: Kendall/Hunt, 1993).

Hildebrandt, Wilf, *An Old Testament Theology of the Spirit of God* (Peabody, MA: Hendrickson, 1995, 1999).

Hollenweger, Walter J., *The Pentecostals* (Peabody, MA: Hendrickson, 1972, 1988).

—'After Twenty Years of Research on Pentecostalism', *IRM* (January 1986), pp. 3-12,

—'Evangelism: A Non-Colonial Model', *JPT* 7 (1995), pp. 107-28.

Hollenweger, Walter J. and Allan Anderson, *Pentecostals after a Century: A Movement in Transition* (JPTSup 15; Sheffield: Sheffield Academic Press, 1999).

Horton, Stanley M. (ed.), *Systematic Theology* (Springfield, MO: Gospel Publishing House, rev. edn, 1995).

—*What the Bible Says about the Holy Spirit* (Springfield, MO: Gospel Publishing House, 1976, 1992).

Horton, Stanley M. and William W. Menzies, *Bible Doctrines: A Pentecostal Perspective* (Springfield, MO: Gospel Publishing House, 1993, 1994).

Hymes, David, 'Japan', in Stanley M. Burgess and Eduard M. Van Der Maas (eds.), *NIDPCM*, pp. 147-50.

Johns, Cheryl Bridges, *Pentecostal Formation: A Pedagogy among the Oppressed* (JPTSup 2; Sheffield: Sheffield Academic Press, 1993, 1998).

Jones, James William, *Blood that Cries Out from the Earth: The Psychology of Religious Terrorism* (New York: Oxford University Press, 2008).

Juergensmeyer, Mark, *Terror in the Mind of God: The Global Rise of Religious Violence* (Berkeley and Los Angeles: University of California, 2001).

Kärkkäinen, Veli-Matti, *Pneumatology: The Holy Spirit in Ecumenical, International, and Contextual Perspective* (Grand Rapids: Baker, 2002).

—*An Introduction to the Theology of Religions: Biblical, Historical, & Contemporary Perspectives* (Downers Grove, IL: InterVarsity Press, 2003).

—*Trinity and Religious Pluralism: The Doctrine of the Trinity in Christian Theology of Religions* (Burlington, VT: Ashgate, 2004).

—(ed.), *The Spirit in the World: Emerging Pentecostal Theologies in Global Contexts* (Grand Rapids: Eerdmans, 2009).

—'Missiology: Pentecostal and Charismatic', in Stanley M. Burgess and Eduard M. Van Der Maas (eds.), *NIDPCM*, pp. 877-85.

Kim, Kirsteen, 'Theologies of Religious Pluralism', in Amos Yong and Clifton Clarke (eds.) *Global Renewal, Religious Pluralism, and the Great Commission: Towards a Renewal Theology of Mission and Interreligious Encounter* (Lexington, KY: Emeth Press, 2011), pp. 117-35.

King, J.H., *From Passover to Pentecost* (Franklin Springs, GA: Advocate Press, 4th edn., 1976).

—*Yet Speaketh* (Franklin Springs, GA: Advocate Press, 1949).

—*Christ – God's Love Gift: Selected Writings of J.H. King,* vol. 1 (Franklin Springs, GA: Advocate Press, 1969).

Küng, Hans, *Christianity and World Religions: Paths to Dialogue with Islam, Hinduism, and Buddhism* (New York: Doubleday, 1986).

Land, Steven J. 'A Passion for the Kingdom: Revisioning Pentecostal Spirituality', *JPT* 1 (October 1992), pp. 19-46.

—*Pentecostal Spirituality: A Passion for the Kingdom* (JPTSup 1; Sheffield: Sheffield Academic Press, 1993).

Land, Steven J., R.D. Moore, and J.C. Thomas (eds.), *Passover, Pentecost, & Parousia: Studies in Celebration of the Life and Ministry of R. Hollis Gause* (JPTSup 35; Dorset, UK: Deo Publishing, 2010).

Lewis, Paul, 'Indonesia', in Stanley M. Burgess and Eduard M. Van Der Maas (eds.), *NIDPCM*, pp. 126-31.

Logan, James C. (ed.), *Theology and Evangelism in the Wesleyan Heritage* (Nashville: Kingswood Books, 1994).

Ma, Julie C., 'Animism and Pentecostalism: A Case Study', in Stanley M. Burgess and Eduard M. Van Der Maas (eds.), *NIDPCM*, pp. 315-18.

Ma, Julie C. and Wonsuk Ma, *Mission in the Spirit: Towards a Pentecostal/Charismatic Missiology* (Regnum Studies in Mission; Eugene, OR: Wipf & Stock, 2010).

Ma, Wonsuk, 'Philippines', in Stanley M. Burgess and Eduard M. Van Der Maas (eds.), *NIDPCM*, pp. 201-207.

Macchia, Frank D. *Baptized in the Spirit: A Global Pentecostal Theology* (Grand Rapids: Zondervan, 2006).

—'Theology, Pentecostal', in Stanley M. Burgess and Eduard M. Van Der Maas (eds.), *NIDPCM*, pp. 1120-40.

Martin, David, *Tongues of Fire: The Explosion of Protestantism in Latin America* (Cambridge, MA: Wiley-Blackwell, 1993).

Martin, Francis (ed.), *Acts* (ACCS; Downers Grove, IL: InterVarsity Press, 2006).

Martin, Lee Roy, *The Unheard Voice of God: A Pentecostal Hearing of the Book of Judges* (JPTSup 32; Dorset, UK: Deo Publishing, 2008).

Marty, Martin E., *When Faiths Collide* (Malden: Blackwell, 2005).

McDermott, Gerald, *Can Evangelicals Learn from World Religions: Jesus, Revelation, & Religious Traditions* (Downers Grove, IL: InterVarsity Press, 2000).

McLung, Jr., Grant L., 'Evangelism', in Stanley M. Burgess and Eduard M. Van Der Maas (eds.), *NIDPCM*, pp. 617-620.

Migliore, Daniel L., *Faith Seeking Understanding: An Introduction to Christian Theology* (Grand Rapids: Eerdmans, 1991, 2004).

Miller, Donald E. and Tetsunao Yamamori, *Global Pentecostalism: The New Face of Christian Social Engagement* (Los Angeles: University of California Press, 2007).

Moltmann, Jürgen, *A Broad Place: An Autobiography* (trans. Margaret Kohl; Minneapolis: Fortress, 2008).

—*The Church in the Power of the Spirit: A Contribution to Messianic Ecclesiology* (London: SCM, 1977).

Mounce, Robert H., *Matthew* (NIBC; Peabody, MA: Hendrickson, 1985, 1991).

Neill, Stephen, *Christianity and Other Faiths: Christian Dialogue with Other Religions* (New York: Oxford University Press, 1961, 1970).

Netland, Harold, *Encountering Religious Pluralism: The Challenge to Christian Faith & Mission* (Downers Grove, IL: InterVarsity Press, 2001).

Newberg, Eric, *Pentecostal Mission in Palestine: The Legacy of Pentecostal Zionism* (Eugene, OR: Pickwick, 2012).

Niebuhr, Reinhold, *The Children of Light and The Children of Darkness: A Vindication of Democracy and A Critique of Its Traditional Defense* (New York: Charles Scribner's Sons, 1944, 1960).

Omenyo, Cephas, 'Renewal, Christian Mission, and Encounter with the Other', in Amos Yong and Clifton Clarke (eds.), *Global Renewal, Religious Pluralism, and the Great Commission: Towards a Renewal Theology of Mission and Interreligious Encounter* (Lexington, KY: Emeth Press, 2011), pp. 137-56.

Ormerod, Neil J. and Shane Clifton, *Globalization and the Mission of the Church* (New York: T & T Clark, 2009).

Parham, Charles F., *The Sermons of Charles F. Parham* (New York: Garland, 1985).
—*A Voice Crying in the Wilderness* (1902).
—*The Everlasting Gospel* (1919).
Pinnock, Clark H. *A Wideness in God's Mercy: The Finality of Jesus Christ in a World of Religions* (Grand Rapids: Zondervan, 1992).
—*Flame of Love: A Theology of the Holy Spirit* (Downers Grove, IL: InterVarsity Press, 1994).
—'The Church in the Power of the Spirit: The Promise of Pentecostal Ecclesiology', *JPT* 14.2 (April 2006), pp. 147-65.
Pinnock, Clark H. *et al.* (eds.), *Four Views on Salvation in a Pluralistic World* (Grand Rapids: Zondervan, 1995).
Plüss, Jean-Daniel, 'Testimony', in William A. Dyrness and Veli-Matti Kärkkäinen (eds.), *GDT* (Downers Grove, IL: InterVarsity Press, 2008), pp. 877-79.
Rahner, Karl, *Foundations of Christian Faith* (New York: Crossroad, 1978, 2002).
Reed, David A., 'Oneness Pentecostalism', in Stanley M. Burgess and Eduard M. Van Der Maas (eds.), *NIDPCM,* pp. 936-44.
Richie, Tony, 'Mr. Wesley and Mohammed: A Contemporary Inquiry Concerning Islam', *ATJ* 58.2 (Fall 2003), pp. 79-99.
—'Revamping Pentecostal Evangelism: Appropriating Walter J. Hollenweger's Radical Proposal', *IRM* 96.382/383 (July/October 2007), pp. 343-54.
—'Hints from Heaven: Can C.S. Lewis Help Evangelicals Hear God in Other Religions?' *ERT* 32.1 (January 2008), pp. 38-55.
—'Approaching Religious Truth in a Pluralistic World: A Pentecostal-Charismatic Contribution', *JES* 43.3 (Summer 2008), pp. 351-69.
—'A Politics of Pluralism in American Democracy: Reinhold Niebuhr's Christian Realism as a National Resource in a Post-9/11 World', *JES* 45.3 (Summer 2010), pp. 471-92.
—*Speaking by the Spirit: A Pentecostal Model for Interreligious Dialogue* (Asbury Seminary Series in World Christian Revitalization Movements in Pentecostal/Charismatic Studies 6; Lexington, KY: Emeth Press, 2011).
Robeck, Cecil M., *The Azusa Street Mission & Revival: The Birth of the Global Pentecostal Movement* (Nashville: Nelson, 2006).
Runyon, Theodore, *The New Creation: John Wesley's Theology Today* (Nashville: Abingdon, 1998).
Sanders, Cheryl, *Saints in Exile: The Holiness-Pentecostal Experience in African American Religion and Culture* (Religion in America; New York: Oxford University Press, 1999).
Shelton, James B., 'Matthew', in French L. Arrington and Roger Stronstad (eds.), *FLBCNT* (Grand Rapids: Zondervan, 1999), pp. 119-253.
Shenk, Wilbert R., 'Gospel', in William A. Dyrness and Veli-Matti Kärkkäinen (eds.), *GDT* (Downers Grove, IL: InterVarsity Press, 2008), pp. 356-58.
Shepperd, Jerry W., 'Sociology of World Pentecostalism', in *NICPCM,* pp. 1083-90.
Simonetti, Manlio (ed.), *Matthew 1-13* (ACCS; Grove, IL: InterVarsity Press, 2001).

Sims, John A., *Our Pentecostal Heritage: Reclaiming the Priority of the Holy Spirit* (Cleveland, TN: Pathway Press, 1995).

Snyder, Howard A., 'Wesleyanism, Wesleyan Theology', in William A. Dyrness and Veli-Matti Kärkkäinen (eds.), *GDT* (Downers Grove, IL: InterVarsity Press, 2008), pp. 929-36.

Spittler, Russell P. (ed.), *Perspectives on the New Pentecostalism* (Grand Rapids: Baker, 1976).

—'Spirituality, Pentecostal', in Stanley M. Burgess and Eduard M. Van Der Maas (eds.), *NIDPCM,* pp. 1096-1102.

Stackhouse, Jr., John G. (ed.), *No Other Gods Before Me? Evangelicals and the Challenge of World Religions* (Grand Rapids: Baker Academic, 2001).

Stephenson, Christopher A., *Types of Pentecostal Theology: Method, System, Spirit* (Oxford: Oxford University Press, 2013).

Synan, Vinson, *The Century of the Holy Spirit: 100 Years of Pentecostal and Charismatic Renewal* (Nashville, TN: Nelson, 2001).

—*Voices of Pentecost: Testimonies of Lives Touched by the Holy Spirit* (Ann Arbor, MI: Servant Books, 2003).

—'Evangelicalism', in Stanley M. Burgess and Eduard M. Van Der Maas (eds.), *NIDPCM,* pp. 613-16.

Tan-Chow, May Ling, *Pentecostal Theology for the Twenty-First Century* (Burlington, VT: Ashgate, 2007).

Taylor, G.F., *The Rainbow* (Franklin Springs, GA: Advocate Press, 1924).

Tennent, Timothy, *Christianity at the Religious Roundtable: Evangelicalism in Conversation with Hinduism, Buddhism, and Islam* (Grand Rapids: Baker Academic, 2002).

Thacker, Kimberly and Timoteo D. Gener, 'Evangelism', in William A. Dyrness and Veli-Matti Kärkkäinen (eds.), *GDT* (Downers Grove, IL: InterVarsity Press, 2008), pp. 297-300.

Thomas, John Christopher, 'Pentecostal Theology in the Twenty-First Century', *Pneuma* 20.1 (1998), pp. 3-19.

—*The Apocalypse: A Literary and Theological Commentary* (Cleveland, TN: CPT Press, 2012).

Tyra, Gary, *The Holy Spirit in Mission: Prophetic Speech and Action in Christian Witness* (Downers Grove, IL: InterVarsity Press, 2011).

Tyson, Paul G., 'Taming the Spirit', *Pneuma* 34.2 (2012), pp. 229-44.

Wacker, Grant, *Heaven Below: Early Pentecostals and American Culture* (London: Harvard University Press, 2001).

—'Sojourners at Home', *Religion in American Life*, in Jon Butler, Grant Wacker, and Randall Balmer (eds.), *Religion in American Life: A Short History* (New York: Oxford University Press, 2008), pp. 212-29.

—'Prophets for a New Nation', in Jon Butler, Grant Wacker, and Randall Balmer (eds.), *Religion in American Life: A Short History* (New York: Oxford University Press, 2008), pp. 155-69.

Walker, Paul L., *Is Christianity the Only Way?* (Cleveland, TN: Pathway Press, 1975).

Warrington, Keith, *Pentecostal Theology: A Theology of Encounter* (New York: T & T Clark, 2008).

Wesley, John, *Complete Works of John Wesley* (Rio, WI: Ages Software, 2002).

Williams, E.S., *Systematic Theology* (3 vols.; Springfield, MO: Gospel Publishing House, 1953).

Williams, J. Rodman, *Renewal Theology: Systematic Theology from a Charismatic Perspective* (3 vols.; Grand Rapids: Zondervan, 1996).

Wilson, Everett A., 'Brazil', in Stanley M. Burgess and Eduard M. Van Der Maas (eds.), *NIDPCM*, pp. 35-42.

Wilson, D.J., 'Eschatology', in Stanley M. Burgess and Eduard M. Van Der Maas (eds.), *NIDPCM*, pp. 601-05.

Wright, Christopher, *Deuteronomy* (NIBC; Peabody, MA: Hendrickson, 1996, 2003).

Yong, Amos, '"Not Knowing Where the Wind Blows ... "': On Envisioning a Pentecostal-Charismatic Theology of Religions', *JPT* 14 (April 1999), pp. 81-112.

—*Discerning the Spirit(s), A Pentecostal-Charismatic Contribution to Christian Theology of Religions* (JPTSup 20; Sheffield: Sheffield Academic Press, 2000).

—*Beyond the Impasse: Toward a Pneumatological Theology of Religions* (Grand Rapids: Baker, 2003).

—*The Spirit Poured Out on All Flesh: Pentecostalism and the Possibility of Global Theology* (Grand Rapids: Baker, 2005).

—'Academic Glossolalia? Pentecostal Scholarship, Multi-disciplinarity, and the Science-Religion Conversation', *JPT* 14.1 (October 2005), pp. 61-80.

—*Hospitality and the Other: Pentecost, Christian Practices, and the Neighbor* (Maryknoll, NY: Orbis, 2008).

—'From Demonization to Kin-domization: The Witness of the Spirit and the Renewal of Mission in a Pluralistic World', in Amos Yong and Clifton Clarke (eds.), *Global Renewal, Religious Pluralism, and the Great Commission: Towards a Renewal Theology of Mission and Interreligious Encounter* (Lexington, KY: Emeth Press, 2011), pp. 157-74.

—*Pneumatology and the Christian-Buddhist Dialogue: Does the Spirit Blow through the Middle Way?* (Leiden and Boston: Brill, 2012).

Index of Biblical References

1 John, cont'd		*Revelation*		13.8	63
4.9	54	3.4	157	20.11-15	60
		3.15-16	153	22.6	161
3 John		12.11	101		
3-4	135				

Index of Names and Subjects

Johns, Cheryl Bridges 97
Jones, C.E. 39
Jones, James William 90
Jones, Scott 129
Judaism 25, 71, 114-17, 119, 124-25, 167, 176, 181
Juergensmeyer, Mark 89-90
Justin Martyr 45

Kärkkäinen, Veli-Matti 11, 14, 16, 21, 23, 27, 57, 75-79, 85-86, 109, 110-12, 132, 137, 140, 145-46, 161, 163
Kim, Kirsteen 4-5
kingdom of God 27, 28, 35, 36, 127, 140, 145, 147, 149, 154, 155, 166, 177
Kinnamon, Michael 95
King, Joseph Hillary 13, 59, 61-66, 163-67, 178
Kireopoulos, Antonios, 107
Knight III, Henry H. 24, 43
Knitter, Paul 56
Koran (Quran) 5, 37, 180, 184,
Kraft, Charles H. 129
Krishna 22

Land, Steven Jack 1, 24, 35-36, 98, 124, 152
Langford, Thomas A. 44
Latin America 99
Lewis, C.S. 56, 187
Lewis, Paul 2
liberation 111, 122, 181

Ma, Julie 29, 31
Ma, Wonsuk 2, 29, 31
MacDonald, William 98
Macchia, Frank D. 22, 24, 28, 73, 74, 102, 152, 159-60
Martin, Lee Roy 183
Marty, Martin E. 89, 93
McClung, Grant, Jr. 132, 151
McDermott, Gerald 92
Mellor, G. Howard 31, 93
Menzies, William W. 26, 33
Migliore, Daniel L. 10, 12, 56, 134

Miller, Donald 31, 118
mission 4, 29-32, 51, 73, 74, 78, 80, 83, 91, 94, 112, 122, 134, 135, 140, 149, 164, 170, 188
Mohammed 22, 45, 59, 60, 119, 184, 185
Moltmann, Jürgen 9, 14, 98, 114-15, 138-61, 162-78, 187-88, 191, 192
monotheism 71, 182
Moreland, J.P. 17, 165
Mounce, Robert H. 94

Neill, Stephen 48, 51-54
Netland, Harod 52
Newberg, Eric 114
Newbigin, Lesslie 8, 48, 57-58, 125, 130, 131, 133, 135-36, 158
Nichols, David R. 21
Niebuhr, Reinhold 9, 89, 92, 115-17, 118, 124-25

Ochs, Peter 114, 181
Olson, Roger E. 162
Omenyo, Cephas 4, 91
Origen 152
Owens, Robert 105

paganism 8, 18, 38, 47, 65, 86, 88, 115, 121, 152, 154, 167
Palestine 114-15, 117, 119-20, 122
Pannenberg, Wolfhart 146, 169
Parham, Charles Fox 13, 59-61
Park, Myung Soo 99
Pinnock, Clark H. 11, 13, 42, 67-70, 72, 75, 158
peace 18, 62, 64, 83, 89-92, 102, 120-22, 153, 187
Pecota, Daniel 33
Plato 165
pluralism 4, 5, 7, 12, 14, 15, 16-19, 22, 31-33, 38, 48, 49, 51, 52, 55-58, 60, 65, 66, 69-70, 73, 76-77, 78-79, 85-86, 90, 112, 116, 123-25, 129-37, 146, 151, 185, 188-92
pneumatological theology of religions 25, 73, 77, 79, 81, 85, 132, 147
pneumatology 23-26, 61, 64, 175

prayer   7, 63, 99, 103-06, 121, 128,
  130
prevenient grace   40-45, 68, 122,
  158-59, 174-75
Protestantism   56, 57, 97, 106, 132,
  192
providence   38, 51, 62, 83, 122, 168,
  183
Plüss, Jean-Daniel   96, 97, 104, 108

Rahner, Karl, 146, 160, 169
reconciliation   32, 164
redemption   25, 26, 34, 59, 60, 62,
  74, 114-15, 116, 164, 172
Reed, David A.   24
regeneration   10, 32, 63
religion of Christ   64, 163, 165, 166,
  167, 168-69, 171, 173, 175, 176-77,
  178, 180, 182, 185
religion of Christianity   22, 142, 163,
  165, 167
resurrection   44, 48, 62, 147, 160,
  166, 169
revelation   17, 33, 36, 38, 49, 50, 55,
  57, 61, 63, 68, 69, 77, 92, 97, 149-
  50, 168
Richie, Tony   5, 8, 23, 25, 45, 57-59,
  61, 68, 88, 93, 100, 101, 110, 118,
  133, 135, 154, 163, 168
Ricoeur, Paul   96-97
Robeck, Cecil M.   96
Runyon, Theodore   44, 93
Rybarczyk, Edmund J.   33

sanctification   10, 32, 39-40, 41, 104
Sanders, Cheryl   103, 106
saving grace   12, 26, 41, 43, 77
second coming of Jesus   10, 40
secularism   86, 92, 114, 116-17, 120,
  124, 136, 186, 187, 190-92
Sepúlveda, Juan   98-99
sharia   192
Shelton, James   94, 125
Shelton, R. Larry   44
Shenk, Wilbert   127
Shepperd, Jerry W.   3

Shintoism   144, 156, 158
Siddiqui, Ataulah   181, 182, 184,
  185-86
Simonetti, Manlio   94, 125
Sims, John A.   40, 41, 43
sinfulness (fallenness)   29, 34, 42,
  49, 116, 156, 172
Snyder, Howard A.   39-40, 41-42
social concerns   30, 31, 36, 58, 69,
  71, 83, 96, 97, 103, 118, 127, 128,
  129, 133, 135, 144, 156, 161, 172,
  186, 187, 191
soteriology   13, 32-35, 44, 45, 51, 54,
  55, 61, 65, 68, 70, 74, 75, 81, 84,
  99, 124, 149, 159
speaking in tongues (glossolalia)   8,
  10, 23, 27, 73, 97, 103, 128
Spirit baptism   7, 8, 10, 24, 30, 73,
  97, 128
Spittler, Russell P.   104, 106, 107
Stackhouse, John G. Jr.   93
Stanley, Susie C.   107
Stephenson, Christopher A.   138,
  150
Sterling, Larry Jr.   32
Studebaker, Steven M.   73-74
Synan, H. Vinson   39, 48, 104, 105
syncretism   48, 50, 51, 58, 144, 156-
  58

Tallman, Frank D.   24, 25, 27, 30, 38
Taoism   8
Tennent, Timothy   93
terrorism   4, 12, 89-90, 94, 120
testimony   14, 67, 88, 95-108, 110,
  111, 112, 114, 119, 121-23, 124,
  126, 127, 137, 169, 179, 193
Thacker, Kimberly   127
Thomas, John Chrisotopher   27, 30,
  98, 101, 152, 153
Tillich, Paul   191-92
tolerance   5, 33, 62, 77, 141, 187
transformation   23, 36, 52, 53, 54,
  69, 83, 97-98, 103, 106, 118, 135-
  36, 141, 144, 147, 148, 156, 157,
  159, 161, 170, 192

9 781935 931348